Expanding Reading Skills

ADVANCED

SECOND EDITION

Linda Markstein

The Borough of Manhattan Community College
The City University of New York
New York, New York

Louise Hirasawa

The University of Washington
Seattle, Washington

HEINLE & HEINLE PUBLISHERS
A Division of Wadsworth, Inc.
Boston, Massachusetts 02116

Director: Laurie E. Likoff
Production Coordinator: Cynthia Funkhouser
Text Design Adaptation and Cover Design: Suzanne Bennett Associates
Compositor: Progressive Typographers, Inc.
Printer and Binder: Malloy Lithographing, Inc.

Photo/illustration credits. p. 1: S. Shargal; pp. 12, 27, 132: © Beryl Goldberg, photographer; p. 44: Gigli/The Record/Sygma; p. 56: U.S. Supreme Court Historical Society; p. 68: Angel Vannoy; p. 86: Spencer A. Burnett; p. 96: Pete Byron; p. 108: News Times, Newport, Oregon, August 6, 1986; p. 120: Craig Fujii/The Seattle Times, August 24, 1986; p. 40, courtesy of Recreational Equipment Inc. (REI); p. 152: ESM Documentations/Art Resouce, Duchamp, *Bicycle Wheel,* 1913, © 1990 ARS N.Y./ADAG; p. 155: Cliché des Musées Nationaux, Picasso, Bull's Head, © 1990 ARS N.Y./SPADEM; pp. 166, 171, 173, 174: Máris Bishofs; pp. 178, 183: reprinted by permission of New Society Publishers, 4527 Springfield Avenue, Philadelphia, PA 19143, from *Through Our Own Eyes: Popular Art and Modern History,* by Guy Brett, 1986.

Expanding Reading Skills — Advanced, Second Edition

Library of Congress Cataloging in Publication Data

Markstein, Linda.
    Expanding reading skills, advanced / Linda Markstein, Louise Hirasawa. — 2nd ed.
        p.   cm.
    Rev. ed. of: Expanding reading skills, advanced / [compiled by] Linda Markstein, Louise Hirasawa.
    Includes bibliographical references.
    ISBN 0-8384-3098-8
    1. English language — Textbooks for foreign speakers.
2. Developmental reading.   I. Hirasawa, Louise.   II. Expanding reading skills, advanced.   III. Title.
PE1128.M3455   1990
428.6'4 — dc20   89-12824
                                                                          CIP

93 92   9 8 7 6 5

428.64
m 346

Contents

Developing Research Writing Skills 187

Introduction

Expanding Reading Skills: Advanced is the second edition of our 1977 book by the same name. However, the second edition is a completely new book, and it reflects a different orientation toward reading. Since the first edition was published in 1977 — more than ten years ago — our philosophy of the nature of reading and our perception of the real reading needs of students have evolved. The new text is based upon an interactive, process model of reading.

Expanding Reading Skills: Advanced (Newbury House Stage 6) is intended for adults who want to refine their reading skills for academic, personal, and/or career purposes. This book was designed for English as a Second Language and English as a Foreign Language students in both academic and nonacademic settings; however, it was also successfully used with native-speaking adults in a developmental reading class in the initial testing.

Expanding Reading Skills: Advanced is part of a reading series by the same authors. It is the most advanced text in the series and can be used as a follow-up or challenging replacement for *Developing Reading Skills: Advanced*.

Expanding Reading Skills: Advanced is composed of five thematic units:

- Families and Childcare
- Technology and Ethics
- Prisons and Punishment
- Leisure Time
- Art

Each unit has three or four readings and a variety of reading, writing, discussion, and structure exercises designed to help the learners develop comprehension and to integrate new ideas with their knowledge and experience of the world. All readings are authentic, original texts on relevant topics. Students and teachers at the Borough of Manhattan Community College, City University of New York, helped us select the unit themes, and they generously offered us feedback on the materials in the experimental stage. All of the materials were thoroughly tested and revised before publication.

Some of the major features of *Expanding Reading Skills: Advanced* are

- **extensive prereading activities:** Before they begin reading, learners work together in guided discussion to activate their awareness of the topic. The prereading activities (1) introduce the text in the context of what is already known by the learners, (2) promote a sharing of information by members of the group, (3) encourage speculation on textual content and, finally, (4) set the stage for the learners' successful integration of new ideas and concepts in the text with their knowledge and experience of the world.

- **the thematic organization:** Each of the five units has at least three readings built around a common theme. The thematic approach allows for a natural recycling and spiraling of concepts, vocabulary, and syntactic structures. The result is that learners develop their reading/thinking/writing skills more quickly and are highly motivated to expand their efforts as they successfully cope with more and more challenging material.

We have carefully selected the thematic readings so that the learners will be exposed to a variety of content demands. For example, we have reading passages about significant current events from newspapers and magazines, selections from college-level textbooks, excerpts from landmark legal opinions, transcripts of discussions reflecting the markers of oral English and, last but not least, selections from significant pieces of fiction.

- **a solid reading-writing connection:** Students write about what they read. They explore their own ideas and feelings about each selection in writing, and they read their writing to their classmates. Furthermore, in the expansion section at the end of every unit, students have the opportunity to develop research and report writing skills through a multistep process approach. They learn how to continue the thematic spiral through their own independent research. The research and report-writing section has been placed at the end of the book so students may refer to it as a resource handbook as needed.

Finally, it is widely recognized in the literature that reading and writing are different aspects of a larger thinking process. Consequently, we believe that reading skills and writing skills can be expanded more efficiently and effectively when the two are carefully integrated within a single instructional context.

■ **a process approach to reading and writing:** Learners are shown how to interact with the text in a logical, systematic manner and how to vary their reading approach to suit their reading purpose and the content demands of the reading. They learn to alter their reading speed according to their reading purpose and to fit the content demands of the material. They learn how to use text features — headings, different print sizes and types — as pointers to meaning and to use context clues to figure out meanings of new words and phrases. They are guided in how to relate their prior knowledge and experience to the text. Finally, they learn that systematic rereading is just as important to reading as systematic rewriting is to writing.

■ **the glossary:** A glossary, with definitions and example sentences, has been added at the end of the text as a quick reference. Students will still need to use their own dictionaries for examining the range of meanings of a word and for words not included in the glossary.

HOW TO USE THE TEXT

We recommend that instructions within the units be followed as closely as possible. For example, every unit begins with an extensive headnote to provide contextual orientation. This headnote helps learners get their bearings before they begin reading by providing useful social and historical information about the topic. Prereading discussion activities follow. We emphasize the importance of giving careful attention to these activities because they help the learners relate the text to their previous knowledge and experience. Furthermore, the prereading activities promote cooperative learning and encourage a sharing of information. In brief, the more attention given to the prereading activities, the more successfully the learners will be able to interact with the text.

In the first unit, we recommend that the teacher work directly with the students in helping them recognize the significance of textual features (e.g., headings, subheadings, different prints) and how these features point to meaning and are essential to effective skimming and scanning. We believe that reading speed is important; however, we have not recommended specific reading times because, in the testing stage, we found that different groups — and individuals within groups — had significantly different reading abilities and could read and comprehend at very different rates. We encourage teachers to evaluate the reading abilities of their students and to set reading times that are challenging, yet not frustrating. We note that ESL and EFL students must be consistently encouraged to break the word-by-word reading habit, which in fact interferes with comprehension. Particularly in the beginning, it is important to emphasize to students that they can understand a reading selection even though they do not understand every word.

The second reading of the passage is designed to give the students time to go back over difficult passages of text and to look up words in their glossaries or dictionaries if they wish. We do not encourage students to look up every unfamiliar word and, in the experimental testing, we noted that very few students attempted to do so. Generally, students chose to confer with each other on the meanings of certain words and to look up other words, or words they were still unsure of, on their own.

The third reading is designed to help the students integrate old and new concepts and vocabulary within the text. It is important to encourage students to recognize the purposes and benefits of rereading because many students are not familiar with a process approach to reading and, in fact, without careful instruction in this area, may consider rereading a sign of poor reading skills. In certain cases of densely packed text, we have recommended more than three readings.

Finally, we recognize that the level of the readings in this book is challenging. Reading is developmental: We learn to read by reading; we learn to read difficult material by reading difficult material, and what at first seems inordinately difficult becomes less so only as we read more and more challenging material. We believe that learners at the advanced level are fully capable of meeting new reading challenges and, indeed, they must, if they are to reach their personal, professional and vocational goals.

Linda Markstein   Louise Hirasawa
New York, New York   *Seattle, Washington*

To Anne Habiby and Dr. Peter Mohai

Acknowledgments

Many people have helped us in the production of this book. First, we would like to thank the students at the Borough of Manhattan Community College with whom we tested the content. Their responses and comments were invaluable in helping us make appropriate revisions. Secondly, we would like to thank Angel Vannoy, Denise Anderson, and Dale Parkhurst. We would also like to thank Shaw & Markstein for the generous use of their fax machine.

And, finally, we would like to thank Laurie Likoff and Cynthia Funkhouser at Newbury House Publishers for their time and painstaking attention to this project.

Unit 1
Families and Childcare

DISCUSSION

Although most if not all societies place the family at the heart of the society, the treatment of families and family concerns varies a great deal from society to society. For example, some regard childcare as a personal matter to be handled entirely by the parents. They do not believe that the government has a role in providing childcare. Others, however, subsidize childcare facilities and, in this way, the government and the family form a partnership in the raising of children. Still others take a middle position, with the government offering some assistance to families for childcare on a limited basis. Using the society of your country as a reference, discuss the answers to these questions.

1. In your country, who usually takes care of the children?
2. Is it common for mothers to work outside the home in your society? Approximately what percentage of middle-class mothers work outside the home? Approximately what percentage of lower-class mothers work outside the home?
3. Does the government encourage women to work in your country? If so, explain and give examples.
4. Does the government offer free or inexpensive childcare facilities for working parents? Does the government have any role in providing childcare?
5. What are your views on childcare? Who should be responsible for childcare? Who should pay for childcare? Should childcare be left entirely up to parents? Why? Why not?

Deleg and Dashnyam, left, at their daughter's wedding

1
One of Many Families

"One of Many Families" by S. Shargal describes a typical family in the Mongolian Peoples Republic, an independent Asian state bounded on the east, south, and west by China and on the north by the U.S.S.R. The Mongolian Peoples Republic is a socialist state. "One of Many Families" appeared in 1987 in a journal called *Women of the Whole World*. Reprinted by permission.

1.1
FIRST READING

Read this article quickly for the main ideas. Pay attention to the title and the text headings as you read. Do *not* stop to look up words in your dictionary.

1. Traditionally, Mongolian families have many children. They have always been regarded as a source of joy and happiness in our country. We would like to introduce you here to one such typical large family.

A HERO OF LABOUR

2. Luvsanzhamzyn Dashnyam works at the leading factory of the Association of Clothing Enterprises. She is a Hero of Labour of the Mongolian Peoples Republic. She was born in 1943, into the family of a cattle breeder in the Central Gobi Region. Like all children living in villages, she was used to working from an early age. When she was four or five years old, she was already entrusted with the task of looking after the herds of cattle on the pastures. This is no exception as rural children in Mongolia usually begin preparing for work in connection with cattle breeding at that early age. Quite frequently children of six or seven years are found among the winners of horse racing events at the "Nadom" national festival.

3. The inhabitants of the Gobi Desert are generally very much appreciated for their dedication to work. This evidently derives from the rough environmental and climatic conditions. Dashnyam, as a typical girl of the Gobi Desert, also developed this fine trait. For her self-sacrificing work, her great skill, and because she is a particularly sympathetic and just sort of person, she is popular with and respected by the large staff of the factory where she works.

DASHNYAM'S FAMILY

4. Dashnyam has a large family. In fact, with seven children, she is a mother heroine. The older ones have started out on their own independent life and also founded families. Her daughter Erdenechimeg has her diploma of education and is working as a teacher in her mother's native village. Dashnyam's son Tuvshinzhargal is a driver. Dashnyam is very pleased with him; she thinks that he has that most important thing, the foundation of a good character, namely a natural dedication to work. Her daughters Tungalagtamir and Tuvshintamir are both students. The three youngest children, Munkhtamir, Enkhtamir and Orkhontamir, are pupils of the secondary school. The new, third generation of the family is either in a creche or a nursery. Dashnyam, although a young grandmother, already has four grandchildren.

HELP FROM THE STATE

5. How did Dashnyam manage to raise and educate so many children and at the same time work so successfully in a production enterprise? What kind of help did she receive from the state?

6. In our country the entire nation regards motherhood with respect and surrounds mothers with care; they are protected and assisted in every way by the state. Women are provided with all the social welfare facilities assuring them a happy motherhood, at the same time allowing them to take an increasingly active and creative part in production, social and political life. Our legislation assures an all-sided protection of the interests of mothers and children and every child a happy childhood.

7. An extensive network of creches, nurseries, schools and other institutions for the education of healthy young people allows the harmonious development of their physical and mental capacities. The state has at its disposal a special fund for the maintenance of creches and nurseries and for children's school education. Dashnyam's family did not have to pay a single tugrik for the accommodation of her children in a creche as these facilities are free of charge in our country. The costs of accommodation at a nursery approximate between 15 and 50 tugrik [approximately $5 – $15] a month, depending on the family income. If a family

has three or more children in a nursery, the third and every further child will be kept free of charge.

8. School education is free of charge in the MPR, as in all socialist countries. All expenses are carried by the state, and they are quite considerable: The education of one child at school for 10 years costs 11 thousand tugrik [approximately $3500]. Thanks to this system of education in our country, Dashnyam was not only able to raise and educate all her children, but also to continue her work with unlimited dedication.

9. As Dashnyam herself said: "Even if I had not continued working and exclusively spent all my time bringing up my children, I could never have provided them with all the things offered by the creche and nursery — the collective spirit and the many-sided harmonious development assured them there."

10. Mothers also receive material aid. After the birth of the fourth and every following child, they receive additional children's allowances up until the time such children are 16 years old. This is apart from the basic monthly children's allowance. Mothers who give birth to four or more children are entitled to retire at the age of 50 years. Mothers of many children also have the right to a stay at a sanatorium or rest home once a year free of charge.

11. As we already mentioned, two of Dashnyam's daughters are students in higher education. Not only is higher education free of charge, as is secondary education, but every student, without exception, receives a scholarship grant, depending on their standards of achievement. The state pays 25,000 to 30,000 tugrik [about $8000 – $10,000] for the higher education of each student in a five-year course.

ADVANTAGES OF A LARGE FAMILY

12. It is a good thing if there are many children in a family, as from their earliest childhood they are accustomed to working. They develop a team spirit; they learn to respect their elders and each other and to feel responsible for other people, not only for themselves.

13. Dashnyam's children all grew up in this way. They are as diligent as their mother. In this family everybody has a precise daily schedule for specific obligations in the household. Tungalagtamir, for example, is the head cook and seamstress of the family, Dashnyam's son Munkhtamir is responsible for keeping the home clean, and so on.

DASHNYAM'S HUSBAND

14. The life, happiness and well-being of any woman and her children depend largely on the husband and father. Deleg, Dashnyam's husband, is a faithful helper and friend of his wife. For the past 25 years he has been actively involved in the upbringing of their children, provid-

ing all conditions for his wife to go about her work without worries. Himself a master in the clothing branch, Deleg is an indispensable assistant, for instance, in drawing up the personal production plans of his wife. They met in 1961 when Deleg, as a young master, was the instructor of a group of girls in the clothes-making industry.

15. "It is not an easy job to have a wife who is a Hero of Labour with many obligations in social life," Deleg said with a smile, "But I try to the best of my ability to assure her of a reliable 'home-front', so to speak. Judging by our children, I think I can say that I managed fairly well. They can all cope with their various obligations."

16. Apart from all other preoccupations, Deleg has another obligation which he took over himself. He is responsible for the "family archive." For 20 years he has collected photos, cuttings from newspapers and magazines about Dashnyam. A large album with her professional biography has been accumulated in this way as a visual example for her children of dedication to her work and for all the things she holds dear in life.

17. This couple is very clearly aware of the outstanding importance of the family in the education of children and the significance of the constant and untiring interest in their activities and, above all, of their own personal example. If children see their parents in a friendly, concerned relationship of respect and mutual assistance towards each other, their relatives, friends and to other people as a whole, if family life is peaceful and calm, they will grow up as friendly and responsive individuals.

DASHNYAM'S VIEWS ON YOUTH

18. When we became acquainted with this friendly family, we were curious to know what Dashnyam felt about youth in general and what were her concerns if any.

19. "Our young people today have excellent qualities: a striving for knowledge and learning. A wonderful generation of young workers is growing up; they can cope with all the tasks confronting them. But unfortunately there are some young people who do not respect the work of workers. They think that they stand above such occupations. In fact, however, they are far below the level of a worker, both in mental and also in physical development. Unfortunately one can quite often find parents who even support such whims in their children; they promote a snobbish, narrowminded attitude of this kind and try to install their offspring in so-called 'clean' work. Undoubtedly this kind of attitude is the cause of the weakening of our magnificent traditional respect for every sort of work and the appreciation of an individual on the basis of work achievements," Dashnyam replied.

HOW DASHNYAM COPES

20. Meeting Dashnyam — a modest Mongolian working woman, in private life mother of many children, loaded with obligations in public life — I wondered from where she derived the inner strength to cope with it all.

21. "Women in our country are active members of society with equal rights today," Dashnyam replied. "They take a fully valid part in socialist construction. They give birth to children, bring them up; they learn, work, look after themselves and carefully uphold their personal dignity. I think that the main thing for a woman is the ability to organise her daily work in the right way. In contrast to professional work, household obligations and the upbringing of children are occupations which keep you busy around the clock. Without a strict schedule, we would simply drown in an overwhelming mass of household work, find no time for our own personal concerns and development. Women in our time are faced with a multitude of preoccupations. They could not manage without endurance, patience and optimism. I believe that without these qualities, a woman could never succeed as a caring mother, an attractive personality, a good housewife, as well as an outstanding worker. And, of course, all our happiness of the present, our dreams of the future for our children, could not be conceivable without the essential precondition of lasting peace in the world and a firm confidence in a peaceful future. That is why we women and mothers should do all we can to ward off the threat of war. Throughout the centuries women were regarded as the main support of the home; this obliges them to say a meaningful word in all matters concerning the peaceful future of our planet."

1756 words

Reading Times
1st reading ____ minutes
3rd reading ____ minutes

Reading Speed
10 minutes = 175 wpm
9 minutes = 195 wpm
8 minutes = 219 wpm
7 minutes = 251 wpm
6 minutes = 293 wpm

1.2
SECOND READING

Go back and read the article again. Take as much time as you need this time. Look up some of the unfamiliar words in the glossary at the end of the book or in your dictionary if you wish.

1.3
THIRD READING

Read the article quickly a third time. Concentrate on understanding the main ideas of the article and the meanings of new vocabulary words in the context in which they appear.

1.4
READER RESPONSE

You, the reader, are part of the reading process. Your ideas and your reactions to what you read are important and valuable because the meaning of the reading depends in part on you and the knowledge and experience that you bring to the reading. In order to explore your response to this reading, take out a pen or pencil and a piece of paper and write for 15 minutes about anything that interested you in this article. You may wish to write about a personal experience this article reminded you of — or you may wish to agree or disagree with something in the article. Try to explore *your own thoughts and feelings* as much as possible. Do *not* merely summarize or restate the ideas in this article. For sample reader responses, turn to page 39. Note: These are authentic writings by real students, and we thank these students for permission to use them.

1.5
RESPONSE SHARING

Read your response to two or three other people in your class. Listen carefully to what the others have written. After you have discussed each other's responses, talk about other points of interest in the article.

1.6
IDENTIFYING MAIN IDEAS

Working with the same small group, make a list of the main ideas in this article. Be sure to state the main ideas in your own words. Don't just copy sentences directly from the text. Think carefully about what the writer is trying to tell you.

> **Example:**
> **Women in the Peoples Republic of Mongolia are able to combine families and work.**

– 1.7
ANALYZING THE TEXT

Work with your group members on this exercise. Discuss the answers carefully, particularly if there are disagreements among members of your group. In some cases, there may be more than one possible interpretation.

1. The writer, Shargal, tells us about Dashnyam because:
   a. Dashnyam has a large family, and her children are generally successful members of society.
   b. Dashnyam is a Hero of Labour of the Mongolian Peoples Republic.
   c. Dashnyam has succeeded in two important roles in Mongolian society: as a mother and as a worker.
2. Shargal wants the reader to see that Dashnyam's success is due to:
   a. her own efforts as a strong, independent woman.
   b. help and support from her husband, Deleg.
   c. help and support from the state.
   d. a combination of the three answers given above.
3. Read paragraph 4 carefully and then write whether these statements are true (*T*) or false (*F*).

   a. __*T*__ Large families are highly valued in the Mongolian Peoples Republic.

   b. _____ Dashnyam is prouder of her daughter who is a teacher than she is of her son who is a driver.

   c. _____ Girls do not have opportunities for education in the Mongolian Peoples Republic.
4. Where is the writer of "One of Many Families" from?

   _____

   Give at least three pieces of evidence to support your answer. (*Hint:* You can find one piece of evidence in paragraph 1.)
5. The writer of "One of Many Families" gives:
   a. a very negative picture of life in the Mongolian Peoples Republic.
   b. a very positive picture of life in the Mongolian Peoples Republic.
   c. a neutral picture of life in the Mongolian Peoples Republic. In other words, she is objective and she mixes praise with criticism.

   Explain your answer and give examples.

1.8
VOCABULARY STUDY

It is important to learn how to figure out word and phrase meanings from the context in which they appear. First, study the italicized words and phrases in their contexts and guess at their meanings. Write your guess in the first blank; then, look up the word or phrase in your dictionary and write the definition in the second blank.

> **Example:**
> **(paragraph 2) Like all children living in villages, she was used to working from an early age. When she was four or five years old, she *was* already *entrusted with* the task of looking after the herds of cattle on the pastures.**
>
> a. (guess) ___was responsible for_____
>
> b. (dictionary) _____

1. (paragraph 1) *Traditionally,* Mongolian families have many children. They have always been regarded as a source of joy and happiness in our country.

   a. (guess) _____

   b. (dictionary) _____

2. (paragraph 7) An extensive network of *creches,* nurseries, schools and other institutions for the education of healthy young people allows the harmonious development of their physical and mental capacities.

   a. (guess) _____

   b. (dictionary) _____

3. (paragraph 10) Mothers also receive *material* aid. After the birth of the fourth and every following child, they receive additional children's allowances up until the time such children are 16 years old. This is apart from the basic monthly children's allowance.

   a. (guess) _____

   b. (dictionary) _____

4. (paragraph 16) Apart from all other preoccupations, Deleg has another obligation which he took over himself. He is responsible for the *"family archive."* For 20 years, he has collected photos, cuttings from newspapers and magazines about Dashnyam. A large album with her professional biography has been accumulated in this way.

   a. (guess) _____

   b. (dictionary) _____

   Note: Look up *archive* and then figure out what a *family archive* would be.

1.9
CLOZE EXERCISE

Choose the correct word for each blank. Discuss your choices with your group.

Dashnyam is _____ a _____ woman in
(1) a an the

_____ the _____ Mongolian Peoples Republic
(2) a an the

_____ who _____ has successfully combined family and work.
(3) who whom that

Dashnyam and _____ husband have seven children,
(4) his her its

all of _____ have turned out very well according to
(5) who whom which

this article. Dashnyam's success _____ been due to
(6) has have had

three main factors: _____ own hard work and dedica-
(7) his her their

tion, help and assistance from _____ state, and
(8) a an the

_____ support of her husband. Dashnyam says that
(9) a an the

women in Mongolian society are _____ members of
(10) active actives

society today.

1.10
APPLICATION, CRITICAL EVALUATION, AND SYNTHESIS

1. Go back to the discussion questions at the beginning of the unit. Using these questions as a guide, compare your society and the Mongolian Peoples Republic on the issues of opportunities for women and child-care arrangements. Discuss both the strong points and the weak points, if any, in both societies.
2. Imagine that you are a government consultant in your country and you are writing a short report recommending changes in your country's childcare system. What are the changes you are recommending? Why are they needed? Who would benefit? Why? Who would pay for the changes? Why? Be sure to explain your recommendations clearly and then give examples to support your recommendations.
3. The writer of "One of Many Families" is from the Mongolian Peoples Republic, a socialist country. How do you think her political views may have affected the content and tone of this article? Why do you think this is so?

2
Day Care: Do We Really Care?

Ruth Sidel, Ph.D., is a professor of sociology at Hunter College of the City University of New York. Dr. Sidel has specialized in studying the roles of women, the care of preschool children, and the provisions of human services by the government in various societies. She has studied childcare policies in Sweden and China as well as in the United States. This excerpt from "Day Care: Do We Really Care?" comes from *Women and Children Last: The Plight of Poor Women in Affluent America* published by Viking Penguin, Inc., in 1986. Reprinted by permission.

2.1
FIRST READING

Read this passage quickly for the main ideas. As you read, pay attention to the title and the opening quote by Pamela Roby. Do *not* stop to look up words in your dictionary.

> Child development advocates stress that what the nation saves by skimping on child care today may seriously harm many individuals and later cost the society much in remedial health, education, penal, welfare, and manpower training bills. . . . The early childhood years comprise one-tenth of humans' lives, and the dignity, respect, and well-being with which persons can live during those years should be of concern to all.
>
> *Pamela Roby*

1. Day care is one of those murky issues on which many Americans do not really know where they stand. Are we for it or against it? Is it good for children or harmful to them? Will it facilitate their social and intellectual development or undermine their emotional well-being? Is it perhaps somewhat "un-American" for a mother to leave her child during the first few years of life? That is what the Russians, the Chinese, and

the Swedes do; is that what we want to do? Why do we seem so very ambivalent about this important topic?

2. Although one child-care specialist has recently stated, "Day care has become as American as apple pie and baseball," the facts do not confirm her optimistic statement. Not only have funds for day care been cut back over the past four years [1982–1986] but, perhaps even more importantly, the rhetoric of the Reagan administration* [1980–1988] and its allies has undermined public perception of the need for day care by nostalgically recalling and mythologizing another era — perhaps the 1950s, more likely the 1920s — and longingly trying to recapture it.

3. In this image of small-town America, we are led to believe that father went to work every morning and returned home every evening to hugs and shouts of joy, that mother had hot cocoa and homemade cookies ready for well-behaved children returning from school, and that in case of an emergency grandmother was down the block, only too glad to help out when needed. Children set up lemonade stands on tree-lined streets, large families gathered for Thanksgiving dinner, and friends of long standing were available to provide mutual aid and support in times of hardship — perhaps a scene out of a Jimmy Stewart movie, with everything working out just fine in the end. There is little evidence that this Norman Rockwell image of America† ever existed except, possibly, for a limited number of middle- and upper-middle-class families; it surely is not the reality of today. But this image, this rhetoric, has been used by an administration that has tried, and succeeded to a remarkable extent, in removing supports from families under the guise that they will be encouraged to return to an idyllic Never-Never Land.

4. Other voices, from other viewpoints, also attack day care. Recent allegations of . . . abuse of children by workers in day-care centers in California and New York have shocked parents, professionals, and the public. These incidents highlight a critical problem that has existed in American society for many years: The flagrant disregard for the well-being of children resulting in the absence of a responsible, coherent child-care policy.

5. First let it be said that thousands of child-care workers across the United States are providing excellent, loving, imaginative care for children, often under extremely difficult circumstances. Reports of various forms of abuse of children in day care centers are, however, not new. Each time such a report surfaces, it is greeted with headlines,

* *The Reagan administration* refers to the years when Ronald Reagan was President of the United States.
† Norman Rockwell was a popular American artist who painted idealized pictures of American families that appeared on the covers of *The Saturday Evening Post* in the 1940s and 1950s.

shocked pronouncements by politicians, and sanctimonious editorials, all of which are forgotten as soon as the headlines fade.

6. Marion Blum, educational director of the Wellesley College Child Study Center, has recently written a powerful critique of day care. She points out that in our extraordinarily materialistic society, children are viewed as things, as commodities around which others can make a profit. She rightly condemns such equipment as cage-like cribs, harnesses and leashes that treat children as though they were animals rather than humans in order to minimize the number of caretakers and to maximize profits. She points out that because of the high turnover of preschool teachers, and the fact that teachers work shifts that may not coincide with the children's hours at the center, children must relate to a variety of adults during their day-care experience. She points out that eight hours or more is a long time for a three- or four-year-old to be away from home and to be required, for the most part, to behave according to preset schedules. She and others have pointed out the difficulties for overworked caregivers trying to maintain proper sanitation, particularly in younger age groups in which the children may not be toilet trained. She points out the higher rates of colds, flu, diarrhea, and even hepatitis A in children who attend day-care centers.

7. Finally, Blum notes that day care has involved a "transfer of roles from one group of exploited women — mothers — to another group of exploited women — day-care staff." Day-care workers are among the lowest paid adult wage earners in our society, with little or no opportunity for advancement, little or no prestige, and very little in the way of benefits. According to the Children's Defense Fund, "Two out of three center-based caregivers earn below poverty level wages and 87 percent of family day-care workers earn below the minimum wage." The status of preschool teachers clearly indicates the lack of value we place on women and children in our society.

8. Why is day care so inadequate in the United States? Why is it so exploitive of children, of day-care workers, of the parents themselves who often have no other choice? Is it because day care is seen as "nonproductive" in a society so geared to materialism and productivity? Is it because it serves the needs of two groups — women and children — who are particularly powerless? Is it because in a system not committed to full employment, decision-makers really do not want women in the labor force possibly taking jobs away from men? Is it because many, particularly people in positions of power, want to maintain the patriarchal family, and day care is seen as a force undermining that power relationship? A brief look at the history of day care in the United States may provide some insights into some of these issues.

9. Part of the hostility, or at best ambivalence, toward day care in this country arises from the fact that it has always been perceived as a service

for the poor. Day care began in the United States in 1854 with the establishment of the Nursery for Children of Poor Women in New York City. This and other early day nurseries, as they were called, were modeled after the French creche, a form of care for the children of working mothers founded in Paris in 1844. The creche, a response to the increased number of French women working in factories, was also used to improve the health of infants and children and to lower the infant mortality rate. Mothers breastfed their infants in the creches and were taught methods of hygienic child care. In 1862 creches received official recognition, and regulations were issued that had to be met in order for the creches to receive government subsidy.

10. Day nurseries in the United States received no such official recognition. Most were sponsored by churches, settlement houses, or voluntary social agencies. Their goals were "to prevent child neglect during a mother's working hours and to eliminate the need to place children of destitute parents in institutions. They served an underprivileged group, handicapped by family problems."

11. The nursery school, on the other hand, evolved out of a middle-class concern that children be given an early childhood educational experience. The first cooperative nursery school in the United States was organized in 1915 by a group of University of Chicago faculty wives in order "to offer an opportunity for wholesome play for their children [and] to give the mothers certain hours of leisure from child care. . . ." A far cry from the goals of the day nurseries — no one talked about hours of leisure for poor women!

12. Nursery schools, influenced by educational pioneers such as Maria Montessori and models such as Robert Owen's infant school in Scotland, were to have an impact on the development of day care; but the two streams remained fundamentally separate. In fact, according to one observer, "In general . . . the day nursery was regarded with a kind of contempt by nursery school people, and the relationship between the two institutions was not always smooth."

13. Day care grew rapidly during the depression of the 1930s when nursery schools were financed by the Federal Emergency Relief Administration and then by the Works Progress Administration (WPA). In 1933 President Roosevelt authorized the establishment of nursery schools to care for "children of needy, unemployed families or neglected, underprivileged homes where preschool age children will benefit from the program offered." All personnel, including teachers, nurses, cooks, clerical workers, and janitors, were to come from relief rolls. By 1937 the centers were serving forty thousand children; this effort is still considered by professionals to have provided excellent care, including health care and nutrition, as well as education.

14. But day care really expanded during World War II, when women now essential to the war effort entered the labor force in large numbers. While the U.S. War Manpower Commission stated in 1942 that "the first responsibility of women, in war as in peace, is to give suitable care in their own homes to their children," the Community Facilities Act (the Lanham Act) passed in June of the same year provided the federal resources necessary to establish day care for the children of working mothers. During this period the federal government spent $51,922,977, matched by $26,008,839 from the states, to fund 3,102 centers that cared for 600,000 children. Though this effort was a significant one, it has been estimated that these centers only served approximately 40 percent of the children in need.

15. World War II was also a time for innovation in day care. The Kaiser Shipbuilding Corporation in Portland, Oregon, for example, opened two centers at the entrance to each shipyard. The Kaiser centers, which were open twelve months a year, twenty-four hours a day, attempted to meet the mothers' needs as well as care for their children. The services provided included shopping for the mothers, mending clothing, caring for children with minor illnesses, and providing "carry-out dinners at low cost to parents who worked long hours." But at the end of the war, when the shipyards closed, the centers closed with them. What this experience indicates, of course, is that when the United States as a society makes day care a priority, it can provide high quality, imaginative services that provide for the needs of children and their parents.

16. Following the war, when women were encouraged to leave their jobs and to return home so that returning veterans could move into existing jobs, the "Lanham centers" were closed in every state but California, where due to the availability of state funds they remained open. In the late 1940s and 1950s, a period noted for its conservatism, particularly its political conservatism, women were encouraged to remain at home and to devote themselves to their children and to homemaking. Moreover, women across the country found themselves increasingly isolated and confined to homogeneous communities by the postwar migration to the suburbs. Hand-in-hand with their geographical isolation was the confinement to home and to the role of mother that stemmed from the wave of popular psychology loosely based on Freudian thinking. Mothers were cautioned that their toddlers would be forever maimed emotionally if they were not toilet trained just right, if separation anxiety got out of hand, or if sibling rivalry was not handled with appropriate sensitivity. The newest version of the domestic code, or the role of supermom, as it was now called, was in its heyday!

17. Nevertheless, the number of working mothers continued to rise. In 1940, 1.5 million mothers were in the labor force; by 1950, there were

4.6 million. By 1959, approximately 7 million mothers were working outside of the home, and there were day-care facilities available for only 2.4 percent of their children. The message was clear: when American society needed women in the labor force, it provided day care for their children; when it wanted women to remain at home, day care was virtually eliminated. . . .

18. Limiting day care to . . . disadvantaged groups, while the middle and upper middle classes are able to purchase care for their children, places the working-class parent in an almost intolerable bind. The working-class mother often can neither qualify for day care nor afford to place her child in a private setting. Since the two-parent working-class family is often just surviving economically, usually because of the wife's income, what are they to do about child care if there is no relative available? . . .

19. Many who learn of the deplorable conditions in some U.S. day-care facilities blame the parents. "How can a mother leave her child in a place like that?" is a common response. Parents must, I believe, bear some of the responsibility for the environment in which their children are cared for when they cannot care for them themselves. Parents must learn what conditions are necessary for their children's healthy development and then demand those conditions. But what are parents to do when adequate care does not exist? What are they to do when adequate care exists but they cannot afford it? Perhaps in an era in which the extended family is rarely a viable, functioning institution — even in the black community, where there is a long tradition of grandmothers caring for grandchildren, the grandmothers today are often in the labor force and unable to help the young working mother; at a time when the traditional nuclear family is frequently not a viable, functioning unit, either; in an era in which communities offer few if any supports, the society must accept the role of monitoring services for children and other dependent groups. Just as we expect the Department of Public Health to monitor conditions in restaurants and health facilities, just as we expect the Board of Education to monitor what goes on in our schools, don't we have the right to expect comparable agencies to monitor the conditions in day-care facilities?

20. As of March 1984, according to the Children's Defense Fund, almost half of all mothers with children under three and almost 52 percent of mothers with children under six were in the labor force. More than 9 million children under six have working mothers, and 67 percent of these mothers work full time. There is grossly insufficient day care for these children; it is estimated, for example, that 7 million children ages thirteen and under may be spending part of each day without adult supervision.

21. Child care is still a two-class system in the United States. Those with adequate income can generally purchase first-rate care for their pre-school children; those without adequate income are left at the mercy of the political and economic forces that determine social policy. While the poor, the near poor, and the working class sometimes have access to good care, more often than not they are faced with long waiting lists, inadequate teacher-child ratios, and a rapid turnover of caregivers.

22. Statistics from the National Center of Education show that 53 percent of children ages three to four whose families had incomes of $25,000 and above attended a preschool program in 1982, while less than 29 percent of children whose families had incomes below $25,000 were in preschool. In addition, approximately half of the three-year-olds and 72 percent of the four-year-olds whose mothers were college graduates were in such programs in 1982. For child care, as for other human services, affordability and accessibility have become key issues.

23. That we still have extremely limited access to child care in the 1980s, twenty years after the War on Poverty and the initiation of Head Start, is particularly shameful since a study has recently been released indicating that a first-rate preschool experience may be of particular value to disadvantaged children. Conducted in Michigan by the High/ Scope Educational Research Foundation, it found that poor black children with low IQs who received preschool education from the age of three "have grown up with markedly greater success in school and in their personal lives than a comparable group without early childhood education. . . ." Following the children from age three through age nineteen, the researchers found that they had better work histories, completed more years of schooling, were involved in less crime, and had fewer teenage pregnancies than a comparable group that did not have early childhood education. Sixty-seven percent of the pre-school education group had graduated from high school by the age of nineteen, compared to 49 percent of the control group.

24. While the preschool education was not inexpensive — the cost adjusted for inflation at 1981 prices was $4,818 per child per year — the long-term savings to the educational system and to society were far greater. But the financial savings is the least important aspect of this project. As Fred Hechinger has stated, "Neglect at an early age has been shown to mean wasted lives, with mounting costs to individuals and society, and the creation of a permanent underclass."

25. There is little doubt that the absence of a high-quality, coherent, comprehensive day-care policy is a key factor in the perpetuation of poverty among women and children. Without access to affordable day care, women with young children are frequently unable to enter the labor force. Without adequate day care, how can a mother receiving AFDC

[Aid for Dependent Children] hope to acquire skills or training necessary to get a decent job? If we are serious about economic equity for women, about stemming the feminization of poverty, and about giving every child a fair chance educationally, emotionally, and economically, one of our first priorities must be accessible, affordable, high-quality day care.

3000 words

Reading Times
1st reading ——— minutes
3rd reading ——— minutes

Reading Speed
20 minutes = 150 wpm
18 minutes = 166 wpm
16 minutes = 187 wpm
14 minutes = 214 wpm
12 minutes = 250 wpm
10 minutes = 300 wpm

2.2
SECOND READING

Go back and read the passage again. Take as much time as you need this time. Look up some of the unfamiliar words in the glossary at the end of the book or in your dictionary if you wish.

2.3
THIRD READING

Read the passage quickly a third time. Concentrate on understanding the main ideas of the passage and the meanings of new vocabulary words in the context in which they appear.

2.4
READER RESPONSE

In order to explore your response to this reading, write for 15 minutes about anything that interested you in this passage. You may wish to write about a personal experience this passage reminded you of — or you may wish to agree or disagree with something in the passage. Try to explore *your own thoughts and feelings* as much as possible. Do *not* merely summarize or restate the ideas in this passage.

2.5
RESPONSE SHARING

Read your response to two or three other people in your class. Listen carefully to what the others have written. After you have discussed each other's responses, talk about other points of interest in the passage.

2.6
IDENTIFYING MAIN IDEAS

Working with the same small group, make a list of the main ideas in this article. Be sure to state the main ideas in your own words. Don't just copy sentences directly from the text. Think carefully about what the writer is trying to tell you.

> **Example:**
> **Day care is generally inadequate in the United States.**

2.7
ANALYZING THE TEXT

Work with your group members on this exercise. Discuss the answers carefully, particularly if there are disagreements among members of your group. In some cases, there may be more than one possible interpretation.

1. Pamela Roby's main point in the introductory quote is that:
   a. there are many ways that the nation could change its childcare policies to save money on childcare.
   b. a big investment by the nation in childcare will eventually save the nation money in social services later on.
   c. childcare is not the responsibility of the government. In fact, the government cannot and should not try to meet childcare needs.

2. According to Sidel, Americans are _____
   _____ day care.
   a. generally in favor of
   b. generally opposed to
   c. unsure about their feelings toward

3. The image of small-town America (paragraph 3), according to Sidel:
   a. never really existed for most Americans.
   b. was used politically by the Reagan administration to remove money from family-support programs.

    c. is accurate and represents the experience of most Americans.
    d. *a, b,* and *c.*
    e. *a* and *b* only.
  4. Write whether these statements are true *(T)* or false *(F)*.

    a. _____ Marion Blum's report on day care in America was very positive.

    b. _____ Day care in the United States has always been seen as a service
       for the poor.

    c. _____ The government encouraged day care during World War II
       because women were needed in the work force.

    d. _____ Working-class parents can easily qualify for day care, but poor
       parents cannot.

    e. _____ According to Sidel, the absence of high-quality, affordable day
       care keeps many women and children in an ongoing state of
       poverty.
  5. In general, Sidel's picture of day care in the United States is:
    a. very positive and optimistic.
    b. neutral — neither positive nor negative.
    c. very negative and highly critical of the government's role in child
       care.
    Explain your answer and give examples.

2.8
VOCABULARY STUDY

Study the italicized words and phrases in their contexts. Guess at their
meanings. Write your guess in the first blank. Then, look up the word or
phrase in your dictionary.

1. (paragraph 1) Day care is one of those *murky* issues on which many
   Americans do not really know where they stand. Are we for it or against
   it? Is it good for children or harmful to them?

   a. (guess) _____

   b. (dictionary) _____

2. (paragraph 7) Finally, Blum notes that day care has involved a "transfer
   of roles from one group of *exploited* women — mothers — to another
   group of *exploited* women — day-care staff." Day-care workers are
   among the lowest paid adult wage earners in our society, with little or no
   opportunity for advancement, little or no prestige, and very little in the
   way of benefits.

　　a. (guess) _____

　　b. (dictionary) _____

3. (paragraph 15) World War II was also a time for *innovation* in day care. The Kaiser Shipbuilding Corporation in Portland, Oregon, for example, opened two centers at the entrance to each shipyard. The Kaiser centers, which were open twelve months a year, twenty-four hours a day, attempted to meet the mothers' needs as well as care for their children. The services provided included shopping for the mothers, mending clothing, caring for children with minor illnesses, and providing "carry-out dinners at low cost to parents who worked long hours."

　　a. (guess) _____

　　b. (dictionary) _____

4. (paragraph 17) In 1940, 1.5 million mothers were in the labor force; by 1950, there were 4.6 million. By 1959, approximately 7 million mothers were working outside of the home, and there were day-care facilities available for only 2.4 percent of their children. The message was clear: when American society needed women in the labor force, it provided day care for their children; when it wanted women to remain at home, day care was *virtually* eliminated.

　　a. (guess) _____

　　b. (dictionary) _____

2.9
CLOZE EXERCISE

Write an appropriate word in each blank. Discuss your word choice with your group. *Note:* In some cases, more than one word may be appropriate, or no word may be needed.

_____ 1949, 31.8 percent of American women worked outside
　　(1)

_____ home. In 1984, 53.5 percent of women _____ work-
　　(2)　　　　　　　　　　　　　　　　　　　　　　　　　(3)

ing outside the home, _____ three out of every five _____
　　　　　　　　　　　　　(4)　　　　　　　　　　　　　　　　(5)

with children were working. _____, it is surprising that
　　　　　　　　　　　　　　　　(6)

_____ United States _____ not have a well-_____
　　(7)　　　　　　　　　　　(8)　　　　　　　　　　　　　　(9)

day-care system to meet the childcare _____ of working parents.
　　　　　　　　　　　　　　　　　　　　　(10)

Ruth Sidel claims this disturbing fact has occurred because Americans are

_____ about day care and also because they have seen day care as a
       (11)

service _____ to the poor.
              (12)

2.10
APPLICATION, CRITICAL EVALUATION AND SYNTHESIS

1. Compare the childcare systems in the Mongolian Peoples Republic and the United States. List the positive and negative features of both. Why do you think the systems are so different? Which system appeals to you more? Do you have questions about either system that are not answered in the text? If so, what are these questions?

2. In the United States, more than half of the women with children work. Why do you think most of these women work? For economic reasons or for professional reasons? Think of people you know to use as examples.

3. Many people in the United States believe that the government should not support day care on a wide scale because they believe that mothers can provide the best care for their children by staying home and taking care of their children in the home. Imagine that you are a government official supporting government-sponsored day care. How would you argue against the above position? Be sure to give reasons and specific examples to support your position in favor of government-supported day care. Use statistics given in this chapter to support your position.

4. The tone of "One of Many Families" and the tone of the excerpt from "Day Care: Do We Really Care?" are very different. How do you explain this difference? Do you think Sidel is too openly critical of the government? Why? Why not? Do you think openness can go too far in a democracy? Please explain your position and give examples.

3
Kramer Versus Kramer

Kramer Versus Kramer is a story about a father, Ted Kramer, who fights his ex-wife, Joanna, to get permanent custody of their five-year-old son, Billy. Ted, a man who was not sure that he even wanted a child when Billy was born, realizes that he cannot live without the boy after taking care of Billy by himself for a year and a half. As this chapter opens, Ted is waiting anxiously by the phone for his lawyer to call him about the judge's decision on custody following a long trial. Ted believes that the trial had gone reasonably well from his point of view — but he realizes that the mother is always in a strong position when the custody of a young child is concerned. *Kramer Versus Kramer,* by Avery Corman, was published by Random House in 1977, and it later became a major motion picture starring Dustin Hoffman and Meryl Streep. Reprinted by permission.

3.1
FIRST READING

Read this chapter quickly to understand the story. Do *not* stop to look up words in your dictionary.

1. He did not permit himself to ever be more than fifteen minutes out of reach by phone. He was also running a switchboard for other people's anxiety. Among the callers, his mother was phoning daily from Florida.
2. "Did you hear yet?"
3. "I'll let you know."
4. "You let me know."
5. "Mother, you're not reducing the tension. Maybe you should call her."
6. "Her? I wouldn't call her. I'll call you."
7. He relived the custody hearing, second-guessed his lawyer's strategy,

critiqued his responses on the witness stand, and in the end, he was satisfied with the presentation of his case.

8. During these days following the hearing, he performed in the manner that had been described in the courtroom, which was the normal conduct of his life. He spent his days at work and his evenings at home with his son. But the hours passed more slowly than any time he had ever known, more slowly than any time of his being unemployed, even more slowly than his first three weeks at Fort Dix when his orders had been misplaced and he remained in the reception center, officially in the Army, but not — time that did not count toward basic training. This was similar, worse — time that did not count toward anything but getting to the judge's decision.

9. A three-day weekend was approaching for Washington's Birthday, and Larry and Ellen offered to open the house on Fire Island. Since there was no water or heat, they would camp out in the house and use sleeping bags. Billy called it "a big adventure," and for Ted it would be a chance to pass a long weekend and get to the next business day, when he would begin to wait again for the lawyer to call.

10. As the time for the trip grew near he was becoming less enthusiastic about spending his nights in an unheated summer cottage by the ocean in the winter, but Billy was very excited, making certain he had fresh batteries for his flashlight so he could see skunks and raccoons outside the house at night, sharpening his plastic scout knife to do battle with wild bears. . . .

11. On Friday, the day before the weekend, his lawyer called.

12. "Ted, it's John."

13. "Yes?"

14. "The decision is in, Ted."

15. "Yes?"

16. "We lost."

17. "Oh, Jesus — "

18. "I can't tell you how sorry I am."

19. "Oh, no."

20. "The judge went for a motherhood ruling straight down the line."

21. "Oh, no. I think my heart is going to break."

22. "I'm upset, too. I'm very sorry, Ted."

23. "How could she win? How?"

24. "She's the mother. Ninety percent of the time, they give it to the mother. It's even higher with little children. I figured this one time, just this time, we could sneak in there."

25. "No!"

26. "It's terrible."

27. "I lost him? I lost him?"

28. "We tried, Ted."

29. "It isn't fair."
30. "I know."
31. "It isn't fair, John!"
32. "Here. Let me read you the decision. It's a very traditional ruling, I'm sorry to say."
33. " 'In the matter of *Kramer v. Kramer,* the petitioner is the natural mother of the child, William, five and a half years of age. The mother in this proceeding is seeking custody of the child from the father, in whose custody the child had been placed one year and a half ago in a prior divorce action. The court is guided by the best interests of the child and rules the best interests of this child, who is of tender age, will be served by his return to the mother.
34. " 'The petitioner now resides in Manhattan and has taken steps to create a suitable home for the child. Prior determination of custody is not considered by the court to be conclusive, *Haskins v. Haskins.** The mother, having experienced stress at the time of the marriage, now shows every sign of being a competent, responsible parent. The father is also deemed a competent, responsible party. As between fit and proper parents, the court must make the best available choice, *Burney v. Burney.** The court rules the best interests of a child this young, *Rolebine v. Rolebine,** dictates a finding for the petitioner.
35. " 'Ordered, adjudged and decreed that the petitioner be awarded care and custody of the minor child, effective Monday the 16th of February. That the respondent pay for the maintenance and support of said child, four hundred dollars each month. That the father shall have the following rights of visitation: Sundays from eleven A.M. to five P.M.; and two weeks during either July or August. No costs.' And that's it, Ted."
36. "That's it? What do I get, Sundays from eleven to five? That's what I get with my boy?"
37. "At least you don't have to pay her court costs."
38. "What's the difference? I lost him. I lost him."
39. "Ted, you'll still be in his life if you want to be. Sometimes the parents fight like hell for custody, and the one who loses doesn't keep up, and never sees the kid that much."
40. "Either way, we become strangers."
41. "Not necessarily."
42. "Monday—it starts Monday. That's right away."
43. "It's not exactly permanent. If conditions should change, you could always bring a petition against her."
44. "Sure."

* Cases involving child custody.

45. "We can also appeal. But you still have to comply. And they usually sustain."
46. "So I just turn him over, right? I just turn him over?"
47. "Ted, I'm so sorry. I honestly believe we gave it our best shot."
48. "My Billy. My little Billy. Oh, Jesus — "
49. "I don't know what else we could have done — "
50. "Terrific. And now the one who's supposed to be unfit to keep him — *I'm* the one who's in charge of telling him. Oh, Jesus — "
51. Ted Kramer left the office for the day, too sick in spirit to work. He went home and rummaged through Billy's room, trying to determine how you managed it. Did you pack up his entire life in boxes? Did you leave pieces behind for when he might come to visit? He tried to plan what he could say to him, how you explained.
52. Ron Willis, serving as an intermediary for Joanna, called after trying to reach Ted in the office. He was courteous on the phone, the party assuming power being gracious to the losing side. He wanted to know if Monday morning at ten would be convenient and if Ted could put together a suitcase or two of Billy's key possessions. They could arrange for any other toys or books later on.
53. Etta returned from food shopping and Ted informed her that Joanna had been awarded custody of the boy. The time she had spent with Billy had been invaluable, he said, and Billy would always have a good foundation from the love she had given him. He had decided to make a request of Joanna that she retain Etta as a housekeeper, and Etta said of course she would be willing to take care of Billy. Then she got busy in the house, putting away food. A little while later he heard her. She was in the bathroom, crying.
54. Billy was to be finished with his school day shortly, and Ted asked Etta to take him to the park for a while. He had unfinished business and he could not bear to see him just now. He began making phone calls to tell people, hoping to reach secretaries, third parties, answering machines, preferring to just leave messages and not have to get into conversations. He thought it would be best to leave the city for the weekend as planned, for Saturday and Sunday anyway. Ted could get away from the phone, and Billy would be deeply disappointed if the adventure were canceled. After he left his messages, spoke to friends, shared their regrets, he called his mother. Dora Kramer did not howl as he expected she might. "Joanna won custody," he told her, and she said quietly, "I was afraid of that."
55. "Will I never see him again?" she asked, and Ted was not clear for the moment how visitation rights worked for grandparents.
56. "I promise you, Mother, you'll see him. If nothing else, on my time."
57. "My poor baby," she said. He was about to answer her with some invented reassurance about Billy, when she said, "What will you do?" and he realized his mother was referring to him.

58. The question of Etta was an immediate concern to Ted. He wanted to get to Joanna before she made plans. If he mailed a special-delivery letter immediately, Joanna would have it in the morning. He did not care to speak to her. There were other things to be communicated about Billy, as well. He could not pin a note to his jacket as though the child were a refugee. He wrote:

> Joanna — This is by way of introducing William Kramer. He is a sweet child, as you will see. He is allergic to grape juice, but will more than make up for the loss in apple juice. He is not, however, allergic to grapes. Don't ask me why. He seems to also be allergic to peanut butter from the health food store, fresh ground, but not the stuff they sell in the supermarket — and don't ask me why. At times, in the night he will be visited by monsters, or one particular monster. It is called The Face. The Face, as best I can determine, looks like a circus clown without a body. . . . His doctor, by the way, is Feinman. His best medicine for colds is Sudafed. His best stories have been Babar and Winnie the Pooh up to now, with Batman moving up. His housekeeper has been Etta Willewska and is a main reason for this note. She is a loving woman, conscientious, very concerned about Billy, experienced, anything you'd want in a housekeeper. Most important, Billy cares for her and is used to her. I hope you don't feel the need to make such a clean slate that you won't consider her. I urge you to retain her. Her number is 555-7306, and I think she will take the job if offered. I'm sure other things will come up. Ask me what you need to and I guess eventually we'll talk. That's all I can think of right now. Try to speak well of me in his presence, and I will try, against my feelings, to do the same for you, since it would be "in the best interests of the child," as they say. Ted.

59. He mailed it special delivery from the post office and then went home to wait for Billy. The boy came into the house, his face rosy from the outdoors. He rushed to Ted — "Daddy, you're home so early," hugging his father around his waist. He could not tell the boy then that he no longer lived there, nor could he tell him at dinner, a last Burger King, or at bedtime, with Billy turning out all the lights to test his "super-powered raccoon-spotting flashlight." Ted delayed through breakfast the next day, and finally, unable to put it off any longer, while waiting for Larry and Ellen to call for them, he made the speech.
60. "Billy, you know your mommy now lives in New York City?"
61. "I know."
62. "Well, sometimes when a mother and a father are divorced, there is a discussion about who the child should live with, the mother or the father. Now, there is a man who is very wise. He's called a judge. And the judge has a lot of experience with divorces and mothers and fathers and children. He decides who it would be best for a child to live with."
63. "Why does he decide?"
64. "Well, that's what he does. He's a very powerful man."

65. "Like a principal?"
66. "Bigger than a principal. The judge sits in robes in a big chair. This judge has thought a lot about us, about you and me and Mommy, and he has decided that it would be best for you if you live with Mommy in her apartment. And I'm very lucky. Because even though you live with Mommy, I'll get to see you every Sunday."
67. And I will, Billy, I promise you. I won't be one of those people Shaunessy talked about.
68. "I don't understand, Daddy."
69. Neither do I.
70. "What part of it don't you understand, honey?"
71. "Where will my bed be, where will I sleep?"
72. "At Mommy's. She'll have a bed for you in your own room."
73. "Where will my toys be?"
74. "We'll send your toys there, and I'm sure you'll get some new ones."
75. "Who will read me my stories?"
76. "Mommy."
77. "Will Mrs. Willewska be there, too?"
78. "Now, that I don't know about. That's still being discussed."
79. "Will you come and say good night to me every night?"
80. "No, Billy, I'll still live here. I'll see you on Sundays."
81. "I'll live in Mommy's house?"
82. "And it will all start this Monday. Your mommy will come for you in the morning and pick you up here."
83. "But we were supposed to go for the weekend! You promised!"
84. "We'll still go. We'll come home a day earlier, that's all."
85. "Oh, that's good."
86. "Yes, that's good."
87. The child took a few minutes to evaluate the information, then he said:
88. "Daddy, does this mean we'll never play monkeys again?"
89. Oh, I don't think I can get through this.
90. "Yes, my honey, we'll play monkeys again. We'll just be Sunday monkeys."
91. On the car ride to Long Island, the grownups worked desperately for a jolly beginning to the weekend, singing "I've Been Working on the Railroad" and other favorites. In the interludes between the forced merriment, Ellen would glance back at Ted and Billy and then turn away, unable to look. Given the slightest break from the songs, everyone above the age of five and a half was solemn. Billy was talking away, fascinated by the off-season life on the island: "Where do the birds go?" "Do children live there?" "Does the ferry crash into the ice like an icebreaker boat?" and then he, too, would fall silent, thinking.

92. "Daddy, I have a secret." And he whispered so the others would not hear. "What if The Face comes when I live at Mommy's?"

93. "Mommy knows about The Face. You and Mommy will tell The Face to beat it."

94. On the ferry ride across, Billy looked out the window, not wanting to miss even a wave in his adventure, and then his interest would drop, apprehensions would take him over again.

95. "Does Mommy know I can't drink grape juice?"

96. "Yes, she knows. She won't give you anything that's not good for you."

97. When they reached the island, Billy converted the empty summer houses into "Ghostland," creating a game which he and Ted played through the morning, searching for ghosts, climbing on and off decks of houses, scaring each other, laughing. Don't make this too wonderful, Ted was thinking.

98. The child's enthusiasm was infectious. After lunch, Larry and Ellen, lightened by the rum the adults had been drinking on this cloudy, cool day, played Ghostland also. Then they all jogged along the beach. After dinner, Billy took his flashlight out to look for small animals, but Ghostland was suddenly legitimate. He lasted outside in the dark for only ten minutes, driven indoors by shadows and night sounds.

99. "Did you see any deer?" Larry asked. "There are deer on the island, you know."

100. "Not in Ocean Bay Park," Ted said. "They won't rent to them."

101. They began to laugh, Billy also, who thought it was very funny.

102. "Can you imagine if the deer shopped in the grocery?" Billy said, a joke by a five-year-old, and on laughter and rum and the long day outside, they all fell asleep in their sleeping bags, chuckling to the end.

103. Sunday, the last day, Ted and Billy bundled up and went down to the beach to build a sandcastle. The beach was empty. They were on an island of their own this one last time. They tossed a ball on the beach, took a walk to the bay and sat on the dock, finally going inside to get away from the raw weather. Ted and Billy played pickup sticks, the boy intent on the game, and then as before, his mind began to drift again. He suddenly turned and looked at his father with lost eyes. Ted Kramer knew that he had to be the daddy now, no matter how deep his own pain, he had to help the boy get through this.

104. "You're going to be fine, Billy. Mommy loves you. And I love you. And you can tell anybody just what it is you want, whatever it is."

105. "Sure, Dad."

106. "You'll be just fine. You're surrounded by people who love you."

107. On the ferry back, no one was laughing any more. For Ted, the pain of their separation was so intense he could hardly breathe.

108. In the city, Larry and Ellen dropped them off at the house. "Hang in, buddy," Larry said to Ted. Then Ellen kissed Billy and told him, "You're welcome to visit us on the island any time. You remember that. We'll look for deer in the grocery."

109. "It will have to be on a Sunday," the boy said, grasping the reality completely.

110. Ted saw that Billy brushed his teeth, got into his pajamas, then he read him a story. He said good night, keeping it cheery. "See you in the morning, Billy." He tried to watch a movie on television, but he was, thankfully, exhausted. And then he took one final look at the boy sleeping. Had he invested too much in the child, he wondered. Perhaps somewhat, he thought. But as he had come to believe, a certain amount of this was inevitable when you were alone with a child. Joanna would find it the same. He decided it was just as it should have been during these many months. He was grateful for this time. It had existed. No one could ever take it away. And he felt he was not the same for it. He believed he had grown because of the child. He had become more loving because of the child, more open because of the child, stronger because of the child, kinder because of the child, and had experienced more of what life had to offer — because of the child. He leaned over and kissed him in his sleep and said, "Goodbye, little boy. Thank you."

3100 words

Reading Times
1st reading ____ minutes
3rd reading ____ minutes

Reading Speed
20 minutes = 155 wpm
18 minutes = 172 wpm
16 minutes = 194 wpm
14 minutes = 221 wpm
12 minutes = 258 wpm
10 minutes = 310 wpm

3.2
SECOND READING

Go back and read the chapter again. Take as much time as you need this time. Look up some of the unfamiliar words in the glossary at the end of the book or in your dictionary if you wish.

3.3
THIRD READING

Read the chapter quickly a third time. Concentrate on understanding the story and the meanings of new vocabulary words in the context in which they appear.

3.4
READER RESPONSE

In order to explore your response to this reading, write for 15 minutes about anything that interested you in this passage. You may wish to write about a personal experience this passage reminded you of — or you may wish to discuss one of the characters. Try to explore *your own thoughts and feelings* as much as possible. Do *not* merely summarize or restate the story line.

3.5
RESPONSE SHARING

Read your response to two or three other people in your class. Listen carefully to what the others have written. After you have discussed each other's responses, talk about other points of interest in the story.

3.6
IDENTIFYING MAIN IDEAS

Working with the same small group, make a list of the main ideas in this article. Be sure to state the main ideas in your own words. Don't just copy sentences directly from the text. Think carefully about what the writer is trying to tell you.

> **Example:**
> **Fathers love their children as much as mothers do.**

3.7
ANALYZING THE STORY

Work with your group members on this exercise. Discuss the answers carefully, particularly if there are disagreements among members of your group. In some cases, there may be more than one possible interpretation.

1. What is the significance of the title *Kramer Versus Kramer?*
   a. Kramer is the name of a family, and this story is about a family.
   b. This is the story of a custody battle, and the case was called *Kramer v.* [versus] *Kramer* in the legal papers.
   c. Ted and Joanna were fighting over the custody of their child, and fights are referred to in this way, for example, "Mike Tyson versus Michael Spinks."
2. Who made this statement? "The judge went for a motherhood ruling straight down the line." (paragraph 20)

   a. Ted Kramer.
   b. The judge.
   c. Ted Kramer's lawyer.
3. What does the statement mean?
   a. The judge's decision was a traditional custody decision favoring the mother.
   b. The judge made up new rules in his decision.
   c. The judge made a highly unusual decision.
4. This statement implies that the judge:
   a. did not think Ted was a good parent.
   b. thought Joanna was a better parent than Ted was.
   c. based his decision on the belief that young children are better off with their mothers than with their fathers.
5. How would you describe Ted's reaction to his lawyer's news?
   a. He was devastated and stunned.
   b. He was disappointed but not surprised.
   c. He was sad but a little relieved.
   Explain your answer.

3.8
VOCABULARY STUDY

Study the italicized words and phrases in their contexts. Guess at their meanings. Write your guess in the first blank. Then, look up the word or phrase in your dictionary and write the definition in the second blank.

1. (paragraph 33) . . . the *petitioner* [in this case] is the natural mother of the child, William, five and a half years of age.

   a. (guess) _____

   b. (dictionary) _____

2. (paragraph 33) The mother in this *proceeding* is seeking custody of the child from the father, in whose custody the child had been placed one year and a half ago in a prior divorce action.

   a. (guess) _____

   b. (dictionary) _____

3. (paragraph 34) The mother, having experienced stress at the time of the marriage, now shows every sign of being a competent, responsible parent. The father is also *deemed* a competent, responsible party.

   a. (guess) _____

   b. (dictionary) _____

4. (paragraph 35) Ordered, adjudged and decreed that the petitioner be awarded care and custody of the minor child, effective Monday the 16th of February. That the *respondent* pay for the maintenance and support of said child, four hundred dollars each month.

   a. (guess) _____

   b. (dictionary) _____

5. (paragraph 45) We can also appeal. But you still have to *comply.* And they usually sustain.

   a. (guess) _____

   b. (dictionary) _____

3.9
CLOZE EXERCISE

Write an appropriate word in each blank. Discuss your word choice with your group. *Note:* In some cases, more than one word may be appropriate, or no word may be needed.

Part of the power _____ *Kramer Versus Kramer* is _____
(1) (2)
it clearly demonstrates the _____ and concern that a _____
(3) (4)
can have for his _____. We are accustomed to _____ mother
(5) (6)
being the primary care-giver _____ the family. In *Kramer Versus*
(7)
Kramer, _____ see a father assuming _____ role of primary
(8) (9)
care-giver. _____ Kramer learns, through trial _____ error,
(10) (11)
to be an exemplary _____. He has to make _____ in his
(12) (13)
professional role _____ succeed in his family _____. He
(14) (15)
willingly makes these sacrifices. _____ is nothing unusual about
(16)
_____ primary care-giver having to _____ these kinds of
(17) (18)
sacrifices. _____ is unusual and therefore dramatic _____
(19) (20)
that in the case of *Kramer Versus Kramer,* the primary care-giver is the father

instead of the mother.

3.10
APPLICATION, CRITICAL EVALUATION, AND SYNTHESIS

1. *Kramer Versus Kramer* is about a father's struggle to gain permanent custody of his young son. Do you believe that fathers can raise children as well as mothers can? Explain and give examples to support your point of view.
2. How do you think Avery Corman, the author of *Kramer Versus Kramer,* feels about Ted Kramer? Look at the last paragraph in the chapter. What do you think Corman is trying to tell you about Ted Kramer? What kind of character has Corman created? Is he an admirable character? Why? Why not? What do you think Corman is trying to tell you about fathers and children?
3. How do you think judges should decide who should receive custody of children? What factors should they consider? Should mothers always be given custody? Why? Why not? Should the children be consulted? At what age? To what extent? Should all of the children always be kept together? Why? Why not?
4. The divorce rate in the United States and in many other countries around the world has increased greatly in the last 30 years. What are some of the factors responsible for this increase? Do you think women's liberation is a factor? Why? Why not? Do you think it is coincidental that many more women are working outside the home now than they were 30 years ago? Could this be tied to the divorce rate? If so, how?
5. You have just read Chapter 19 of *Kramer Versus Kramer.* Chapter 20, the final chapter, ends on a dramatic and surprising note. What do you think happens? Why? You may wish to go to a library and find out by reading this chapter or, better yet, the whole book!

AT THE END OF EVERY UNIT, YOU ARE INVITED TO TURN TO THE EXPANSION SECTION ON PAGE 187. THIS SECTION CONCENTRATES ON THE FUNDAMENTALS OF LIBRARY RESEARCH AND REPORT WRITING.

SAMPLE READER RESPONSE #1 (See Ex. 1.4, page 8)

I think women in the Mongolian People's Republic have a pretty good deal. The society really helps them out a lot by giving them all those benefits. I feel a little envious. I have a couple of kids and let me tell you, it's a hassle. Nobody helps me out. Daycare is so expensive. I'm working two jobs and going to school. I'm separated and my husband - you can forget about him. No help from him. So I think those mothers in Mongolia should be thankful for all the help they get. Don't get me wrong - this is a great country but women don't count for much here. That's the way I feel.

SAMPLE READER RESPONSE #2

When I was reading this article, I was thinking, "This is too good to be true." It might be true to a certain extent, but I'm sure it's not the complete picture. In socialist countries, a lot of times writers don't give you the whole picture. They can't because the government won't let them. The government just wants the good things reported, so I don't believe all of this. There's another part that we aren't told about. How here in the U.S., writers can write just about anything. They don't just give you the rosy picture. They tell you the dirt too maybe even too much. But anyway it's better if you know the whole truth, I don't think this article is the whole truth. It's just a part of the truth — so I don't really buy it.

Unit 2
Technology and Ethics

DISCUSSION

In the twentieth century, in particular, there have been many advances in technology. Scientists have sent people out into space and even to the moon. Television, cars, and computers have changed our lives profoundly. New medicines and medical treatments have offered hope and even life itself to severely ill people. We have come a long way because of technology. Yet the great possibilities of technology have created equally troubling problems involving ethics. More and more, these questions are being asked: Is everything that is technologically possible desirable from an ethical point of view? Should there be ethical limits to technological development? If so, how do we decide where to draw the ethical lines? And who should decide? Before you begin reading, think about the following questions and discuss your answers.

1. What does *technology* mean to you?
2. Give an example of technology that you think has been particularly good for people in this century. In what specific ways has this technological development changed people's lives for the better?
3. Give an example of technological development that has been bad, or at least not entirely good, for people. In what specific ways has this techno-logical development changed people's lives for the worse?
4. It is now technologically possible to produce children in new ways, e.g., test-tube fertilization, artificial insemination either inside or outside the womb. The new reproductive technology has raised some questions about how we should define familiar terms like *father* and *mother*. How would you define *father* and *mother*? Have you heard of "surrogate

mothers?" Do you think the surrogate mothers should have any rights to the children they bear for other people?

5. Do you see anything wrong, or objectionable, in a woman agreeing to bear a child for an infertile couple for a certain sum of money? Do you think that ethics come into conflict with reproductive technology in such cases? Why? Why not? Should there be laws concerning surrogate parenting? Why? Why not?

Mary Beth Whitehead and "Baby M"

1
Who Keeps "Baby M"?

The "Baby M" case brought up all kinds of new and deeply troubling questions concerning parents, children, and families in the age of technology. "Who Keeps 'Baby M'?" appeared in *Newsweek* in January, 1987, and in this article, the authors discuss some of the perplexing problems created by new means of reproduction. The "Baby M" case received enormous attention in newspapers, magazines, and on television and radio. It raised questions of how we define parents and the rights of parents. And, more troubling perhaps, it raised the question of how we are going to define *mother*, — certainly one of the most basic words in any language — in an age of technology. "Who Keeps 'Baby M'?" was written when the baby's biological mother and father went to court to fight each other for the child's custody. Judge Harvey R. Sorkow made his decision on this case several months after this article appeared. His decision — and the decision of a higher court in 1988 — will be presented later in this unit. Reprinted by permission.

1.1
FIRST READING

Read this article quickly for the main ideas. Pay attention to the title and the text headings as you read. Do *not* stop to look up words in your dictionary.

A SURROGATE MOTHER FIGHTS FOR CUSTODY OF A CHILD—AND THE CASE RAISES NEW ETHICAL ISSUES

1. *The mother.* She already had a son and a daughter when she agreed to carry a stranger's child and give it to him as soon as it was born. She called it "the most loving gift of happiness," but she also saw the practical side; her $10,000 fee would help subsidize her older children's education. But as the baby grew inside her, she began to have doubts. When the little girl was born, the mother realized she had made a terrible mistake. She wanted to keep her child.

2. *The father.* He is a 40-year-old biochemist, married for 12 years to a pediatrician. He still remembers the night that he came home from a business trip and found the exultant message his wife had scrawled in shaving cream on the bathroom mirror: "She's pregnant." They had been waiting years for a child. Maybe this time. Maybe.

3. *The baby.* She is the reason for the heartache. Nine months old now [January 1987]—blond, blue-eyed, a perfect little girl. The public gets only occasional glimpses of her; photographers snap a few furtive shots as she is shuttled between parents for regularly scheduled visits. The court has given her the pseudonym Baby M in a futile attempt to protect her privacy. Her mother calls her Sara. Her father calls her Melissa. Someday soon, she will probably speak her first words. *Mama. Dada.* Who will answer?

4. The parents have turned to the courts to resolve their battle over Baby M. In a few months a judge will decide who will keep the child. But there is more at stake here than a custody fight. The drama being played out in room 217 of the Bergen County Courthouse in Hackensack, New Jersey, has captured national attention because it tests the adaptability of the law to radical social change and challenges traditional definitions of parenthood.

5. [In 1985] Mary Beth Whitehead, a 29-year-old homemaker from Brick Town, New Jersey, signed a contract to bear a child for Elizabeth and William Stern in exchange for money. It was strictly business, a transaction undertaken by hundreds of women who have become surrogate mothers in the past decade. But the six-page document that Whitehead and William Stern signed placed them in a gray area of the law; although the practice of surrogate motherhood has grown dramatically in the past few years, it is still so new that no states have yet enacted regulations making it legal. But it isn't exactly illegal, either. Laws that might apply to surrogate-motherhood arrangements are usually meant to cover other situations—such as outright baby selling. Surrogate agencies claim they are selling a woman's services, not the baby. . . .

6. *Controversy will continue:* No matter what the decision in the Baby M trial, the controversy will not end. . . . The trial, which began last week [January 1987], provides a compelling forum for the ongoing debate about surrogate motherhood as well as other new forms of reproductive technology. "This case really crystallizes the issues," says Nadine Taub, a professor at Rutgers Law School who has studied the case.

7. Baby M doesn't only raise legal questions. There are complex ethical issues in this case as well. Should women be encouraged to conceive children they will never raise? Are they really mothers—or manufacturers of a product? If conceiving and bearing a child doesn't make a woman its mother, then what does? One surrogate mother who used to

be a strong advocate of the arrangement says she has changed her mind. "All you're doing is transferring the pain from one woman to another, from a woman who is in pain from her infertility to a woman who has to give up her baby," says the Pekin, Illinois, housewife who uses the pseudonym Elizabeth Kane.

8. *Moral nightmare.* Critics say that surrogate motherhood is just the first step toward a virtual revolution in methods of conception — and the end result may be a legal and moral nightmare. It is now possible to implant a fertilized embryo in the womb of a woman who has not supplied the egg for it. Barbara Katz Rothman, author of "The Tentative Pregnancy," thinks that this technique, in particular, makes it possible to create a class of "breeder women," probably poor women, who would rent their wombs to wealthier people. Rothman thinks that the growing public acceptance of surrogacy is the result of clever "marketing," including the use of the term surrogate motherhood to represent the biological mother. Says Rothman: "A mother is a mother is a mother. . . . These are surrogate wives, not surrogate mothers. He is hiring himself an extra wife."

9. Surrogate motherhood is not new. Even the Bible offers an example: when Sarah was unable to give her husband, Abraham, a child, she told him to visit her handmaiden Hagar. The process has been refined since then. With artificial insemination, the mother and father don't even have to meet. The procedure takes some of the moral stigma out of the process — although surrogate motherhood is condemned by some religious groups, including Roman Catholics and Orthodox Jews. . . .

10. *Desperate need:* There aren't enough women willing to be surrogates to satisfy the demand for them, and the cost to the couple — $25,000 or more — makes their services available only to well-off couples. Robert Coreas, a 35-year-old electronics technician from San Jose, California, and his wife, Amalas, 38, a nurse, have been trying to save the money from their combined income of $40,000. "It's an expensive purchase," says Coreas. The shortage of healthy, white infants available for adoption only enhances the appeal of surrogate mothers. In the past decade around a dozen agencies that match surrogates and couples have sprung up around the country. The surrogates say they are responding to a desperate need for babies; approximately one out of every six couples is infertile. Becky McKnight, a 35-year-old Los Angeles mother of three, decided to become a surrogate four years ago when she was working for three obstetricians who specialize in infertility. "I saw the disappointment and the anguish that accompanies infertility," she recalls. "It was so unfair, and surrogate parenting seems to me a marvelous alternative to all the other options that were available to infertile couples." She delivered a baby girl by Caesarean section. . . .

11. In a 1983 study of 125 surrogate candidates, Michigan psychiatrist

Philip J. Parker described [the typical surrogate] — a 25-year-old Christian married woman with at least one child and a high-school education, a woman like Mary Beth Whitehead.

12. "If you asked me to give you a profile of a perfect surrogate, I would give you Mary Beth Whitehead," says Noel Keane, the lawyer who arranged the Whitehead-Stern contract at his New York office. Whitehead's application for the job, filled out [in 1984], is poignantly naive in retrospect.

13. "Having an infertile sister," she wrote, "I understand the feeling of a childless couple. I feel giving the gift of a child would be more rewarding than working at a conventional job." Keane's application form also asked if Whitehead anticipated any emotional difficulties handling the surrogate-mother procedure. "I have been blessed with two happy, healthy children and a loving husband," she wrote. "I am content with my life and would not have any emotional problems."

14. The Sterns, too, fit the profile of couples who choose surrogacy. They were both in their late 30s — too old to be acceptable to most adoption agencies, which prefer couples under 35. They were well educated; both have graduate degrees. Although they wanted children very much, they felt that a pregnancy was medically risky for Elizabeth Stern. She has been diagnosed as having a mild form of multiple sclerosis, and she and her husband worried that pregnancy would aggravate the disease and leave her paralyzed. William Stern wanted a child that was his own flesh and blood because he had lost most of his family in the Holocaust.

15. *Two homes:* In January 1985 Whitehead and her husband, Richard, 37, met the Sterns for dinner in New Brunswick, New Jersey, about halfway between their two homes. The Sterns told the Whiteheads that pregnancy would endanger Elizabeth Stern's life. Mary Beth Whitehead, William Stern recalls, "said she had no intention of showing up on our doorstep after the baby was born," though she said she hoped that when the child was 18, she could meet it. "Before we left the restaurant," Stern recalls, "we agreed Mary Beth would be our surrogate."

16. The couples signed a contract negotiated by Keane on Feb. 6, 1985. Stern and the Whiteheads agreed that for $10,000 plus more than $10,000 in fees and expenses, Mary Beth Whitehead would be inseminated with William Stern's sperm. The $10,000 fee was to go into an escrow account until he got custody. The contract also stipulated that Stern would assume all legal responsibilities for the baby, even if it was born with serious defects. Whitehead was required to undergo amniocentesis; if the results showed problems, she agreed to have an abortion if Stern insisted. The Whiteheads would give the baby to the Sterns.

Mary Beth Whitehead acknowledged that the child would be conceived "for the sole purpose of giving said child to William Stern."

17. That day the first artificial insemination was conducted at a New York sperm bank. It was unsuccessful. After that a regular routine developed. Several times a month Stern and Whitehead drove together from New Jersey into New York for insemination. Sometimes Elizabeth Stern went with them. On July 2 Whitehead conceived. . . . When Stern found out [a month later], he turned to a stranger . . . and announced proudly, "I'm going to be a father."

18. That was one of the high points of the relationship between the Sterns and the Whiteheads, as it is with many surrogate arrangements. . . . [However], the two families had a good relationship during the course of the pregnancy. "When I talked to Mary Beth, it was like talking to my sister," Elizabeth Stern recalls. They were an unlikely pair — the quiet, self-contained pediatrician and the housewife who had dropped out of high school at 16 to marry a 22-year-old she met in the luncheonette where she worked. During the years when the Sterns were struggling through graduate school and beginning their scientific careers, the Whiteheads were barely getting by with two small children — Tuesday, now 10 [in 1987], and Ryan, 12. There were rough times. In 1978 Mary Beth Whitehead was on welfare for a while. Her husband, who now works as a garbage collector, was arrested for marijuana possession 14 years ago and acknowledges that he is an alcoholic; he says, however, that he has had his problem under control for eight months.

19. *Turning point:* The differences in the two couples' backgrounds and personal styles seemed insignificant in the beginning, but as the baby's due date approached, conflicts began to surface. Mary Beth Whitehead says she felt that Elizabeth Stern was trying to take over her life. When Stern insisted that Whitehead go ahead with amniocentesis against her obstetrician's advice, Whitehead retaliated by not telling the Sterns the sex of the baby. Richard Whitehead was also beginning to have doubts about the arrangement. He says he was troubled by "the thought of taking $10,000 for Ryan and Tuesday by selling their sister." Mary Beth Whitehead says that her first moments alone with her child after the March 27 birth were intensely emotional. "Seeing her, holding her. She was my child," Whitehead recalls. "It overpowered me. I had no control. I had to keep her."

20. That was the turning point, Whitehead says. The real struggle was ahead. At first Whitehead gave the child to the Sterns. But her first night without the baby was agony. The next morning she called the Sterns and pleaded with them to let her have her for just a week. When the week ended, she didn't want to give the baby back. She had a plan.

Would the Sterns agree to let her have the child one weekend a month and two weeks during the summer? They insisted that Whitehead stick to the original agreement and went to court to enforce it. The money was still in the escrow account. On May 5 the Sterns were awarded temporary custody by a Bergen County [New Jersey] Family Court judge. The next day the Whiteheads fled to Florida with the baby.

21. The Sterns spent more than $20,000 on a private investigator who found the Whiteheads three months later at Mary Beth's mother's home in Holiday, Florida. Tuesday Whitehead was at home the day the FBI and the private investigator came to take the baby away. "I heard a strange man's voice," she recalls. "I ran out of the bathroom to see what was going on. There were three men in the hallway in front of my sister's room. They saw the crib immediately, grabbed my sister and ran out the front door. I screamed and said, 'No.' I beat the back of a man who was holding the door with my hairbrush. They did not look back."

22. *Daily routine:* The Sterns sued and regained custody of the little girl they called Melissa. Every morning now William Stern gets up at 5 a.m. to feed the baby. Then he showers while she plays in her playpen. Before he leaves for work, he wakes up his wife, who stays with the baby for the rest of the day. Mary Beth Whitehead visits the baby at a county office building for two hours twice a week.

23. The trial is expected to take weeks, maybe months. In the end Judge Harvey R. Sorkow will decide whether the contract the two couples signed was valid. If he finds that it is not, he must decide which couple will get custody. A preliminary court investigation has already found that both couples would make "more than adequate parents." No matter which way the decision goes, both sides have pledged to appeal. They are already facing more than $250,000 each in legal bills. But then, who would put a price on the life of a child?

2330 words

Reading Times	Reading Speed
1st reading ___ minutes	15 minutes = 155 wpm
3rd reading ___ minutes	13 minutes = 179 wpm
	11 minutes = 212 wpm
	9 minutes = 259 wpm
	7 minutes = 333 wpm

1.2
SECOND READING

Go back and read the selection again. Take as much time as you need this time. Look up some of the unfamiliar words in the glossary at the end of the book or in your dictionary if you wish.

1.3
THIRD READING

Read the selection quickly a third time. Concentrate on understanding the main ideas of the selection and the meanings of new vocabulary words in the context in which they appear.

1.4
READER RESPONSE

In order to explore your response to this reading, write for 15 minutes about anything that interested you in this selection. You may wish to write about your feelings about the Baby M case — or you may wish to disagree with something in the article. Try to explore *your own thoughts and feelings* as much as possible. Do *not* merely summarize or restate the ideas in this article.

1.5
RESPONSE SHARING

Read your response to two or three other people in your class. Listen carefully to what the others have written. After you have discussed each other's responses, talk about other points of interest in the article.

1.6
IDENTIFYING MAIN IDEAS

Working with the same small group, make a list of the main ideas in this article. Be sure to state the main ideas in your own words. Don't just copy sentences directly from the text. Think carefully about what the writer is trying to tell you.

1.7
ANALYZING THE TEXT

Work with your group members on this exercise. Discuss the answers carefully, particularly if there are disagreements among members of your group. In some cases, there may be more than one possible interpretation.

1. The Baby M case is important and, consequently, received a lot of media attention because it:
   a. shows how a child's life can be disrupted as a result of a bitter custody fight.
   b. illustrates the ethical and legal questions involved in the new reproductive technology.

    c. shows how surrogate parenting can work successfully to the benefit of all concerned.

2. Barbara Katz Rothman (paragraph 8), author of "The Tentative Pregnancy," is obviously:
    a. critical of the new reproductive technology.
    b. in favor of the new reproductive technology.
    c. neutral on the subject.
Look back at paragraph 8 and give specific examples to explain your answer.

3. The "turning point" in Mary Beth Whitehead's feelings about the child and her subsequent decision to try to keep the child occurred:
    a. when she signed the contract to bear a child for William Stern.
    b. when she became pregnant with Baby M.
    c. immediately after she gave birth to Baby M.
Explain your answer.

4. It is implied in this article that Mary Beth Whitehead:
    a. truly intended to honor the contract she signed with the Sterns at the time that she signed the contract.
    b. never intended to honor the contract that she signed with the Sterns.
    c. was more interested in keeping the $10,000 than in keeping the baby after Baby M was born.
Explain your answer.

5. The writers of "Who Keeps 'Baby M'?":
    a. give a more sympathetic picture of Mary Beth Whitehead than they do of the Sterns.
    b. give a more sympathetic picture of the Sterns than they do of Mary Beth Whitehead.
    c. try to give a fair and impartial picture of both Mary Beth Whitehead and the Sterns.
Explain your answer and give examples.

1.8
VOCABULARY STUDY

Study the italicized words and phrases in their contexts and guess at their meanings. Write your guess in the first blank. Then, look up the word or phrase in your dictionary and write the definition in the second blank.

1. (paragraph 2) The father. . . . He still remembers the night that he came home from a business trip and found the *exultant* message his wife had scrawled in shaving cream on the bathroom mirror: "She's pregnant."

a. (guess) _____

b. (dictionary) _____

2. (paragraph 3) The court has given [the baby] the *pseudonym* Baby M in a futile attempt to protect her privacy. Her mother calls her Sara. Her father calls her Melissa.

a. (guess) _____

b. (dictionary) _____

3. (paragraph 5) [In 1985] Mary Beth Whitehead . . . signed a contract to bear a child for Elizabeth and William Stern in exchange for money. It was strictly business, a transaction undertaken by hundreds of women who have become *surrogate* mothers in the past decade.

a. (guess) _____

b. (dictionary) _____

4. (paragraph 9) With artificial insemination, the mother and father don't even have to meet. The procedure takes some of the moral *stigma* out of the process — although surrogate motherhood is condemned by some religious groups, including Roman Catholics and Orthodox Jews.

a. (guess) _____

b. (dictionary) _____

5. (paragraphs 12 and 13) Whitehead's application for the job, filled out [in 1984], is *poignantly naïve* in retrospect. "Having an infertile sister," she wrote, "I understand the feeling of a childless couple. I feel giving the gift of a child would be more rewarding than working at a conventional job."

a. (guess) _____

b. (dictionary) _____

1.9
CLOZE EXERCISE

Write an appropriate word in each blank. Discuss your word choice with your group. *Note:* In some cases, more than one word may be appropriate, or no word may be needed.

The Baby M case _____ a sensation, not because two parents
                        (1)

_____ fighting   over   custody   of   their   _____
      (2)   (3)

— unfortunately, that happens all the time _____ this day and age
(4)
— but because the _____ was asked to look at _____ validity
(5) (6)
_____ surrogate motherhood. The court was being _____ to
(7) (8)
decide who the parents _____ and what their rights were.
(9)
_____ was even being asked to define _____ term *parent.*
(10) (11)
The Baby M case _____ us how complicated — and _____
(12) (13)
painful and varied — the results _____ modern technology can be.
(14)
The Baby M _____ calls into question some of our deepest values.
(15)
Where _____ we draw the line in technology? _____ will
(16) (17)
protect us from our ingenuity?

1.10
APPLICATION, CRITICAL EVALUATION, AND SYNTHESIS

1. The new reproductive technology allows infertile couples to have children if they can afford to pay for the expensive procedures. Some people object strongly because the technology is expensive and, therefore, it is limited to people with money. How do you feel about this issue? Why? Please explain and give examples.

2. One of the dangers of surrogate motherhood, according to people who oppose it, is that it could lead to the development of a "breeder class" of women — a group of women, most of them poor, who would be paid to bear children for the rich. This is a severe form of exploitation of women, again according to the critics of surrogate motherhood. How real do you think this danger is? How many women do you think would go into the business of bearing children for rich people? Do you find this concept objectionable? Why? Why not?

3. How is surrogate parenting similar to adoption? How is it different? Do you think it raises more — or fewer — ethical questions than adoption? Can the mother change her mind in the case of adoption? Up until what point? How does this differ from the case of a surrogate mother such as Mary Beth Whitehead?

4. Do you think that Mary Beth Whitehead had the right to change her mind about giving up Baby M — or do you think she should have been bound by the contract she signed? Do you think that Whitehead should

have to give up all parental rights (such as visitation) — as she agreed to do in the contract?

5. What do you think the judge's decision was in this case? Do you think he ruled in favor of Whitehead or the Sterns? Why? What would you have done if you had been the judge? Why? Give specific reasons and examples.

The U.S. Supreme Court may eventually rule on the validity of surrogacy.

2
The Opinion of the New Jersey Supreme Court

After a 32-day trial, Judge Harvey R. Sorkow ruled that the contract between Mary Beth Whitehead and the Sterns was valid. This meant that Whitehead had to give up all parental rights to Baby M, including visitation. Furthermore, Judge Sorkow allowed Elizabeth Stern to adopt Baby M. Whitehead's lawyer immediately appealed the decision, and the case went to the New Jersey Supreme Court, the highest court in that state. The case was heard by seven justices, and they came to a unanimous agreement. Excerpts from their opinion follow. This opinion was written by Chief Justice Robert N. Wilentz. It was dated February 3, 1988, and it was immediately considered a landmark opinion because it dealt forcefully with important issues in the new reproductive technology.

2.1
FIRST READING

Read this court opinion quickly for the main ideas. Think about (1) what the judges decided, and (2) why they made these decisions. In particular, what does the decision say about surrogate motherhood? Does it make it legal or illegal? In what situations? Do not worry about understanding every word or detail.

1. *Wilentz, C. J.* — In this matter the Court is asked to determine the validity of a contract that purports to provide a new way of bringing children into a family. For a fee of $10,000, a woman agrees to be artificially inseminated with the semen of another woman's husband; she is to conceive a child, carry it to term, and after its birth surrender it to the natural father and his wife. The intent of the contract is that the child's natural mother will thereafter be forever separated from her child. The wife is to adopt the child, and she and the natural father are to be regarded as its parents for all purposes. The contract providing

for this is called a "surrogacy contract," the natural mother inappropriately called the "surrogate mother."

2. We invalidate the surrogacy contract because it conflicts with the law and public policy of this State. While we recognize the depth of the yearning of infertile couples to have their own children, we find the payment of money to a "surrogate" mother illegal, perhaps criminal, and potentially degrading to women. Although in this case we grant custody to the natural father, the evidence having clearly proved such custody to be in the best interests of the infant, we void both the termination of the surrogate mother's parental rights and the adoption of the child by the wife/stepparent. We thus restore the "surrogate" as the mother of the child. We remand the issue of the natural mother's visitation rights to the trial court, since that issue was not reached below and the record before us is not sufficient to permit us to decide it *de novo.*

3. We find no offense to our present laws where a woman voluntarily and without payment agrees to act as a "surrogate" mother, provided that she is not subject to a binding agreement to surrender her child. . . .

INVALIDITY AND UNENFORCEABILITY OF SURROGACY CONTRACT

4. We have concluded that this surrogacy contract is invalid. Our conclusion has two bases: direct conflict with existing statutes and conflict with the public policies of this State, as expressed in its statutory and decisional law.

5. One of the surrogacy contract's basic purposes, to achieve the adoption of a child through private placement, though permitted in New Jersey "is very much disfavored." *Sees v. Baber,* 74 N.J. 201, 217 (1977)*. Its use of money for this purpose — and we have no doubt whatsoever that the money is being paid to obtain an adoption and not, as the Sterns argue, for the personal services of Mary Beth Whitehead — is illegal and perhaps criminal. *N.J.S.A. 9:3-54.* In addition to the inducement of money, there is the coercion of contract: the natural mother's irrevocable agreement, prior to birth, even prior to conception, to surrender the child to the adoptive couple. Such an agreement is totally unenforceable in private placement adoption. *Sees,* 74 N.J. at 212–14.* Even where the adoption is through an approved agency, the formal agreement to surrender occurs only *after* birth . . . and then, by regulation, only after the birth mother has been counseled. . . .

6. Under the contract, the natural mother is irrevocably committed before she knows the strength of her bond with her child. She never makes

---

* These are legal citations. They refer to specific legal cases. Legal decisions are always based upon previous cases.

a totally voluntary, informed decision, for quite clearly any decision prior to the baby's birth is, in the most important sense, uninformed. . . . Her interests are of little concern to those who controlled this transaction.

7. Although the interest of the natural father and adoptive mother is certainly the predominant interest, realistically the *only* interest served, even they are left with less than what public policy requires. They know little about the natural mother, her genetic makeup, and her psychological and medical history. Moreover, not even a superficial attempt is made to determine their awareness of their responsibilities as parents.

8. Worst of all, however, is the contract's total disregard of the best interests of the child. There is not the slightest suggestion that any inquiry will be made at any time to determine the fitness of the Sterns as custodial parents, of Mrs. Stern as an adoptive parent, their superiority to Mrs. Whitehead, or the effect on the child of not living with her natural mother.

9. This is the sale of a child, or, at the very least, the sale of a mother's right to her child, the only mitigating factor being that one of the purchasers is the father. Almost every evil that prompted the prohibition of the payment of money in connection with adoptions exists here.

10. The long-term effects of surrogacy contracts are not known, but feared — the impact on the child who learns her life was bought, that she is the offspring of someone who gave birth to her only to obtain money; the impact on the natural mother as the full weight of her isolation is felt along with the full reality of the sale of her body and her child; the impact on the natural father and adoptive mother once they realize the consequences of their conduct. . . .

11. The surrogacy contract creates, it is based upon, principles that are directly contrary to the objectives of our laws. It guarantees the separation of a child from its mother; it looks to adoption regardless of suitability; it totally ignores the child; it takes the child from the mother regardless of her wishes and her maternal fitness; and it does all of this, it accomplishes all of its goals, through the use of money.

12. Beyond that is the potential degradation of some women that may result from this arrangement. In many cases, of course, surrogacy may bring satisfaction, not only to the infertile couple, but to the surrogate mother herself. The fact, however, that many women may not perceive surrogacy negatively but rather see it as an opportunity does not diminish its potential for devastation to other women.

CUSTODY

13. Having decided that the surrogacy contract is illegal, and unenforceable, we now must decide the custody question. . . . Our custody

conclusion is based on strongly persuasive testimony contrasting both the family life of the Whiteheads and the Sterns and the personalities and characters of the individuals. The stability of the Whitehead family life was doubtful at the time of trial. Their finances were in serious trouble. . . . Mr. Whitehead's employment, though relatively steady, was always at risk because of his alcoholism, a condition that he seems not to have been able to confront effectively. Mrs. Whitehead had not worked for quite some time, her last two employments having been part-time. One of the Whiteheads' positive attributes was their ability to bring up two children, and apparently well, even in so vulnerable a household. Yet substantial question was raised even about that aspect of their home life. . . .

14. The Sterns have no other children, but all indications are that their household and their personalities promise a much more likely foundation for Melissa to grow and thrive. There is a track record of sorts — during the one-and-a-half years of custody Baby M has done very well, and the relationship between both Mr. and Mrs. Stern and the baby has become very strong. The household is stable, and likely to remain so. Their finances are more than adequate, their circle of friends supportive, and their marriage happy. Most important, they are loving, giving, nurturing, and open-minded people. They have demonstrated the wish and ability to nurture and protect Melissa. . . . All in all, Melissa's future appears solid, happy, and promising with them.

15. Based on all of this we have concluded, independent of the trial court's identical conclusion, that Melissa's best interests call for custody in the Sterns. . . .

VISITATION

16. We have decided that Mrs. Whitehead is entitled to visitation. . . . The trial court will determine what kind of visitation shall be granted to her, with or without conditions, and when and under what circumstances it should commence.

CONCLUSION

17. This case affords some insight into a new reproductive arrangement: the artificial insemination of a surrogate mother. The unfortunate events that have unfolded illustrate that its unregulated use can bring suffering to all involved. Potential victims include the surrogate mother and her family, the natural father and his wife, and most importantly, the child. Although surrogacy has apparently provided positive results for some infertile couples, it can also, as this case demonstrates, cause suffering to participants, here essentially innocent and well-intended.

18. We have found that our present laws do not permit the surrogacy contract used in this case. Nowhere, however, do we find any legal prohibition against surrogacy when the surrogate mother volunteers, without any payment, to act as a surrogate and is given the right to change her mind and to assert her parental rights. Moreover, the Legislature remains free to deal with this most sensitive issue as it sees fit, subject only to constitutional constraints.

19. If the Legislature decides to address surrogacy, consideration of this case will highlight many of its potential harms. We do not underestimate the difficulties of legislating on this subject. In addition to the inevitable confrontation with the ethical and moral issues involved, there is the question of the wisdom and effectiveness of regulating a matter so private, yet of such public interest. Legislative consideration of surrogacy may also provide the opportunity to begin to focus on the overall implications of the new reproductive biotechnology — *in vitro* fertilization, preservation of sperm and eggs, embryo implantation and the like. The problem is how to enjoy the benefits of the technology — especially for infertile couples — while minimizing the risk of abuse. The problem can be addressed only when society decides what its values and objectives are in this troubling, yet promising, area.

1593 words

Reading Times	Reading Speed
1st reading _____ minutes	15 minutes = 106 wpm
3rd reading _____ minutes	13 minutes = 123 wpm
	11 minutes = 145 wpm
	9 minutes = 177 wpm
	7 minutes = 228 wpm

2.2
SECOND READING

Go back and read this opinion again. Take as much time as you need this time. Look up some of the unfamiliar words in the glossary at the end of the book or in your dictionary if you wish.

2.3
THIRD READING

Read the passage quickly a third time. Concentrate on understanding the main points of the opinion: the invalidity of the contract and why it is invalid, who gets custody and why, the dangers of surrogacy and why, when surrogacy is permissible and why. Since this legal opinion may be difficult for you to understand, do not hesitate to read it over a fourth and even a fifth time.

2.4
READER RESPONSE

In order to explore your response to this reading, write for 15 minutes about anything that interested you in this passage. You may wish to write about a point that you strongly agreed — or disagreed — with. Try to explore *your own thoughts and feelings* as much as possible. Do *not* merely summarize or restate the ideas in this passage.

2.5
RESPONSE SHARING

Read your response to two or three other people in your class. Listen carefully to what the others have written. After you have discussed each other's responses, talk about other points of interest in the passage.

2.6
IDENTIFYING MAIN IDEAS

Working with the same small group, make a list of the main points in this opinion. *In this case, you may quote directly from the opinion,* if you wish.

2.7
ANALYZING THE TEXT

Work with your group members on this exercise. Discuss the answers carefully, particularly if there are disagreements among members of your group. In some cases, there may be more than one possible interpretation.

1. Write whether these statements are true *(T)* or false *(F)*.

    a. _____ The New Jersey Supreme Court ruled that surrogacy is illegal in every situation.

    b. _____ The New Jersey Supreme Court ruled that surrogate mothers cannot be paid and that they must be allowed to change their minds after the baby is born.

    c. _____ The same court said that Mary Beth Whitehead was the mother of Baby M and that she had parental rights.

    d. _____ The New Jersey Supreme Court gave custody of Baby M to the Whiteheads.

    e. _____ The Court said the contract showed no regard for the best interests of the child.

2. There were two court opinions in the Baby M case: the lower court and

the New Jersey Supreme Court. The opinion of the New Jersey Supreme Court:

    a. agreed with the opinion of the lower court; it upheld the surrogacy contract between Whitehead and the Sterns and said that this contract was legal and binding.

    b. disagreed with the opinion of the lower court; it declared the surrogacy contract between Whitehead and the Sterns illegal and unenforceable.

    c. took no position on the validity of the surrogacy contract.

    Explain your answer.

3. In the matter of custody, the New Jersey Supreme Court gave custody of Baby M to:

    a. the Sterns because the Court found them to be more stable and better able to provide for the child's needs.

    b. Mary Beth Whitehead because she was the natural mother.

    c. both the Sterns and Whitehead in a divided custody arrangement.

    What did the Court consider in deciding who should have custody?

4. The Court invalidated the surrogacy contract because:

    a. it involved baby selling.

    b. it required the mother to agree to give up her child before the child was born or even conceived.

    c. it did not consider the best interests of the child.

    d. the mother was forced to sign the contract against her will.

    e. *a, b, c* — but not *d*.

5. The implication of the last paragraph in the Court's opinion is that:

    a. people know what they think about the new reproductive technology, i.e., their values and objectives are clear.

    b. people do not know exactly what they think about the new reproductive technology, i.e., their values and objectives are unclear.

    Explain your answer.

2.8
VOCABULARY STUDY

Study the italicized words and phrases in their contexts. Guess at their meanings. Write your guess in the first blank. Then, look up the word or phrase in your dictionary.

1. (paragraph 2) . . . we find the payment of money to a "surrogate" mother illegal, perhaps criminal, and potentially *degrading* to women.

    a. (guess) _____

    b. (dictionary) _____

2. (paragraph 3) We find no offense to our present laws where a woman voluntarily and without payment agrees to act as a "surrogate" mother, provided that she is not subject to a *binding* agreement to surrender her child.

   a. (guess) _____

   b. (dictionary) _____

3. (paragraph 6) Under the contract, the natural mother is *irrevocably* commited before she knows the strength of her bond with her child. She never makes a totally voluntary, informed decision. . . .

   a. (guess) _____

   b. (dictionary) _____

4. (paragraph 8) Worst of all, however, is the contract's total disregard of the *best interests* of the child. There is not the slightest suggestion that any inquiry will be made at any time to determine the fitness of the Sterns as custodial parents, of Mrs. Stern as an adoptive parent, their superiority to Mrs. Whitehead, or the effect on the child of not living with her natural mother.

   a. (guess) _____

   b. (dictionary) _____

5. (paragraph 11) The surrogacy contract . . . is based upon principles that are *directly contrary* to the objectives of our laws. It guarantees the separation of a child from its mother; it looks to adoption regardless of suitability; it totally ignores the child; it takes the child from the mother regardless of her wishes and her maternal fitness; and it does all of this, it accomplishes all of its goals, through the use of money.

   a. (guess) _____

   b. (dictionary) _____

2.9
CLOZE EXERCISE

Write an appropriate word in each blank. Discuss your word choice with your group. *Note:* In some cases, more than one word may be appropriate.

_____ decision of the New Jersey Supreme Court _____
　　(1)　　　　　　　　　　　　　　　　　　　　　　　　(2)
the Baby M case was _____ great importance, not only
　　　　　　　　　　　　(3)
_____ New Jersey, but throughout _____ country, because
　(4)　　　　　　　　　　　　　　　　　　　(5)

it took a _____ position against surrogacy for money. _____
(6)   (7)
Court also declared that _____ mothers cannot be required
                                        (8)
_____ give up all rights to _____ child before the child is
       (9)   (10)
_____ and before they receive counseling. _____ addition,
      (11)   (12)
the Court stated that the Whitehead-Stern _____ involved baby-
                                                          (13)
selling, which is _____ the law. The Court went _____ to say
                         (14)   (15)
that the best _____ of the child were not _____ in the con-
                     (16)   (17)
tract. This decision _____ a landmark decision because
                              (18)
_____ addressed many of the troubling issues _____ in the
      (19)   (20)
new reproductive technology.

2.10
APPLICATION, CRITICAL EVALUATION, AND SYNTHESIS

1. After the decision of the New Jersey Supreme Court on the Baby M case, many people have said that surrogacy is finished because very few women would agree to become surrogates if no money were involved. What is your position? Do you think this decision has ended the surrogacy movement? If so, how do you feel about that? Why? If not, how do you feel about that? Why?

2. Many people have said that Mary Beth Whitehead knew what she was doing when she signed away her parental rights in the contract with the Sterns. No one forced her to sign the contract, and she said that she understood the conditions. Later, she changed her mind. The New Jersey Supreme Court said she could not possibly have given "informed consent" at the time she signed the contract and that no contract is legal without informed consent. What do you think is meant by "informed consent"? Do you think that Whitehead was able to give "informed consent" when she signed the contract? Why? Why not?

3. On many issues, the women's movement has been in conflict with the Roman Catholic Church (e.g., on the issue of birth control). However, in the case of surrogacy, the women's movement and the Roman Catholic Church and other religious groups as well have been strongly opposed to surrogacy. Why would these very different groups join together against this issue? What are the dangers they feared from surrogacy?

4. How would you define *mother* and *father* after reading the passages in this unit? Do you think the definitions for these words are going to

change or, possibly, are in the process of change now? Is it in society's best interest to have the meanings of these words change? Why? Why not? Explain.

5. The New Jersey Supreme Court stated, "The problem is how to enjoy the benefits of [the new reproductive biotechnology] — especially for infertile couples — while minimizing the risk of abuse. The problem can be addressed only when society decides what its values and objectives are in this troubling, yet promising, area." How do you think society can decide what its values and objectives are in this "troubling, yet promising, area"? Who should make these decisions?

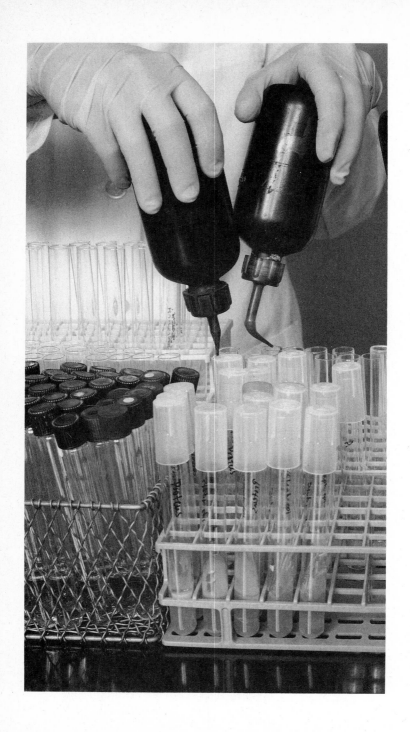

3
Brave New World

Aldous Huxley, an English novelist, essayist, and satirist, wrote his most famous novel, *Brave New World,* in 1932. In this book, Huxley paints a grim picture of the world in the future, a world created by scientific technology and social planning on a massive scale. All phases and stages of reproduction are carried out in the laboratory in *Brave New World,* and people are programmed and completely controlled from the moment of conception on. The passage that follows is the first chapter of the novel and is reprinted by permission of Harper & Row, Inc.

3.1
FIRST READING

Read this chapter and try to understand the story. Do *not* stop to look up words in your dictionary.

1. A squat grey building of only thirty-four stories. Over the main entrance the words, CENTRAL LONDON HATCHERY AND CONDITIONING CENTRE, and, in a shield, the World State's motto, COMMUNITY, IDENTITY, STABILITY.
2. The enormous room on the ground floor faced towards the north. Cold for all the summer beyond the panes, for all the tropical heat of the room itself, a harsh thin light glared through the windows, hungrily seeking some draped lay figure, some pallid shape of academic goose-flesh, but finding only the glass and nickel and bleakly shining porcelain of a laboratory. Wintriness responded to wintriness. The overalls of the workers were white, their hands gloved with a pale corpse-coloured rubber. The light was frozen, dead, a ghost. Only from the yellow barrels of the microscopes did it borrow a certain rich and living substance, lying along the polished tubes like butter, streak after luscious streak in long recession down the work tables.

3. "And this," said the Director opening the door, "is the Fertilizing Room."

4. Bent over their instruments, three hundred Fertilizers were plunged, as the Director of Hatcheries and Conditioning entered the room, in the scarcely breathing silence, the absent-minded, soliloquizing hum or whistle, of absorbed concentration. A troop of newly arrived students, very young, pink and callow, followed nervously, rather abjectly, at the Director's heels. Each of them carried a notebook, in which, whenever the great man spoke, he desperately scribbled. Straight from the horse's mouth. It was a rare privilege. The D.H.C. for Central London always made a point of personally conducting his new students round the various departments.

5. "Just to give you a general idea," he would explain to them. For of course some sort of general idea they must have, if they were to do their work intelligently — though as little of one, if they were to be good and happy members of society, as possible. For particulars, as every one knows, make for virtue and happiness; generalities are intellectually necessary evils. Not philosophers but fret-sawyers* and stamp collectors compose the backbone of society.

6. "To-morrow," he would add, smiling at them with a slightly menacing geniality, "you'll be settling down to serious work. You won't have time for generalities. Meanwhile . . ."

7. Meanwhile, it was a privilege. Straight from the horse's mouth into the notebook. The boys scribbled like mad.

8. Tall and rather thin but upright, the Director advanced into the room. He had a long chin and big, rather prominent teeth, just covered, when he was not talking, by his full, floridly curved lips. Old, young? Thirty? Fifty? Fifty-five? It was hard to say. And anyhow the question didn't arise; in this year of stability, A.F. 632,† it didn't occur to you to ask it.

9. "I shall begin at the beginning," said the D.H.C. and the more zealous students recorded his intention in their notebooks: *Begin at the beginning.* "These," he waved his hand, "are the incubators." And opening an insulated door he showed them racks upon racks of numbered test-tubes. "The week's supply of ova. Kept," he explained, "at blood heat; whereas the male gametes," and here he opened another door, "they have to be kept at thirty-five instead of thirty-seven. Full blood heat sterilizes." Rams wrapped in thermogene beget no lambs.

---

* Carpenters who do fancy design work with a saw.

† In *Brave New World,* the years are counted from the death of Henry Ford. A.F. 632 signifies 632 years after Ford's death. Henry Ford mass-produced the automobile. He developed the factory assembly line and was very much involved in the technological development of the twentieth century. It is obvious that Huxley believed that Ford was largely responsible for the decline in human values in the technological era.

10. Still leaning against the incubators he gave them, while the pencils scurried illegibly across the pages, a brief description of the modern fertilizing process; spoke first, of course, of its surgical introduction — "the operation undergone voluntarily for the good of Society, not to mention the fact that it carries a bonus amounting to six months' salary"; continued with some account of the technique for preserving the excised ovary alive and actively developing; passed on to a consideration of optimum temperature, salinity, viscosity; referred to the liquor in which the detached and ripened eggs were kept; and, leading his charges to the work tables, actually showed them how this liquor was drawn off from the test-tubes; how it was let out drop by drop onto the specially warmed slides of the microscopes; how the eggs which it contained were inspected for abnormalities, counted and transferred to a porous receptacle; how (and he now took them to watch the operation) this receptacle was immersed in a warm bouillon containing free-swimming spermatozoa — at a minimum concentration of one hundred thousand per cubic centimetre, he insisted; and how, after ten minutes, the container was lifted out of the liquor and its contents re-examined; how, if any of the eggs remained unfertilized, it was again immersed, and, if necessary, yet again; how the fertilized ova went back to the incubators; where the Alphas and Betas remained definitely bottled; while the Gammas, Deltas and Epsilons were brought out again, after only thirty-six hours, to undergo Bokanovsky's Process.

11. "Bokanovsky's Process," repeated the Director, and the students underlined the words in their little notebooks.

12. One egg, one embryo, one adult — normality. But a bokanovskified egg will bud, will proliferate, will divide. From eight to ninety-six buds, and every bud will grow into a perfectly formed embryo, and every embryo into a full-sized adult. Making ninety-six human beings grow where only one grew before. Progress.

13. "Essentially," the D.H.C. concluded, "bokanovskification consists of a series of arrests of development. We check the normal growth and, paradoxically enough, the egg responds by budding."

14. *Responds by budding.* The pencils were busy.

15. He pointed. On a very slowly moving band a rack-full of test-tubes was entering a large metal box, another rack-full was emerging. Machinery faintly purred. It took eight minutes for the tubes to go through, he told them. Eight minutes of hard X-rays being about as much as an egg can stand. A few died; of the rest, the least susceptible divided into two; most put out four buds; some eight; all were returned to the incubators, where the buds began to develop; then, after two days, were suddenly chilled, chilled and checked. Two, four, eight, the buds in their turn budded; and having budded were dosed

almost to death with alcohol; consequently burgeoned again and having budded — bud out of bud out of bud — were thereafter — further arrest being generally fatal — left to develop in peace. By which time the original egg was in a fair way to becoming anything from eight to ninety-six embryos — a prodigious improvement, you will agree, on nature. Identical twins — but not in piddling twos and threes as in the old viviparous days, when an egg would sometimes accidentally divide; actually by dozens, by scores at a time.

16. "Scores," the Director repeated and flung out his arms, as though he were distributing largess. "Scores."
17. But one of the students was fool enough to ask where the advantage lay.
18. "My good boy!" The Director wheeled sharply round on him. "Can't you see? Can't you *see*?" He raised a hand; his expression was solemn. "Bokanovsky's Process is one of the major instruments of social stability!"
19. *Major instruments of social stability.*
20. Standard men and women; in uniform batches. The whole of a small factory staffed with the products of a single bokanovskified egg.
21. "Ninety-six identical twins working ninety-six identical machines!" The voice was almost tremulous with enthusiasm. "You really know where you are. For the first time in history." He quoted the planetary motto. "Community, Identity, Stability." Grand words. "If we could bokanovskify indefinitely the whole problem would be solved."
22. Solved by standard Gammas, unvarying Deltas, uniform Epsilons. Millions of identical twins. The principle of mass production at last applied to biology.
23. "But, alas," the Director shook his head, "we can't bokanovskify indefinitely."
24. Ninety-six seemed to be the limit; seventy-two a good average. From the same ovary and with gametes of the same male to manufacture as many batches of identical twins as possible — that was the best (sadly a second best) that they could do. And even that was difficult.
25. "For in nature it takes thirty years for two hundred eggs to reach maturity. But our business is to stabilize the population at this moment, here and now. Dribbling out twins over a quarter of a century — what would be the use of that?"
26. Obviously, no use at all. But Podsnap's Technique had immensely accelerated the process of ripening. They could make sure of at least a hundred and fifty mature eggs within two years. Fertilize and bokanovskify — in other words, multiply by seventy-two — and you get an average of nearly eleven thousand brothers and sisters in a hundred and fifty batches of identical twins, all within two years of the same age.

27. "And in exceptional cases we can make one ovary yield us over fifteen thousand adult individuals."

28. Beckoning to a fair-haired, ruddy young man who happened to be passing at the moment, "Mr. Foster," he called. The ruddy young man approached. "Can you tell us the record for a single ovary, Mr. Foster?"

29. "Sixteen thousand and twelve in this Centre," Mr. Foster replied without hesitation. He spoke very quickly, had a vivacious blue eye, and took an evident pleasure in quoting figures. "Sixteen thousand and twelve; in one hundred and eighty-nine batches of identicals. But of course they've done much better," he rattled on, "in some of the tropical Centres. Singapore has often produced over sixteen thousand five hundred; and Mombasa has actually touched the seventeen thousand mark. But then they have unfair advantages. You should see the way a negro ovary responds to pituitary! It's quite astonishing, when you're used to working with European material. Still," he added, with a laugh (but the light of combat was in his eyes and the life of his chin was challenging), "still, we mean to beat them if we can. I'm working on a wonderful Delta-Minus ovary at this moment. Only just eighteen months old. Over twelve thousand seven hundred children already, either decanted or in embryo. And still going strong. We'll beat them yet."

30. "That's the spirit I like!" cried the Director, and clapped Mr. Foster on the shoulder. "Come along with us and give these boys the benefit of your expert knowledge."

31. Mr. Foster smiled modestly. "With pleasure." They went.

32. In the Bottling Room all was harmonious bustle and ordered activity. Flaps of fresh sow's peritoneum already cut to the proper size came shooting up in little lifts from the Organ Store in the sub-basement. Whizz and then, click! another flap of peritoneum had shot up from the depths, ready to be slipped into yet another bottle, the next of that slow interminable procession on the band.

33. Next to the Liners stood the Matriculators. The processions advanced; one by one the eggs were transferred from their test-tubes to the larger containers; deftly the peritoneal lining was slit, the morula dropped into place, the saline solution poured in . . . and already the bottle had passed, and it was the turn of the labellers. Heredity, date of fertilization, membership of Bokanovsky Group — details were transferred from test-tube to bottle. No longer anonymous, but named, identified, the procession marched slowly on; on through an opening in the wall, slowly on into the Social Predestination Room.

34. "Eighty-eight cubic metres of card index," said Mr. Foster with relish, as they entered.

35. "Containing *all* the relevant information," added the Director.

36. "Brought up to date every morning."
37. "And co-ordinated every afternoon."
38. "On the basis of which they make their calculations."
39. "So many individuals, of such and such quality," said Mr. Foster.
40. "Distributed in such and such quantities."
41. "The optimum Decanting Rate at any given moment."
42. "Unforeseen wastages promptly made good."
43. "Promptly," repeated Mr. Foster. "If you knew the amount of over-time I had to put in after the last Japanese earthquake!" He laughed good-humouredly and shook his head.
44. "The Predestinators send in their figures to the Fertilizers."
45. "Who give them the embryos they ask for."
46. "And the bottles come in here to be predestinated in detail."
47. "After which they are sent down to the Embryo store."
48. "Where we now proceed ourselves."
49. And opening a door Mr. Foster led the way down a staircase into the basement.
50. The temperature was still tropical. They descended into a thickening twilight. Two doors and a passage with a double turn insured the cellar against any possible infiltration of the day.
51. "Embryos are like photograph film" said Mr. Foster waggishly, as he pushed open the second door. "They can only stand red light."
52. And in effect the sultry darkness into which the students now followed him was visible and crimson, like the darkness of closed eyes on a summer's afternoon. The bulging flanks of row on receding row and tier above tier of bottles glinted with innumerable rubies, and among the rubies moved the dim red spectres of men and women with purple eyes and all the symptoms of lupus. The hum and rattle of machinery faintly stirred the air.
53. "Give them a few figures, Mr. Foster," said the Director, who was tired of talking.
54. Two hundred and twenty metres long, two hundred wide, ten high. He pointed upwards. Like chickens drinking, the students lifted their eyes towards the distant ceiling.
55. Three tiers of racks: ground floor level, first gallery, second gallery.
56. The spidery steel-work of gallery above gallery faded away in all directions into the dark. Near them three red ghosts were busily unloading demi-johns from a moving staircase.
57. The escalator from the Social Predestination Room.
58. Each bottle could be placed on one of fifteen racks, each rack, though you couldn't see it, was a conveyor travelling at the rate of thirty-three and a third centimetres an hour. Two hundred and sixty-seven days at eight metres a day. Two thousand one hundred and thirty-six metres in all. One circuit of the cellar at ground level, one on the first gallery,

half on the second, and on the two hundred and sixty-seventh morning, daylight in the Decanting Room. Independent existence — so called.

59. "But in the interval," Mr. Foster concluded, "we've managed to do a lot to them. Oh, a very great deal." His laugh was knowing and triumphant.

60. "That's the spirit I like," said the Director once more. "Let's walk round. You tell them everything, Mr. Foster."

61. Mr. Foster duly told them.

62. Told them of the growing embryo on its bed of peritoneum. Made them taste the rich blood surrogate on which it fed. Explained why it had to be stimulated with placentin and thyroxin. Told them of the *corpus luteum* extract. Showed them the jets through which at every twelfth metre from zero to 2040 it was automatically injected. Spoke of those gradually increasing doses of pituitary administered during the final ninety-six metres of their course. Described the artificial maternal circulation installed on every bottle at Metre 112; showed them the reservoir of blood-surrogate, the centrifugal pump that kept the liquid moving over the placenta and drove it through the synthetic lung and waste-product filter. Referred to the embryo's troublesome tendency to anemia, to the massive doses of hog's stomach extract and foetal foal's liver with which, in consequence, it had to be supplied.

63. Showed them the simple mechanism by means of which, during the last two metres out of every eight, all the embryos were simultaneously shaken into familiarity with movement. Hinted at the gravity of the so-called "trauma of decanting," and enumerated the precautions taken to minimize, by a suitable training of the bottled embryo, that dangerous shock. Told them of the tests for sex carried out in the neighbourhood of Metre 200. Explained the system of labelling — a T for the males, a circle for the females and for those who were destined to become freemartins a question mark, black on a white ground.

64. "For of course," said Mr. Foster, "in the vast majority of cases, fertility is merely a nuisance. One fertile ovary in twelve hundred — that would really be quite sufficient for our purposes. But we want to have a good choice. And of course one must always leave an enormous margin of safety. So we allow as many as thirty per cent of the female embryos to develop normally. The others get a dose of male sex-hormone every twenty-four metres for the rest of the course. Result: they're decanted as freemartins — structurally quite normal (except," he had to admit, "that they *do* have just the slightest tendency to grow beards), but sterile. Guaranteed sterile. Which brings us at last," continued Mr. Foster, "out of the realm of mere slavish imitation of

nature into the much more interesting world of human invention."

65. He rubbed his hands. For of course, they didn't content themselves with merely hatching out embryos: any cow could do that.

66. "We also predestine and condition. We decant our babies as socialized human beings, as Alphas or Epsilons, as future sewage workers or future . . ." He was going to say "future World controllers," but correcting himself, said "future Directors of Hatcheries," instead.

67. The D.H.C. acknowledged the compliment with a smile.

68. They were passing Metre 320 on Rack 2. A young Beta-Minus mechanic was busy with screwdriver and spanner on the blood-surrogate pump of a passing bottle. The hum of the electric motor deepened by fractions of a tone as he turned the nuts. Down, down . . . A final twist, a glance at the revolution counter, and he was done. He moved two paces down the line and began the same process on the next pump.

69. "Reducing the number of revolutions per minute," Mr. Foster explained. "The surrogate goes round slower; therefore passes through the lung at longer intervals; therefore gives the embryo less oxygen. Nothing like oxygen-shortage for keeping an embryo below par." Again he rubbed his hands.

70. "But why do you want to keep the embryo below par?" asked an ingenuous student.

71. "Ass!" said the Director, breaking a long silence. "Hasn't it occurred to you that an Epsilon embryo must have an Epsilon environment as well as an Epsilon heredity?"

72. It evidently hadn't occurred to him. He was covered with confusion.

73. "The lower the caste," said Mr. Foster, "the shorter the oxygen." The first organ affected was the brain. After that the skeleton. At seventy per cent of normal oxygen you got dwarfs. At less than seventy eyeless monsters.

74. "Who are no use at all," concluded Mr. Foster.

75. Whereas (his voice became confidential and eager), if they could discover a technique for shortening the period of maturation what a triumph, what a benefaction to Society!

76. "Consider the horse."

77. They considered it.

78. Mature at six; the elephant at ten. While at thirteen a man is not yet sexually mature; and is only full-grown at twenty. Hence, of course, that fruit of delayed development, the human intelligence.

79. "But in Epsilons," said Mr. Foster very justly, "we don't need human intelligence."

80. Didn't need and didn't get it. But though the Epsilon mind was mature at ten, the Epsilon body was not fit to work till eighteen. Long years of superfluous and wasted immaturity. If the physical develop-

ment could be speeded up till it was as quick, say as a cow's, what an
enormous saving to the Community!

81. "Enormous!" murmured the students. Mr. Foster's enthusiasm was
infectious.

82. He became rather technical; spoke of the abnormal endocrine co-
ordination which made men grow so slowly; postulated a germinal
mutation to account for it. Could the effects of this germinal mutation be undone? Could the individual Epsilon embryo be made to
revert, by a suitable technique, to the normality of dogs and cows?
That was the problem. And it was all but solved.

83. Pilkington, at Mombasa, had produced individuals who were sexually
mature at four and full-grown at six and a half. A scientific triumph.
But socially useless. Six-year-old men and women were too stupid to
do even Epsilon work. And the process was an all-or-nothing one;
either you failed to modify at all, or else you modified the whole way.
They were still trying to find the ideal compromise between adults of
twenty and adults of six. So far without success. Mr. Foster sighed and
shook his head.

84. Their wanderings through the crimson twilight had brought them to
the neighborhood of Metre 170 on Rack 9. From this point onwards
Rack 9 was enclosed and the bottles performed the remainder of their
journey in a kind of tunnel, interrupted here and there by openings
two or three metres wide.

85. "Heat conditioning," said Mr. Foster.

86. Hot tunnels alternated with cool tunnels. Coolness was wedded to
discomfort in the form of hard X-rays. By the time they were decanted
the embryos had a horror of cold. They were predestined to emigrate
to the tropics, to be miners and acetate silk spinners and steel workers.
Later on their minds would be made to endorse the judgment of their
bodies. "We condition them to thrive on heat," concluded Mr. Foster. "Our colleagues upstairs will teach them to love it."

87. "And that," put in the Director sententiously, "that is the secret of
happiness and virtue — liking what you've *got* to do. All conditioning
aims at that: making people like their unescapable social destiny."

88. In a gap between two tunnels, a nurse was delicately probing with a
long fine syringe into the gelatinous contents of a passing bottle. The
students and their guides stood watching her for a few moments in
silence.

89. "Well, Lenina," said Mr. Foster, when at last she withdrew the syringe and straightened herself up.

90. The girl turned with a start. One could see that, for all the lupus and
the purple eyes, she was uncommonly pretty.

91. "Henry!" Her smile flashed redly at him — a row of coral teeth.

92. "Charming, charming," murmured the Director, and giving her two

or three little pats, received in exchange a rather deferential smile for himself.

93. "What are you giving them?" asked Mr. Foster, making his tone very professional.

94. "Oh, the usual typhoid and sleeping sickness."

95. "Tropical workers start being inoculated at Metre 150," Mr. Foster explained to the students. "The embryos still have gills. We immunize the fish against the future man's diseases." Then, turning back to Lenina, "Ten to five on the roof this afternoon," he said, "as usual."

96. "Charming," said the Director once more, and with a final pat, moved away after the others.

97. On Rack 10 rows of next generation's chemical workers were being trained in the toleration of lead, caustic soda, tar, chlorine. The first of a batch of two hundred and fifty embryonic rocket-plane engineers was just passing the eleven hundred metre mark on Rack 3. A special mechanism kept their containers in constant rotation. "To improve their sense of balance," Mr. Foster explained. "Doing repairs on the outside of a rocket in mid-air is a ticklish job. We slacken off the circulation when they're right way up, so that they're half starved, and double the flow of surrogate when they're upside down. They learn to associate topsy-turvydom with well-being; in fact, they're only truly happy when they're standing on their heads.

98. "And now," Mr. Foster went on, "I'd like to show you some very interesting conditioning for Alpha Plus Intellectuals. We have a big batch of them on Rack 5. First Gallery level," he called to two boys who had started to go down to the ground floor.

99. "They're round about Metre 900," he explained. "You can't really do any useful intellectual conditioning till the foetuses have lost their tails. Follow me."

100. But the Director had looked at his watch. "Ten to three," he said. "No time for the intellectual embryos, I'm afraid. We must go up to the Nurseries before the children have finished their afternoon sleep."

101. Mr. Foster was disappointed. "At least one glance at the Decanting Room," he pleaded.

102. "Very well then." The Director smiled indulgently. "Just one glance."

3611 words

Reading Times	Reading Speed
1st reading ____ minutes	20 minutes = 181 wpm
3rd reading ____ minutes	18 minutes = 201 wpm
	16 minutes = 226 wpm
	14 minutes = 258 wpm
	12 minutes = 301 wpm

3.2
SECOND READING

Go back and read the chapter again. Take as much time as you need this time. Look up some of the unfamiliar words in the glossary at the end of the book or in your dictionary if you wish.

3.3
THIRD READING

Read the chapter quickly a third time. Concentrate on understanding the story and the meanings of new vocabulary words in the context in which they appear. *Note:* You may wish to reread parts of this chapter a fourth or even a fifth time.

3.4
READER RESPONSE

In order to explore your response to this reading, write for 15 minutes about anything that interested you in this passage. You may wish to write about one of the characters — or something you strongly agreed or disagreed with — and why this caused such a strong reaction in you. Try to explore *your own thoughts and feelings* as much as possible. Do *not* merely summarize or restate the story line.

3.5
RESPONSE SHARING

Read your response to two or three other people in your class. Listen carefully to what the others have written. After you have discussed each other's responses, talk about other points of interest in the story.

3.6
IDENTIFYING MAIN IDEAS

Working with the same small group, make a list of the main ideas in this article. Be sure to state the main ideas in your own words. Don't just copy sentences directly from the text. Think carefully about what the writer is trying to tell you.

3.7
ANALYZING THE TEXT

Work with your group members on this exercise. Discuss the answers carefully, particularly if there are disagreements among members of your group. In some cases, there may be more than one possible interpretation.

1. *Brave New World* opens at the CENTRAL LONDON HATCHERY AND CONDITIONING CENTRE. What is this place?
   a. a place where fish are scientifically produced to fit specialized environments
   b. a place where human beings are scientifically produced to fit specialized environments
   c. a combination hospital and research laboratory
2. What kind of atmosphere is created in paragraph 2?
   a. a vast, cold, deathlike atmosphere
   b. a cozy, warm, and inviting atmosphere
   c. a light and airy atmosphere
   Explain your answer by referring to particular words and phrases.
3. What is Bokanovsky's Process? (paragraphs 11 – 13)
   a. a new laboratory process by which one egg divides to produce as many as 96 embryos, which subsequently become 96 human beings
   b. a new laboratory process by which one egg produces one embryo, which subsequently becomes one human being
   c. a new laboratory process by which 96 eggs divide human beings.
4. Write whether these statements are true *(T)* or false *(F)*.

   a. _____ According to the Director, Bokanovsky's Process represents progress because it means that reproduction can be more carefully controlled, and this control leads to greater social stability.

   b. _____ In *Brave New World,* people are mass produced as if they were cars.

   c. _____ *Brave New World* presents a favorable picture of social control through scientific technology.

   d. _____ People have no control over their own lives in *Brave New World.*

   e. _____ People are conditioned in utero to be satisfied with their lives in *Brave New World.*
5. In *Brave New World,* the picture Aldous Huxley presents of social control through technology is:
   a. idealized and positive

b. grim and frightening
c. interesting and amusing
Explain your answer with specific examples from the text.

3.8
VOCABULARY STUDY

Study the italicized words and phrases in their contexts. Guess at their meanings. Write your guess in the first blank. Then, look up the word or phrase in your dictionary.

1. (paragraph 1) A *squat* grey building of only thirty-four stories.

    a. (guess) _____

    b. (dictionary) _____

2. (paragraph 4) A troop of newly arrived students, very young, pink and *callow,* followed nervously, rather abjectly, at the Director's heels.

    a. (guess) _____

    b. (dictionary) _____

3. (paragraph 20) Standard men and women; in *uniform batches.* The whole of a small factory staffed with the products of a single bokanovskified egg.

    a. (guess) _____

    b. (dictionary) _____

4. (paragraph 21) "Ninety-six identical twins working ninety-six identical machines!" The voice was almost *tremulous* with enthusiasm.

    a. (guess) _____

    b. (dictionary) _____

5. (paragraph 86) Hot tunnels alternated with cool tunnels. Coolness was wedded to discomfort in the form of hard X-rays. By the time they were decanted the embryos had a horror of cold. They were *predestined* to emigrate to the tropics, to be miners and acetate silk spinners and steel workers. . . . "We condition them to thrive on heat," concluded Mr. Foster. "Our colleagues upstairs will teach them to love it."

    a. (guess) _____

    b. (dictionary) _____

3.9
CLOZE EXERCISE

Write an appropriate word in each blank. Discuss your word choice with
your group. *Note:* In some cases, more than one word may be appropriate,
or no word may be needed.

COMMUNITY, IDENTITY, STABILITY. It _____ hard to be-
(1)
lieve that _____ three words could be _____ chilling. But in
(2)   (3)
Brave New World _____ are the motto of _____ Central
(4)   (5)
London Hatchery and _____ Centre, and they stand _____
(6)   (7)
a complete and rigidly _____ life. People have no _____ will
(8)   (9)
and   no   free   choice.   _____   are   programmed   before   they
(10)
_____ born to be whatever they _____. In fact, they are so
(11)   (12)
_____ programmed that they do _____ even have the free-
(13)   (14)
dom _____ dislike their situation in _____. Before they are
(15)   (16)
born, _____ are conditioned to like _____ they will become,
(17)   (18)
to _____ satisfied with all aspects _____ their life. The re-
(19)   (20)
sult: COMMUNITY, IDENTITY, STABILITY — but the price is very

high. Most people don't want to give up their freedom to choose at that

cost.

3.10
APPLICATION, CRITICAL EVALUATION, AND SYNTHESIS

1. *Brave New World* starts off in A.F. 632. "A.F." stands for "After Ford".
   What does this mean? Who was Ford? What did he or she do? What does
   this have to do with *Brave New World*? In other words, how was the
   world changed by Ford? Do you think Huxley thought the world was
   changed for the better by Ford?
2. The title *Brave New World* is "ironic." What does the word *ironic* mean?
   Did Huxley really admire the world he described? Did he really believe
   that this was indeed a "brave new world"? Explain your answers and give
   examples.
3. In *Brave New World,* embryos are conditioned for certain types of lives.

Mechanics are conditioned to like being mechanics, engineers to being engineers, clerks to being clerks; as the Director sums it up, "And that . . . is the secret of happiness and virtue — liking what you've *got* to do. All conditioning aims at that: making people like their unescapable social destiny." What do you think about this social conditioning? Would you rather have social conditioning or free choice? Why? In your opinion, which makes for a better society? Why?

4. Later in *Brave New World,* a "savage" is found in New Mexico. He is imported by the authorities and used in experiments. The "savage" has educated himself by reading Shakespeare, and he believes in spirituality and moral choice. In the "brave new world," he soon goes insane, and he kills himself. Why do you think he could not live in the "brave new world"? What do you think Huxley was trying to tell you, the reader?

5. You cannot judge a book by its cover — or even by its first chapter. If possible, get a copy of *Brave New World* and read the whole book. You won't regret it!

TURN TO THE EXPANSION SECTION ON PAGE 187 FOR PRACTICE IN DOING LIBRARY RESEARCH AND REPORT WRITING.

Unit 3
Prisons and
Punishment

DISCUSSION

One of the major concerns in many countries today is the question of prisons. What are prisons for? Who should go to prison — and for how long? In some societies, the general feeling is that almost everyone who commits a crime should be "locked up," regardless of the reason for the crime or the individual's past experiences. Other societies think there may be other ways to punish people for certain types of crimes and that each offender's situation is different. This chapter looks at prisons, at the experience of a woman who is going to be living in prison for a long time, and at some alternative ways to punish criminals. Before you begin reading, think about the following questions and discuss your answers.

1. In your country, is there a lot of crime? If yes, what types of crimes are typical and why do you think there is so much crime? If no, why do you think your country has so little crime?
2. When people commit crimes in your country, what kind of punishment do they get? Are most people sent to prison? If yes, is it for a long time or a short time? Are fines (money penalties) common? What other kinds of punishments are common in your country?
3. Who decides how a person is punished? What kind of system does your country use to make the decisions about punishment?
4. What are prisons like in your country? Are there many of them? Do they provide any job training or work for the prisoners? How do prisoners get food, clothing, and personal items? What do the newspapers and magazines write about the conditions in these prisons?
5. What are your views on prisons and punishment? How harshly should persons be punished? Should there be different kinds of punishment for different crimes (for example, stealing a car vs. murder) or for different circumstances (for example, a first-time offender vs. someone who has committed many crimes)?

Officer escorting work detail

1
Prison

How did the modern prison develop? What are the problems of prisons today? This reading is from *The World Book Encyclopedia* entry entitled "Prison." (Excerpted from *The World Book Encyclopedia.* © 1988 World Book, Inc.) Reprinted by permission.

1.1
FIRST READING

Read this selection quickly for the main ideas. Pay attention to the title and the text headings as you read. Do *not* stop to look up words in your dictionary.

1. PRISON is an institution for confining and punishing people who have been convicted of committing a crime. Prisons punish criminals by severely restricting their freedom. For example, prisons limit where *inmates* (prisoners) may go, what they may do, and with whom they may associate. Inmates serve prison sentences ranging from a year to the rest of their lives. Prisons are also important because they help protect society from its most dangerous criminals.

TYPES OF CORRECTIONAL INSTITUTIONS

2. Various names have been used for prisons and other institutions that confine convicted lawbreakers or persons awaiting trial. The most common terms include *penitentiaries, correctional centers, correctional facilities,* and *reformatories.* Women form about 5 per cent of all inmates in the United States. Most of them are held in prisons that house only women.
3. Experts classify prisons by the degree of security or control they pro-

vide. The main types are (1) maximum security prisons, (2) medium security prisons, and (3) minimum security prisons.

HOW PRISONS OPERATE

4. Prisons have four major purposes. These purposes are (1) retribution, (2) incapacitation, (3) deterrence, and (4) rehabilitation. *Retribution* means punishment for crimes against society. Depriving criminals of their freedom is a way of making them pay a debt to society for their crimes. *Incapacitation* refers to the removal of criminals from society so they can no longer harm innocent people. *Deterrence* means the prevention of future crime. It is hoped that prisons provide warnings to people thinking about committing crimes, and that the possibility of going to prison will discourage people from breaking the law. *Rehabilitation* refers to activities designed to change criminals into law-abiding citizens, and may include providing educational courses in prison, teaching job skills, and offering counseling with a psychologist or social worker.

5. The four major purposes of prisons have not been stressed equally through the years. As a result, prisons differ in the makeup of their staffs, the design of their buildings, and their operations.

HISTORY

6. **Early Prisons.** Before the 1700's, governments seldom imprisoned criminals for punishment. Instead, people were imprisoned while awaiting trial or punishment. Common punishments at that time included branding, imposing fines, whipping, and *capital punishment* (execution). The authorities punished most offenders in public in order to discourage people from breaking the law. Some criminals were punished by being made to row the oars on ships called *galleys.*

7. However, English and French rulers kept their political enemies in such prisons as the Tower of London and the Bastille in Paris. In addition, people who owed money were held in *debtors' prisons.* In many such cases, offenders' families could stay with them and come and go as they pleased. But the debtors had to stay in prison until their debts were settled.

8. During the 1700's, many people criticized the use of executions and other harsh punishments. These critics included the British judge Sir William Blackstone. As a result, governments turned more and more to imprisonment as a form of punishment.

9. **Early Prison Reform.** Early prisons were dark, dirty, and overcrowded. They locked all types of prisoners together, including men, women, and children, plus dangerous criminals, debtors, and the insane. During the late 1700's, the British reformer John Howard toured

Europe to observe prison conditions. His book *The State of the Prisons in England and Wales* (1777) influenced the passage of a law that led to the construction of the first British prisons designed partly for reform. These prisons attempted to make their inmates feel *penitent* (sorry for doing wrong) and became known as *penitentiaries.*

10. In 1787, a group of influential Philadelphians, mostly Quakers, formed the Philadelphia Society for Alleviating the Miseries of Public Prisons (now the Pennsylvania Prison Society). They believed that some criminals could be reformed through hard work and meditation. The Quakers urged that dangerous criminals be held separately from nonviolent offenders and men and women prisoners be kept apart. These ideas became known as the Pennsylvania System, and were put into practice in 1790 at Philadelphia's Walnut Street Jail. This jail is considered the first prison in the United States.

11. The Pennsylvania System was the first attempt to rehabilitate criminals by classifying and separating them on the basis of their crimes. As a result, the most dangerous inmates spent all their time alone in their cells. In time, however, the system failed, chiefly because overcrowding made such separation impossible.

12. **During the 1800's,** New York prison officials developed two major systems of prison organization — the Auburn System and the Elmira System. The Auburn System, introduced at Auburn (N.Y.) Prison in 1821, became widely adopted. Under this system, prisoners stayed in solitary confinement at night and worked together during the day. The system emphasized silence. Prisoners could not speak to, or even look at, one another. Prison officials hoped that this silence and isolation would cause inmates to think about their crimes and reform. They believed that the prisoners' spirit must be broken before reform could take place. However, the system failed partly because the rigid rules and isolation drove inmates insane.

13. In 1876, the Elmira (N.Y.) Reformatory opened as a model prison for offenders between the ages of 16 and 30. The Elmira System made use of *indeterminate* (flexible) sentences and allowed prisoners to earn *parole* (early release) for good behavior. It also offered physical and military training and an educational program. The reformatory's emphasis on rehabilitation through education became its major contribution. But the institution did not fully achieve its high expectations, largely because it judged inmates on their prison behavior instead of on their actual fitness for release. Studies showed that most reformatory inmates committed new crimes after their release.

14. **Reforms in the 1900's** have led to further improvement of prisons. In the 1930's, for example, prisons began to develop rehabilitation programs based on the background, personality, and physical condition of the individual inmate. This approach made rehabilitation programs

more meaningful. But despite such efforts, attempts to rehabilitate offenders had disappointing results. Many failed because of poorly trained staffs, lack of funds, and ill-defined goals.

15. By the 1960's, many people felt that criminals could be helped better outside prison. As a result, federal and state governments began to set up *community correctional centers* and *halfway houses*. Offenders lived in these facilities just before release and received counseling to help them adjust to life outside prison. The number of prison inmates declined. But community correction programs also failed to meet expectations, and prisons again became the most preferred institution.

PRISONS TODAY

16. **Current Problems.** Severe overcrowding now ranks as the major problem in most prisons. The U.S. prison population, for example, more than doubled between the early 1970's and the early 1980's. The overcrowding has developed because of new laws requiring longer sentences, eliminating parole for certain crimes, and increasing the number of crimes that require imprisonment.

17. Judges have ruled that many prisons are so crowded that they violate prisoners' constitutional protection from "cruel and unusual punishment." Conditions have become so bad that prisoners have been held in warehouses, tents, and house trailers in some places. Many states have had to build more prisons or release inmates early to make room for new prisoners.

18. Prisons face other problems as well. A lack of adequate funding has made improvements difficult. In addition, tensions among prisoners and between prisoners and the prison staff often run high and lead to brutal attacks. Such conditions, worsened by overcrowding, have contributed to a number of prison riots since the late 1960's. Thirty-three inmates and 10 prison staff members were killed during a rebellion at the Attica (N.Y.) Correctional Facility in 1971. A two-day riot at the New Mexico State Penitentiary in Santa Fe in 1980 left 33 inmates dead.

19. **Continuing Debate.** The current concern with crime and the problems of prisons have helped focus public attention on the continuing debate about the purposes and effectiveness of prisons. Studies have shown that even good rehabilitation programs fail to reform many released prisoners. The apparent failure of such programs had led many people to stress imprisonment as punishment rather than as treatment. On the other hand, experts also have failed to prove that prisons reduce the crime rate either by incapacitating offenders or by discouraging people from breaking the law. For this reason, some experts believe that it would be cheaper, more humane, and more productive to keep most offenders in community correctional centers rather than in

prisons. They argue that only the most dangerous criminals should be imprisoned.

20. Some courts are experimenting with sentences that allow criminals to remain out of prison. Some of these sentences require criminals to repay the victims of their crimes, and others make offenders perform various public services in the community.

James O. Finckenauer

1432 words

Reading Times	Reading Speed
1st reading ____ minutes	9 minutes = 159 wpm
3rd reading ____ minutes	8 minutes = 179 wpm
	7 minutes = 205 wpm
	6 minutes = 239 wpm

1.2
SECOND READING

Go back and read the selection again. Take as much time as you need this time. Look up some of the unfamiliar words in the glossary at the end of the book or in your dictionary if you wish.

1.3
THIRD READING

Read the selection quickly a third time. Concentrate on understanding the main ideas of the selection and the meanings of new vocabulary words in the context in which they appear.

1.4
READER RESPONSE

In order to explore your response to this reading, write for 15 minutes about anything that interested you in this selection. You may wish to write about another description of prison that this selection reminded you of — or you may wish to disagree with something in the selection. Try to explore *your own thoughts and feelings* as much as possible. Do *not* merely summarize or restate the ideas in this article.

1.5
RESPONSE SHARING

Read your response to two or three other people in your class. Listen carefully to what the others have written. After you have discussed each other's responses, talk about other points of interest in the selection.

1.6
IDENTIFYING MAIN IDEAS

Working with the same small group, make a list of the main ideas in this selection. Be sure to state the main ideas in your own words. Don't just copy sentences directly from the text. Think carefully about what the writer is trying to tell you.

1.7
ANALYZING THE TEXT

Work with your group members on this exercise. Discuss the answers carefully, particularly if there are disagreements among members of your group. In some cases, there may be more than one possible interpretation.

1. The main purpose of this encyclopedia selection is:
   a. to make the reader think about his or her attitude towards prisons.
   b. to convince the reader that prisons are necessary for certain crimes.
   c. to give the reader some facts about prisons.
2. A number of words in this selection are printed in italics. Match the items in italics with one of these uses of italics. (You will need to choose some of the uses more than once): (1) Italics indicate the word being defined; (2) italics note the title of a book; (3) italics emphasize new ideas or items.
   a. *inmates* (prisoners)
   b. *Retribution* means punishment for crimes against society.
   c. The most common terms include *penitentiaries, reformatories, correctional centers,* and *correctional facilities.*
   d. ships called *galleys*
   e. Federal and state governments began to set up *community correctional centers* and *halfway houses.*
   f. *The State of Prisons in England and Wales*
3. The language used throughout this selection is:
   a. neutral. It tries to remain objective and fair.
   b. inflammatory. It tries to make us angry about prisons.
   c. persuasive. It tries to make us agree with the author's statements.
   Why did you choose your answer? Give some examples.
4. Read the section on "History" carefully. Then write whether these statements are true *(T)* or false *(F)*.

   a. _____ Progress has been made throughout the years in prison reform.

   b. _____ Rehabilitation and reform occur when inmates are placed in halfway houses.

   c. _____ In the 1700's authorities thought that if they punished offenders in public, people would be discouraged from breaking the law. This article states that this concept is also true today.

    d. _____ Many ideas for prison reform have been tried but all seem to have some drawbacks.

5. The final section, "Continuing Debate,":
    a. draws some firm conclusions about the future of prisons.
    b. is pessimistic about the future of prisons.
    c. summarizes the current ideas about prisons today.

1.8
VOCABULARY STUDY

Study these italicized words and phrases in their contexts and guess at their meanings. Write your guess in the first blank. Then, look up the word or phrase in your dictionary and write the definition in the second blank.

1. (paragraph 1) PRISON is an institution for *confining* and punishing people who have been convicted of committing a crime. Prisons punish criminals by severely restricting their freedom. For example, prisons limit where inmates may go, what they may do, and with whom they may associate.

    a. (guess) _____

    b. (dictionary) _____

2. (paragraph 4) It is hoped that prisons provide warnings to people thinking about committing crimes, and that the possibility of going to prison will *discourage* people from breaking the law.

    a. (guess) _____

    b. (dictionary) _____

3. (paragraph 12) Prisoners could not speak to, or even look at, one another. Prison officials hoped that this silence and *isolation* would cause inmates to think about their crimes and reform.

    a. (guess) _____

    b. (dictionary) _____

4. (paragraph 13) It also offered physical and military training and an educational program. The reformatory's emphasis on *rehabilitation* through education became its major contribution.

    a. (guess) _____

    b. (dictionary) _____

5. (paragraph 17) Judges have ruled that many prisons are so crowded that they *violate* prisoners' constitutional protection from "cruel and unusual punishment." Conditions have become so bad that prisoners have been held in warehouses, tents, and house trailers in some places.

   a. (guess) _____

   b. (dictionary) _____

1.9
DICTIONARY SKILLS

All the words in bold type have several different meanings. Look up each word in your dictionary, evaluate the different meanings, and decide which one fits *in the context* of the sentence.

1. As a result, prisons differ in the **makeup** of their staffs, the designs of their buildings, and their operations.

   cosmetics   special examinations
   structure

2. **Common** punishments at that time included imposing fines, whipping and capital punishment.

   ordinary   public
   shared   prevalent

3. His book influenced the **passage** of a law that led to the construction of the first British prisons designed partly for reform.

   enactment   movement from one place to another
   hallway   portion of a written work

4. The Quakers **urged** that dangerous criminals be held separately from nonviolent offenders and men and women prisoners be kept apart.

   desired   insisted
   strongly advocated

5. The apparent failure of such programs has led many people to **stress** imprisonment as punishment rather than as treatment.

   exert   use the pressure of
   emphasize

1.10
APPLICATION, CRITICAL EVALUATION, AND SYNTHESIS

1. The reading describes the development and current situation of prisons in the United States. Compare your society and the United States on the issues of prisons. How are they similar? How are they different? Are certain aspects of prisons better or worse in your society? In the United States?

2. If you were in charge of the prison system in your country, what kind of system do you think would work best? How would you handle different types of criminals? What would you want prisoners to do while they were in prison? What would you want prisoners to be like when they left prison? What would you recommend to the court system regarding sentencing?

3. The final paragraph in the selection describes some new types of sentences that permit criminals to receive their punishment outside of prison. They might have to repay their victims, pay fines, perform public service to their community, and stay close to home (although they would be allowed to work). Does this sound like a good idea to you? Why or why not? Please give some examples of what you think about this idea.

Jean Harris, Bedford Hills, 1986

2
Stranger in Two Worlds

Jean Harris was, for many years, the headmistress of an elite girls' school in Virginia. In 1981, at age 58, she was convicted for the murder of Dr. Herman Tarnower, a well-known physician and her companion of 14 years. She was sentenced to "15 years to life." Mrs. Harris now lives in a women's prison, the Bedford Hills Correctional Facility, where she is active in the Children's Center and in improving educational opportunities for incarcerated women. These excerpts are from *Stranger in Two Worlds,* the book she has written about the grim realities of prison life and about her own experience there. (By permission of Macmillan Publishing Company, 1986)

2.1
FIRST READING

Read this passage quickly for the main ideas. Pay attention to the title and the main ideas as you read. Do *not* stop to look up words in your dictionary.

1. On February 28, 1981, I was found guilty of murdering Dr. Herman Tarnower. Judge Leggett congratulated the jury on their verdict. "The evidence substantiates the verdict," he assured them. On March 20 I was sentenced to prison for fifteen years to life, with no hope of parole for at least fifteen years. This leaves me with the questionable distinction of being one of the most dangerous women in the state of New York. The average stay in this top security prison is less than three years. I was given a few moments to remove my jewelry and hug the boys goodbye, and then Vivian and Dolf, who had served as the officers of the court during the trial, drove me to Bedford Hills Correctional Facility. . . . I was wearing all my own clothes, probably for the last time in my life.
2. Except for the clothes I was wearing I had brought a toothbrush and a

book. I was left in the hands of a corrections officer (C.O.) those grim
initials that were soon to become the bane of my existence. She quickly
took me upstairs and told me to take off all my clothes. She handed me
some disinfectant soap and led me to a grim, grimy shower. Having
made sure that I washed my hair with the disinfectant, just in case I had
lice, she permitted me to dry myself, then handed me a yellow jumper
that zipped up the front and came about three inches above my knees.
A secondhand, sickly green blouse completed the ensemble, and since
they had no shoes my size, I was permitted to wear my own.

3. I went downstairs to a little room to have my picture taken in my new
   yellow and green costume. It was developed and laminated on the spot,
   so that I would not have to venture any further without my ID. I was
   now 81 G 98, meaning I was the ninety-eighth prisoner to enter the
   facility that year, 1981. My next stop was the state store where I was
   issued:

   1 dark green winter coat, very heavy and size 46. They said it was the
   smallest one they had and I wore it for a year, all ninety-eight pounds of
   me. The tag which reads "10 percent wool, 90 percent unidentified
   fibers" is a treasure I have saved.

   1 lightweight coat, dark green

   1 dark green jumper

   1 yellow jumper

   2 dark green slacks, double knit

   4 blouses, all used

   2 pairs of pajamas

   1 brown flannel robe

   various undergarments

   2 pairs of shoes

   1 pair of boots

   When my new wardrobe was complete, and everything had been
   stamped with my name, 81 G 98, it was all tossed into a large black
   garbage bag and handed to me.

4. How do you pass the time in prison? Options are few, especially in a
   women's prison. You must keep your eyes and ears open for whatever
   opportunities may come up. The soap, clothes, furniture, and much of
   the baked goods used at Bedford are made by incarcerated men. At
   Bedford we do the laundry for one of the male prisons, nothing more.
   Here a woman can clean hallways, lobbies, kitchens, classrooms, toi-
   lets and rec rooms, do some cooking in the staff kitchen, take arts and
   crafts, IBM data processing, electronics, baby-sit with infants in the

nursery, go to educational courses starting with Adult Basic Education through what is called college, or go to various self-help courses like Alcoholics Anonymous, Narcotics Anonymous, Down on Violence, Money Addiction, Reality House.

5. The list doesn't sound too bad, but you must remember that each group is limited in number. Seventy percent of the state's prison population, about 24,000 people, have had a history of drug and/or alcohol abuse, and the Department of Corrections treatment programs can accommodate only two thousand inmates.

6. Here at Bedford there are high levels of teacher absenteeism in some courses, for whatever reasons, and substitutes don't exist. Obviously, improving one's level of education is an essential first step, but the GED itself, or even a sociology degree from Mercy College, may not open many doors for these women. Reading, writing, and the true discipline of learning get short shrift. The most useful program is the inmate maintenance program. In it a woman can learn something about plumbing, electrical work, bricklaying, virtually all the building skills. They learn by doing, but only fifteen women at a time can avail themselves of it, and there are almost six hundred women here.

7. There is an electronics course which I am told is a pretty good course when it meets, but many days it doesn't meet. And women are not permitted to put most of what they learn into practice. At Bedford, any inmate possession that needs fixing, like a lamp, hot pot, radio or TV, must be sent out to be fixed, and paid for by women who haven't any money, and who would profit by learning how to fix things themselves.

8. Not only are the number of useful things a prisoner may do limited, the time in which she is permitted to do them is limited still further. She is often physically, forcefully, deliberately not permitted to be on time. She stands in line to get through the door to get in line for the next door, in order to get in line to be fed and to get medication. She stands in line to sign into the clinic and to sign out of the clinic in order to get into the line to the nurse, which will get her into the line to see the doctor — not all in one day, but sometime in the future, at which time she will go through the whole thing all over again.

9. The only time she can go to the commissary is during the work day. She cannot stop early in the morning, or during lunch or dinner break, or in the evening. She must miss work if she wishes to shop, usually half a day of work. And since she can only shop once every two weeks, at an assigned time, she has no control over what day of work she misses.

10. There are some C.O.s who will only open a door on the hour and half hour, and since every clock in the facility says a different time, she can often wait for half an hour while she is hurrying to work, until the C.O.'s clock says "go" again. When this happens she doesn't just stop where she is and wait. She must go back to her floor and repeat the

whole process again. Unfortunately, for many women this modus operandi is quite satisfactory. If they get to work an hour late, because breakfast is an hour late, or the count is an hour late, or just about anything is an hour late, they get paid anyway — nickels and dimes, but the same amount they would have been paid for working. The message they get is simple, "Work is just another way to kill time . . . it don't mean nothin'."

11. Before I was moved to Fiske honor cottage, a housing unit the existence of which I thank God for on my knees every day, it was not unusual for me to stop as many as seventy-five times during the day to wait at a locked door. On Fridays it could be as high as ninety, since Friday evenings I go to Bedford Annex to play Bingo with the ladies there, and that has some extra doors. Here was my door schedule:

Doors to meals, 6 and return	18
Doors to work, 7 and return	14 A.M.
	14 P.M.
Doors to medication and return	8
Doors to a visit and return	14
Doors to commissary and return	6
Doors to volunteer work in the annex	16
	90

12. In prison one works in the moments one can snatch from the system. It suddenly seems easy to understand why prison industries lose money.

13. I have worked at a number of different positions in here, with varying degrees of success. As soon as an inmate has been checked by doctors and "medically cleared," she is assigned to eight weeks of maintenance work. After that she can, if she wishes, classify into other activities.

14. I did my first maintenance work in the hospital kitchen. This involved dishing out food, taking it around to patients, and then cleaning the kitchen. The best thing about it for me was that I had to go from one building to another to get to the kitchen, so I got a little exercise and fresh air.

15. "Security" is the great prison dumping ground. Whatever you do in here, wise or asinine, is always in the name of "security." Last year you could get home-cooked chicken through the package room, but you couldn't have corn on the cob. This year you can have corn on the cob, but you can't have home-cooked chicken.

16. Last year you could wear your own sweaters in the visiting room, but you couldn't wear your own blouses. Then you couldn't wear anything but prison issue. Now you can wear your own shirts and sweaters, but the sweaters can only be a solid color. Two years ago the state issue was in yellow, blue, and green. This year blue is contraband, and yellow is all right for your own clothes, but not for state issue. I was summarily

removed from graduation exercises one year, by a lieutenant, because I was wearing a yellow state-issued jumper. I was made to turn it in to the state store the next day. Yellow state issue was permitted the rest of the inmates for the next year, but not for me.

17. About six months ago inmates at Bedford were told to turn in all their metal hangers and get plastic ones. One can see the sense in that and only wonder why we had metal ones for as long as we did. We asked family and friends to bring us plastic hangers and this they did. As of June 30 of this year plastic hangers were listed as "contraband" and anyone found with a round plastic hanger would be issued a charge sheet.

18. A total lack of consistency and judgment is known to play a role in mental illness. There is no way it could not. I have finally come to terms with this by simply not caring what I am allowed to have and what I am not allowed to have. As long as I am permitted to stay at Fiske, and to read and to write, away from the worst of the obscenities, away from some of the constant C.O. harassment, I don't care what else I am allowed to have, what clothes, what food, or what creature comforts. When we were told that we could now wear our own sweaters again (I had given most of mine away to an inmate's daughter when they said we couldn't) I made two new ones for myself. One is a rose colored one into which I knit my initials. Less than two months after it was finished we were told, starting April 1, that any sweater or blouse with a monogram on it would be contraband.

19. My first "regular" job was as a teacher's aide in the high school equivalency class. The classroom I went to work in was a double room with anywhere from forty to forty-seven students in it, morning and afternoon, a different group each time. When I arrived, and for most of the time that I worked there, there was only one teacher for all the subjects. There had been an English teacher previously, but for over a year the math teacher had taught alone. Students came and went constantly. They still do. Ethel is transferred to Albion; Charlene gets parole; Tootsie "max's out," Dawn's "in lock." Each student works at her own speed, in workbooks. Grammar, fractions, and percentages are the hardest subjects. Some go as far as beginning algebra. There are no reading assignments at all. Graduation comes when you get 225 on the GED graduation equivalency exam.

20. If a student has a question, she raises her hand, and the teacher goes over to her and answers the question. My function was that of a teacher's aide. Teaching to a test, out of workbooks, is a most undesirable way to teach or learn; but, given the conditions that prevail here, it is the most practical way to approach the job. You don't know whether the class will arrive at 8:00 or 9:00, or anytime in between; you don't know which member will be on "call out" to go to commissary, to get her hair fixed, to see a counselor, to go to the nurse, or to a visit.

21. The only thing the students have in common, other than their incarceration, is their ability to read at a sixth-grade level or above. Some spent four years in high school outside, and didn't graduate; some left to hang out or to have a baby in the ninth or tenth grade. Some are just killing time on something they hope will look good to their parole board. They do virtually no work at all, and they disrupt all the others. Some seriously want to work and pass the exam. The women deserve medals for working conscientiously under very difficult conditions, sticking to the job, rising above all the distractions and finally passing. Even under the best conditions, it's hard to go back to school when you remember it as little more than a series of failures. And even when they have passed the GED exam with the magic 225, they are often a long way from being prepared to do college work, that is, honest to God, college level work. Nevertheless, they are allowed to go on.

22. Selena was my prize pupil. She had been here for thirteen years when we began to work together. She still hadn't passed her GED exam, which was sinfully wasteful because she read better than most of the women who had. At the end of her fourteenth year here Selena got Work Release. One of the first things she did outside was take the GED exam and pass it, not because of anything I had taught her. I had only convinced her that she was capable of passing it. It is that assurance, that they are people of value and ability, that is so completely missing in some of their lives.

23. It was a combination of frustration and depression, and just plain boredom that made me decide to leave being a teacher's aide and find something new. I was classified into South Forty in the morning, and the Children's Center in the afternoon.

24. The South Forty program was begun in 1968 at one New York prison, Greenhaven, by William Vanderbilt of the Vanderbilt family. He was interested in the American prison system from the standpoint of rehabilitation. He believed, from what he had observed in his visits to prisons, that much time and talent were wasted there, and not enough was being done to help prisoners get a decent start on the outside. Today the program is still active in six New York State prisons, Bedford among them.

25. It is both publicly and privately funded, and its primary goal is still to help prisoners prepare for re-entry into society, to help them discover where their interests and talents lie, to offer them the chance to develop appropriate skills, and to put them in touch with individuals or groups on the outside who can steer them toward housing and employment. Workshops are offered by volunteers from the outside in subjects as varied as tatting and accounting. One volunteer has organized and manages a small boutique outlet on Long Island where prisoners may sell their work.

26. Much of the newest equipment in the room, including the kiln, was

purchased by the inmates themselves with money they earned selling their work. The ceramic artwork of one of the women, who had never done it before coming to Bedford, has had a showing in New York. South Forty is the only program in the prison I know of that encourages women to create, at a professional level, and then helps them to sell their wares and support themselves.

27. I hope there will be other programs here in which women who want to work can earn more than the $1.55 per day which is the prison's maximum! You start at $.70 per day if you work morning and afternoon. The prison feeds and clothes a prisoner, and provides toothpaste, when it's available, and a bar of very strong soap made by the men in another prison.

28. I have reached the maximum salary now, $7.76 a week, but with family and friends constantly asking me what I need, I have plenty of shampoo, deodorant, snacks, fresh fruit, tea, books, pens, pencils, and writing paper. Many women here have no one on the outside to visit them or send them packages. And for well over half the women, cigarettes are like oxygen. Many came in addicted to drugs and alcohol, and cigarettes play a very important role. Earning the maximum prison wage they can buy one carton of cigarettes every month but that leaves little for toiletries or coffee or Cremora. Since some women will spend anywhere from five to twenty-five years in here, that is a mighty meager existence.

2904 words

Reading Times	Reading Speed
1st reading ____ minutes	15 minutes = 194 wpm
3rd reading ____ minutes	14 minutes = 207 wpm
	13 minutes = 223 wpm
	12 minutes = 242 wpm
	11 minutes = 264 wpm

2.2
SECOND READING

Go back and read the passage again. Take as much time as you need this time. Look up some of the unfamiliar words in the glossary at the end of the book or in your dictionary if you wish.

2.3
THIRD READING

Read the passage quickly a third time. Concentrate on understanding the main ideas of the passage and the meanings of new vocabulary words in the context in which they appear.

2.4
READER RESPONSE

In order to explore your response to this reading, write for 15 minutes about anything that interested you in this passage. You may wish to write about some aspect of prison life — or you may wish to disagree with something in the passage. Try to explore *your own thoughts and feelings* as much as possible. Do *not* merely summarize or restate the ideas in this passage.

2.5
RESPONSE SHARING

Read your response to two or three other people in your class. Listen carefully to what the others have written. After you have discussed each other's responses, talk about other points of interest in the passage.

2.6
IDENTIFYING MAIN IDEAS

Working with the same small group, make a list of the main ideas in this passage. Be sure to state the main ideas in your own words. Don't just copy sentences directly from the text. Think carefully about what the writer is trying to tell you.

2.7
ANALYZING THE TEXT

Work with your group members on this exercise. Discuss the answers carefully, particularly if there are disagreements among members of your group. In some cases, there may be more than one possible interpretation.

1. How would you describe Mrs. Harris's account of life in prison?
   a. angry (describing the difficulties of being an inmate)
   b. positive (looking at the good points of prison education and training)
   c. neutral (telling us the facts in an objective way)
2. At the end of paragraph 4, Mrs. Harris lists a number of self-help courses that are available (Alcoholics Anonymous, Down on Violence, and others). How do you know these courses are needed in prison?
   a. from the following description of the inmate maintenance program
   b. from information at the beginning of the same paragraph
   c. from information in the next paragraph
   Document your answer with one or more specific sentences.
3. In paragraphs 8 to 11, Mrs. Harris describes the process for getting from

one place to another and for going through doors. Why do you think she describes all the steps in such great detail?
   a. She wants the reader to sympathize with her when she has to go back to her floor and repeat the whole process.
   b. She wants the reader to visualize what a long, time-wasting process it is.
   c. She wants the reader to understand how excellent the security is in the whole prison.
4. In paragraph 18, Mrs. Harris says "A total lack of consistency and judgment is known to play a role in mental illness." This sentence refers to the example(s) given in:
   a. paragraph 15.
   b. paragraph 16.
   c. paragraph 17.
   d. *a* and *b* only.
   e. *b* and *c* only.
   f. *a*, *b*, and *c*.
   What is she trying to show in these examples?
5. Mrs. Harris wants the reader to see that:
   a. life in prison is very rigid and frustrating.
   b. most women can learn new skills in prison.
   c. she is not guilty of committing any crime.
   Explain your answer and give examples.

2.8
VOCABULARY STUDY

Study the italicized words and phrases in their contexts and guess at their meanings. Write your guess in the first blank. Then look up the word or phrase in your dictionary and write the definition in the second blank.

1. (paragraph 1) On February 28, 1981, I was found guilty of murdering Dr. Herman Tarnower. Judge Leggett congratulated the jury on their *verdict.*

   a. (guess) _____

   b. (dictionary) _____

2. (paragraph 3) It was developed and laminated on the spot, so that I would not have to *venture* any further without my ID. . . . My next stop was the state store.

   a. (guess) _____

   b. (dictionary) _____

3. (paragraph 6) In it a woman can learn something about . . . virtually all the building skills. They learn by doing, but only fifteen women at a time can *avail* themselves of it, and there are almost six hundred women here.

   a. (guess) ————————————————————————————

   b. (dictionary) ————————————————————————

4. (paragraph 20) Teaching to a test, out of workbooks, is a most undesirable way to teach or learn; but, given the conditions that *prevail* here, it is the most practical way to approach the job.

   a. (guess) ————————————————————————————

   b. (dictionary) ————————————————————————

5. (paragraph 21) Some seriously want to work and pass the exam. These women deserve medals for working *conscientiously* under very difficult conditions, sticking to the job, rising above all the distractions and finally passing.

   a. (guess) ————————————————————————————

   b. (dictionary) ————————————————————————

6. (paragraph 28) Earning the maximum prison wage they can buy one carton of cigarettes every month but that leaves little for toiletries or coffee or Cremora. Since some women will spend anywhere from five to twenty-five years in here, that is a mighty *meager* existence.

   a. (guess) ————————————————————————————

   b. (dictionary) ————————————————————————

2.9
SPECIAL EXPRESSIONS

The phrases in bold type have special meanings. Study these phrases in their contexts. Then choose the definition from the list below that means the same thing and write it over the phrase. Be sure to use correct verb tenses and singular or plural forms for nouns. Check your answers in your glossary or dictionary.

be alert	little attention
establish contact with	loiter
give something up	realize and accept
provide opportunities	spend time doing nothing

1. Options are few, especially in a women's prison. You must **keep your eyes and ears open** for whatever opportunities may come up.
2. Obviously, improving one's level of education is an essential first step, but the GED itself may not **open many doors** for these women.
3. Here at Bedford there are high levels of teacher absenteeism and substitutes don't exist. Reading, writing, and the true discipline of learning get **short shrift.**
4. "Work is just another way to **kill time** . . . it don't mean nothin'."
5. Yellow is all right for your own clothes. I was summarily removed from graduation exercises one year because I was wearing a yellow state-issued jumper. I was made to **turn it in** the next day.
6. A total lack of consistency is known to play a role in mental illness. I have finally **come to terms with** this by simply not caring what I am allowed to have and what I am not allowed to have.
7. Some spent four years in high school, some left to **hang out** or to have a baby.
8. The South Forty program helps prepare prisoners for re-entry into society and to **put them in touch with** groups on the outside who can steer them toward housing and employment.

2.10
APPLICATION, CRITICAL EVALUATION, AND SYNTHESIS

1. Look back at your answers to the questions in the first reading. What are your impressions of prison life after reading Mrs. Harris's description? Are any of your attitudes about prison getting stronger, changing, remaining about the same? Describe and compare. Do you think life is too easy, too hard, or the way it should be for prisoners? Why? Give some examples.
2. If you were running the prison Mrs. Harris is in, what would you keep the same? What would you change? How does Bedford Prison compare to the description of prisons in the first reading? Find several specific points where Mrs. Harris' experience clarifies or gives examples of something that was mentioned in the first reading.
3. Later in her book, Mrs. Harris describes how difficult it is for incarcerated mothers to have some meaningful contact with their children and her efforts to teach these women how to be good mothers. From this reading, can you get some impression of the problems that many of the women in prison have? How did many of them fit into society before they came to prison? Give some examples.
4. Mrs. Harris is a very well educated woman. She can write about prison in a way that many inmates could not. Do you think Mrs. Harris is being totally objective about prison life? Or is she describing prison from her own personal perspective? Give some examples.

CRIMINAL'S APOLOGY

Roger Smith was originally arrested for theft in the First Degree, for selling salvaged building materials. The defendant failed to appear in court on 3-3-86 as ordered by the Circuit Court. He was subsequently arrested and plead guilty to Felony Failure to Appear. He was placed on probation by the court, and the judge stated at the time of sentencing that he would have probably sent the defendant to prison, but that prison overcrowding prevented this.

APOLOGY

NOTE: This apology was submitted by the defendant without editing prior to publication.

I apologize to the citizens of Newport for my improper business dealings in connection with the Jump-Off Joe condominiums. I was arrested because of these business dealings. After my arrest, I was released from jail after agreeing to appear in court. I then failed to appear in court. I urge the citizens of Lincoln County to pass a bond measure authorizing the construction of a new jail.

Roger a. Smith

CRIME STOPPERS TIP: Based upon a Federal consent decree signed by the county in 1984 the maximum capacity of the Lincoln County Jail was reduced from approximately 70 beds with an average of 43 inmates, to 26 beds including four spaces for females. Lincoln County has no secure facilities for juveniles. Lincoln County currently pays $36,000 per year for one bed at the Mid-Valley Detention Center in Salem for juvenile detention. In 1985 Lincoln County conditionally released 2015 defendants from custody. An adequate jail is necessary for a well functioning criminal justice system.

This announcement appeared in the News Times, Newport, Oregon, on August 6, 1986

3
Considering the Alternatives

True or *False:* If a person commits a crime, he or she should always go to prison. This reading from *Time* magazine (February 2, 1987) answers this question "false." It contends that there are alternative ways to punish people. The alternatives range from paying fines to paying back the victim to performing public service. While these are fairly new concepts in the United States, they are already widely practiced in other countries, such as Sweden and Britain. Reprinted by permission.

3.1
FIRST READING

Read this article quickly for the main ideas. Pay attention to the title and the alternative sentences as you read. Do *not* stop to look up words in your dictionary.

1. Jim Guerra sells cars today in Dallas. He used to sell cocaine in Miami. In 1984, after being robbed and even kidnapped by competitors, he decided it was time for a career change. He gave up drugs — and the drug trade — and headed out to Texas for a new law-abiding life. The old life caught up with him anyway. In December, 1985, federal agents arrested him on charges connected to his Florida coke dealing. After pleading guilty last spring Guerra faced 15 years in prison.

2. He never went. These days Guerra, 32, is putting in time instead of doing it, by logging 400 hours over $2\frac{1}{2}$ years as a fund raiser and volunteer for Arts for People, a nonprofit group that provides artists and entertainers for the critically ill at Dallas-area hospitals and institutions. His sentence, which also includes a $15,000 fine, means that a prison system full to bursting need not make room for one more. He sees a benefit to the community too. "I just love the job," he says. "I'll probably continue it after the sentence is up."

3. The work may be admirable, but is a stint of public service the just deserts of crime? Many people would say no, but they may not be the same ones who must contend with the bedlam of American prisons. In recent years, a get-tough trend toward longer sentences and more of them has had a predictable consequence. The nation's prison population now stands at a record 529,000, a total that grows by 1,000 each week; new cells are not being built in matching numbers. While virtually everyone convicted is a candidate for prison, many experts believe perhaps half the inmate population need not be incarcerated at all.

4. In courts across the nation, people convicted of nonviolent crimes, from drunken driving and mail fraud to car theft and burglary, are being told in effect to go to their rooms. Judges are sentencing them to confinement at home or in dormitory halfway houses, with permission to go to and from work but often no more — not even a stop on the way home for milk. The sentences may also include stiff fines, community service and a brief, bracing taste of prison.

5. Some supporters of alternative schemes look to the day when prison cells will be reserved exclusively for career criminals and the violent, with extramural penalties held out for the wayward of every other variety. "We're all against crime," says Herbert Hoelter, director of the National Center on Institutions and Alternatives, a nonprofit group that designed Guerra's package of penalties and persuaded the judge in his case to accept them. "But we need to convince people that there are other ways to get justice."

6. Anyway, who can afford to keep all offenders behind bars? Depending on the prison, it can cost from $7,000 to more than $30,000 to keep a criminal in a cell for a year. Most alternative programs, their backers argue, allow lawbreakers to live at home, saving tax dollars while keeping families intact and off welfare. Since the detainees can get or keep jobs, part of their salaries can be paid out as fines or as compensation to victims. And alternatives give judges a sentencing option halfway between locking up offenders and turning them loose.

7. It remains to be seen, however, whether the new programs will have much appeal for a crime-wary public and law-enforcement establishment. That prison time can be harrowing is to some minds its first merit. The living-room sofa is by comparison a painless instrument of remorse. "Until the alternatives are seen by the public as tough, there won't be support for them," says Thomas Reppeto of the Citizens' Crime Commission in New York City. The problem is even plainer when the offenders are well heeled. Will justice be served if crooked stock traders are confined to their penthouses?

8. The experience of Ron Rusich, 29, a house painter in Mobile, was typical. In 1984 he received a 15-year sentence for burglary. But an intensive probation scheme used in his state since 1982 eventually sent

him back outside, and back to work, under strict supervision. A 10 p.m.-to-6 a.m. curfew was enforced during the first three months after release by at least one surprise visit each week from the corrections officer. There were three other weekly meetings, with restrictions eased as his time in the program increased. Living at home, as he was required to do for 2½ years, Rusich cost the state $8.72 a day, less than a third the expense of keeping him in prison. The experience was a "lifesaver," says Rusich, who is now on parole.

9. A few localities have resorted to the most low-tech deterrent of all: shame. Sarasota County, Fla., is trying the "scarlet letter"* approach, by requiring motorists convicted of drunk driving to paste bumper stickers on their cars announcing the fact. In Lincoln County, Ore., a few felons have even been given a choice between prison and publishing written apologies, accompanied by their photographs, in local newspapers. Roger Smith, 29, paid $294.12 to announce his contrition in two papers after a guilty plea growing out of a theft charge. A published apology "takes the anonymity out of crime," insists Ulys Stapleton, Lincoln County district attorney. "People can't blend back into the woodwork."

10. Do alternatives work? That depends on what they are asked to accomplish. If the goal is cost efficiency, the answer is a qualified yes. If the goal is a society with fewer criminals, then firm judgments are even harder to draw. No criminal sanction, no matter how strict, no matter how lenient, seems to have much impact on the crime rate. But prison does at least keep criminals off the street. Home confinement cannot guarantee that security. Some data, tentative and incomplete, do suggest, however, that felons placed on intensive probation are less likely to commit crimes again than those placed on traditional probation or sent to prison. Joan Petersilia, a Rand Corp. researcher, says the recidivism† rate of such offenders is impressively low, "usually less than 20%." And many keep their jobs, she adds. "That's the real glimmer of hope — that in the long run these people will become functioning members of the community."

11. One essential for getting courts to consider alternative sentencing, says University of Chicago Law Professor Norval Morris, is to develop a publicly understood "exchange rate" between prison time and other forms of punishment, a table of penalties that judges can use for guidance on how to sentence offenders. "We should be able to say that for this crime by this criminal, either x months in prison, or a $50,000 fine plus home detention for a year plus x number of hours in community service," Morris contends.

---

* *scarlet letter:* a public announcement
† *recidivism:* committing another crime after getting out of prison

12. A similar table is already in use in Minnesota, where alternative sentencing has become well established since the 1978 passage of a law that limits new sentences to ensure that prison capacity is not exceeded by the total number of inmates. The crime rate has not increased, supporters boast. Other states remain far more hesitant. Still, the present pressures may yet bring a day when the correctional possibilities will be so varied and so widely used that prison will seem the "alternative" form of punishment.

1271 words

Reading Times
1st reading ——— minutes
3rd reading ——— minutes

Reading Speed
8 minutes = 159 wpm
7 minutes = 182 wpm
6 minutes = 212 wpm
5 minutes = 254 wpm
4 minutes = 318 wpm

3.2
SECOND READING

Go back and read the article again. Take as much time as you need this time. Look up some of the unfamiliar words in the glossary at the end of the book or in your dictionary if you wish.

3.3
THIRD READING

Read the article quickly a third time. Concentrate on understanding the main ideas of the article and the meanings of new vocabulary words in the context in which they appear.

3.4
READER RESPONSE

In order to explore your response to this reading, write for 15 minutes about anything that interested you in this article. You may wish to write about your reactions to some of the ideas presented here — or you may wish to disagree with something in the article. Try to explore *your own thoughts and feelings* as much as possible. Do *not* merely summarize or restate the ideas in this article.

3.5
RESPONSE SHARING

Read your response to two or three other people in your class. Listen carefully to what the others have written. After you have discussed each other's responses, talk about other points of interest in the article.

3.6
IDENTIFYING MAIN IDEAS

Working with the same small group, make a list of the main ideas in this article. Be sure to state the main ideas in your own words. Don't just copy sentences directly from the text. Think carefully about what the writer is trying to tell you.

3.7
ANALYZING THE TEXT

Work with your group members on this exercise. Discuss the answers carefully, particularly if there are disagreements among members of your group. In some cases, there may be more than one possible interpretation.

1. The writer of this magazine article seems to be:
   a. in favor of alternative sentencing.
   b. opposed to alternative sentencing.
   c. undecided about alternative sentencing.
   Discuss your answer and give some examples.
2. Concerning the description of Roger Smith (who published an apology in his local newspaper), the reason the local district attorney gave for the success of this method of punishment is:
   a. the cost of the announcement was so expensive that a person would not want to pay for another one in the future.
   b. announcing a guilty plea in public discourages a person from committing another crime.
   c. punishing a person in public is very embarrassing because everyone will know who he is and what he did.
3. Read paragraph 10 carefully. Then write whether these statements are true *(T)* or false *(F)*.

   a. _____ Alternative sentences seem to be cost effective, but it is still not certain whether they lower the crime rate.

   b. _____ Putting offenders in prison lowers the crime rate.

c. _____ Typically, the rate of recidivism (committing another crime after getting out of jail) is over 20%.

4. Some data suggest that felons placed on intensive probation are less likely to commit crimes again than **those** placed on traditional probation or sent to prison. Joan Petersilia says the recidivism rate of **such offenders** is impressively low. And **many** keep **their** jobs, she adds. "That's the real glimmer of hope — that in the long run **these people** will become functioning members of the community.

For each answer choose either

(a) felons placed on intensive probation OR

(b) felons placed on traditional probation or sent to prison

those refers to _____

such offenders refers to _____

many refers to _____

their refers to _____

these people refers to _____

5. The stories of Jim Guerra, Ron Rusich, and Roger Smith are used in this article to show:

a. the variety of crimes that guilty people commit.

b. examples of several different types of alternative sentences.

c. the difficulty of knowing whether alternative sentences are successful or unsuccessful.

3.8
VOCABULARY STUDY

Study the italicized words and phrases in their contexts and guess at their meanings. Write your guess in the first blank. Then, look up the word or phrase in your dictionary and write the definition in the second blank.

1. (paragraph 7) It remains to be seen, however, whether the new programs will have much appeal for a crime-*wary* public and law enforcement establishment. That prison time can be harrowing is to some minds its first merit.

a. (guess) _____

b. (dictionary) _____

2. (paragraph 8) But an intensive probation *scheme* used in his state since 1982 eventually sent him back outside, and back to work, under strict supervision. A 10 p.m.-to-6 a.m. curfew was enforced. . . . there were three other weekly meetings.

a. (guess) _____

b. (dictionary) _____

3. (paragraph 9) Roger Smith, 29, paid $294.12 to announce his contrition in two papers. . . . A published apology "takes the *anonymity* out of crime," insists . . . the Lincoln County district attorney. "People can't blend back into the woodwork."

a. (guess) _____

b. (dictionary) _____

4. (paragraph 10) Joan Petersilia . . . says the recidivism rate of such offenders is *impressively* low, "usually less than 20%."

a. (guess) _____

b. (dictionary) _____

5. (paragraph 10) And many keep their jobs, she adds. "That's the real glimmer of hope — that *in the long run* these people will become functioning members of the community."

a. (guess) _____

b. (dictionary) _____

3.9
READING GRAPHS

Look at the graphs and answer these questions. Discuss your answers with your small group.

1. Graph A shows:
   a. why the criminal homicide (murder) rate was highest in the Netherlands from 1979 to 1984.
   b. the criminal homicide rates from 1975 to 1984 in various countries.
   c. both a and b.
2. The numbers in the left-hand column (1, 2, 3 . . .) represent:
   a. the seriousness of the crimes committed.
   b. the populations of the countries shown per 100,000 people.
   c. the number of homicides per 100,000 people.
3. After the Netherlands, which country had the highest homicide rate of the countries shown

   a. in 1979? _____

   b. in 1980? _____

   c. in 1982? _____

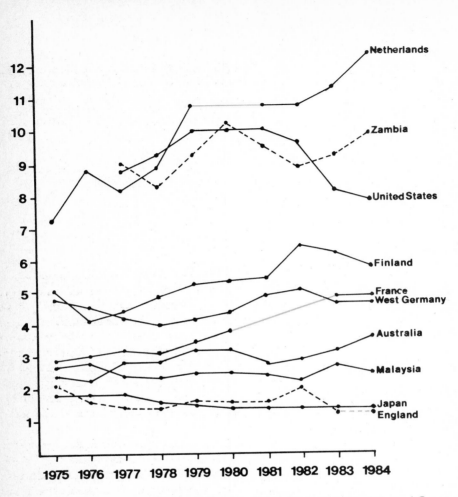

Graph A: Variation in Reported Criminal Homicide Rate for Selected Countries, 1975–1984 [rates per 100,000 population]. *Source:* INTERPOL, International Crime Statistics, 1975–1984 (Paris: General Secretariat of the International Criminal Police Organization). Lighter line represents missing data.

4. What can you conclude about England from Graph A?
   a. England is the smallest country represented and therefore has had fewer homicides.
   b. England, along with Japan, has consistently had the lowest yearly homicide rate of any country shown.
   c. England and Japan have the same population size.
5. Now look at Graph B, "Reported Aggravated Theft Rates." Does Graph B show all aggravated thefts in each country?

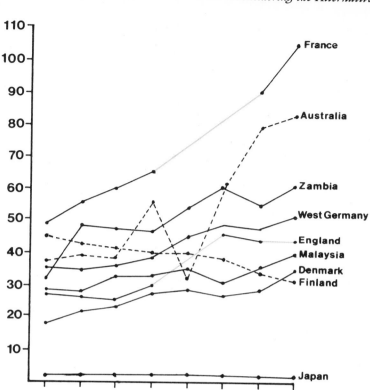

Graph B: Variation in Reported "Aggravated Theft" (Robbery and Violent Theft) Offense Rates, Selected Countries, 1977–1984 [rates per 100,000 population]. *Source:* INTERPOL, International Crime Statistics, 1977–1984 (Paris: General Secretariat of the International Criminal Police Organization). Lighter line represents missing data.

    a. No, it shows only the reported thefts.
    b. Yes, it shows all thefts that occurred.
    c. It is impossible to tell from the information given.

6. Which two countries, in your opinion, had the most dramatic changes in aggravated theft rates over these 8 years? Why do you think so?

    a. _____

    b. _____

7. What is notable about the country with the highest theft rate? About the one with the lowest rate? Discuss your opinion with your small group.

    a. Highest: _____

    b. Lowest: _____

8. Where did the basic data for these graphs come from?
   a. selected countries
   b. national police organizations
   c. INTERPOL

3.10
APPLICATION, CRITICAL EVALUATION, AND SYNTHESIS

1. In this final selection, the general message seems to be that prison is necessary for career criminals (repeat offenders) and for the violent, but there might be better ways to punish other kinds of offenders. Do you agree or disagree with this statement? Give examples from the three readings in this unit and from your own knowledge to support your answer.
2. This reading raises several questions about whether alternative sentencing is really "punishment." How would you answer the following questions? Give several reasons and examples. Reread the paragraph noted in parentheses before you answer each question.
   a. Will justice be served if crooked stock traders are confined to their penthouses? (What is implied in this question? Does it really refer only to stock traders or to other wealthy criminals too?) (paragraph 7)
   b. Can the "scarlet letter" approach (a public announcement) be effective? (For what type of criminal might it work? What do you think of the sentences described here?) (paragraph 9)
   c. Do you think a fair "exchange rate" can be developed between prison sentences and other forms of punishment? Why or why not? (paragraph 11)
3. Go back to the first reading in this unit and look at your answers to exercise 1.10, question 3. Do you still agree with what you said there? Would you like to add anything to your answer? Would you change any of your opinions? Why or why not?
4. Do you think the three readings in this chapter have provided a fair view of prison concerns? Are they too idealistic? Too pessimistic? Are there other aspects of the realities of offenders, prisons, the courts, and law enforcement that you think should be discussed? Describe these topics and some of the specific concerns that need to be addressed.

TURN TO THE EXPANSION SECTION ON PAGE 187 FOR PRACTICE IN DOING LIBRARY RESEARCH AND REPORT WRITING.

Unit 4
Leisure Time

DISCUSSION

People everywhere need to work — and need to play. However, research has found that different cultures have different definitions of "leisure" and handle their leisure time differently. Even within a culture, individuals do very different kinds of things for enjoyment. This chapter investigates some of the many ways that people think about their leisure time and what they do with it. Before you begin reading, discuss these questions.

1. In your country, what do people like to do for enjoyment in their free time?
2. Do men and women participate in the same types of activities? If they do, do they participate equally, or do men do some things more and women do others more? If not, what are the differences between the activities that men and women do?
3. Is there a popular national sport in your country? Why do you think it is so popular? Please explain and give some examples.
4. What do you personally like to do in your leisure time? Do you do these things well? Do you care if you are good at these activities (is it important to you that you do them well)? Why or why not?
5. Have you ever tried to do something extremely difficult in your leisure time (for example, learning to parachute or running a 25-kilometer marathon)? If you did, why did you do it? How did you feel while you were trying to do it? If not, would you ever try to do something very difficult? Why or why not?

People practicing golf in Tokyo, Japan

1
How Japan, Inc., Plays

The Japanese are known around the world as serious, hard workers. But did you know that they treat their leisure time seriously too? This reading, taken from a special newspaper report on life in "Pacific Rim" countries, looks at the differences between how the Japanese view leisure time and how Westerners view it. (*The Seattle Times,* August 24, 1986) Reprinted by permission.

1.1
FIRST READING

Read this selection quickly for the main ideas. Think about the title as you read. Do *not* stop to look up words in your dictionary.

1. Eiji Hamada, who once hit a famous hole-in-one, says he can't fathom the attitude of Americans when they play golf. "Sometimes they have a whiskey bottle in their pocket, or they sing, or they talk about their families or sex," Hamada says. "However, the Japanese, we never have alcohol and we don't talk about anything but golf. We aim to improve our scores." Hamada, who meets Americans through his work for the advertising agency, Dentsu, has pondered this. "There is a very serious difference between foreigners and Japanese, and you can apply it to any sport," he says.

2. A relentlessness propels the typical Japanese. Dedication to the task at hand is its own reward. This determination is reflected in leisure activities and in the flip side of leisure — work. The average American works 1,930 hours a year and often treasures time away from the job. The average Japanese man works 2,100 hours a year, including at least half of most Saturdays. When not in the office with his colleagues, he's probably drinking or golfing with them.

3. "How do you explain that you have more than one family in Japan?" asks Dick Bush, an American who has lived here more than 20 years. "I have the feeling that the family that's most important is the family you spend your time with, the people at the office," Bush says. "I don't know any Japanese who go home at 5 o'clock."

4. Income levels in both countries are among the highest in the world, but in Japan comparatively little is spent on personal comforts. While America is a nation of consumers, Japan is a nation of savers, and the average citizen here banks 17 percent of his or her income. The savings pool is a vast reservoir of low-cost capital, which Japan uses for economic development. But recently this formula of hard work and self-denial has become a political burden internationally, and a source of some concern among Japanese who peer into the future and wonder about Japan's suitability for success in a changing world.

5. "The time has come for Japan to make a historical transformation in its traditional policies on economic management and the nation's life-style," Prime Minister Yasuhiro Nakasone declared in April 1986. Japan must become a bit less competitive internationally, Nakasone said. Work a little less and play a little more, and spend more, especially on goods from abroad, he suggested to his countrymen. Young Japanese are more inclined to leisure and consumption than their elders, but it is unclear how much such urgings as Nakasone's will cause things to change — or who will benefit if the Japanese become less productive.

6. One reflection of Japanese concern is the quasi-governmental Leisure Development Center, founded 14 years ago to promote leisure in Japan. Managing Director Motoyuki Miyano acknowledges looking at the issue from a Japanese rather than an American perspective. Miyano says a U.S. diplomat he knew in Moscow couldn't wait to retire to a comfortable life in the American Southwest. "Honestly speaking," Miyano says, "I, as a Japanese, could not understand why he would want to quit his life's work and move to the Southwest. That is a difference in the way of thinking."

7. It becomes clear in conversations with the Japanese that while many are passionate about their work, others do not appreciate the long hours, nor do they gladly forgo vacations. Some might prefer not to spend their free time with the people from the office, nor to tee off for golf on a rainy Sunday at 4:30 a.m. — after an hour-long ride by taxi from Tokyo. But these activities are expected, and Japan is a nation where people perform to expectations. One must at least appear to work hard, and this requires sacrifice. Spending evenings with peers, the same ones year after year, may lead to success in a company. Playing golf and talking about it may enhance a man's status. Even if it isn't sincerely enjoyed, golf is prestigious because it is expensive — a land-intensive game in a nation with little land to spare.

8. As in adult work and leisure, Japanese show a compulsion to perform in school and retirement. "Gateball" is the pastime of choice among many retirees. Four hundred thousand people play it in Tokyo alone, according to the Japan Gateball Federation. Physically it is a gentle sport, adapted from croquet just after World War II. But like many Western things that have been "Japanized," gateball has assumed elements of ritual and intensity.

9. The elderly players wear numbered jerseys, address each other by number rather than name, line up and bow at prescribed moments, and follow rules regarding where they may stand, to whom they may speak, and what they must say before taking a shot. But the most striking difference between gateball and croquet is the spirit in which it is played.

10. Watch an hour of recreational gateball, and you see that it really matters who wins and who loses. Recently, an elderly Japanese committed suicide because his gateball score wasn't sufficiently improved. "You don't have to commit suicide over gateball," chides Moroi Suzuki, general director of the Shinjuku Ward of the Gateball Federation. But Suzuki understands how it could happen. "In any sport, you need intensity," he explains.

11. To some Japanese, the laxness with which Westerners pursue their leisure activities reflects a laxness that carries over into the work place. This image contributes to suspicions about the quality of Western products and services. "When I go fishing, what I care about is how many fish I catch," Hamada says. "But in the U.S. they enjoy nature or talk with friends or take a nap."

12. Hamada never takes a nap when he fishes, so how does he relax? "I go drinking and singing at karaoke bars every night after work. This releases frustrations," Hamada says. "I go out with my friends." Hamada, who is 49, is not alone. On the contrary, the typical Japanese "salaryman" leaves work sometime between 5 and 8 p.m., and gets home sometime between 9 and dawn — five or six nights a week, year after year.

13. As in many other things, in the pursuit of relaxation the Japanese husband and wife are not together. Women, wrote Edwin O. Reischauer in his highly regarded book *The Japanese,* "have virtually no extra-family social life. Except for a very few at the top of society, who may participate stiffly and unhappily in formal banquets, . . . married women do not go out with their husbands to dinners and parties or entertain outsiders in their homes, which are usually so small as to preclude this sort of entertainment. Their life is likely to be limited to husband, children, a few close relatives, some old schoolday girl friends, and possibly the activities of the PTA."

14. The man has his office colleagues, with whom he may dine and drink

most nights for decades. However, it isn't uncommon for a man to have never met his best friend's wife, even after decades of friendship.

15. Young women may go out on the town, patronize fashionable cafes, or dabble in tennis, skiing or scuba diving. Such activities almost invariably are undertaken in groups. "They do a whole lot until they get married, and then they do nothing," a young Tokyo woman says. "Once they are married and have children, their leisure amounts to talking to other mothers." The married woman has her children and the family budget to manage, and possibly she takes a daytime class in such things as flower arranging, the Japanese tea ceremony, or English. And there always are television programs, which tend to be gossipy during the day.

16. The pattern shows signs of change; some younger married couples go out to dinner together, and there may be less tolerance of a double standard. Still, the overall contrast of Japanese attitudes with those in the United States remains stark.

17. "I understand that in the U.S. you enjoy time with your wife, so it's entirely different," Hamada says. Unless he's working, Hamada tries to reserve Saturday for his family. Sundays are for golf. To him, this reflects a balance in life. He says his wife wouldn't know what to do with him during the week if he came home for dinner. She never cooks dinner, because he never eats it with her. Their only child is away at college.

18. Hiroto Nakayama doesn't know Eiji Hamada, but he says Hamada's description of Japanese work, leisure and relaxation is candid. But Nakayama, a social science researcher and author of a book on leisure in Japan, says attitudes are changing. Men and women under about 30 have a different outlook toward each other and toward leisure because they were raised in relative affluence, he says. Nakayama sees other changes in the offing. Greater affluence means more time and individuality, and spending figures already suggest a steady increase in interest in leisure, he says.

19. According to the Leisure Development Center, nearly 16 percent of the nation's Gross National Product is devoted to leisure pursuits. Fifty to 60 percent of the total is for after-work entertainment, Miyano says. He cites a poll that says the most popular form of leisure is eating out, followed by driving and domestic tourism.

20. One doesn't need a poll or a study to discern the importance of after-work entertainment. Some city blocks have literally hundreds of bars —a single narrow building may have 40 or more separate establishments, most tiny and catering to a known clientele. There are places to eat, places to drink, places to sing, places to be entertained, and places that provide various combinations of these services. The karaoke bar,

for example, is a place where men (and occasionally women) gather to listen to each other sing to recorded instrumental backgrounds. There may even be a stage.

21. By night, while their husbands troupe through the streets and bars of Tokyo together, the wives are at home. By day, when the men are at work, women may be taking classes from some place such as the Asahi Cultural Center. The center takes up three floors of a downtown Tokyo office building, and has 40,000 members, mostly middle-aged women and retirees of both sexes. The average student is a 43-year-old married woman. She pays a one-time $4,100 membership fee and monthly dues, and this month can choose from among 1,280 classes on 530 subjects.

22. The students come "just to kill time," in the opinion of Tamio Okada, director of the division of language. "Japanese women now are getting leisure time more and more," he says. "Their houses are more electrified. When their children get married, the mothers are free to do anything. They seek a purpose in life, a satisfaction."

23. Why is there such intensity in golf, gateball and other leisure? "That's the habit we acquired during the poor period," researcher Nakayama says. "People say Japanese society is wealthy, but that happened recently. To avoid feeling guilty, we work hard." Even the Japanese family vacation reflects intensity. Tours streak through foreign cities. To a people bent on efficiency, it is an "efficient" way to vacation. "Later, the Japanese will relax and spend more time in a single area," Nakayama predicts.

24. Miyano of the Leisure Development Center hasn't been looking so far into the future. He's been charting the here and now — charting the extent to which Japanese actually use earned vacation. It is an indication of how interested the nation is in leisure, he says. Presently, Miyano says, only 60 percent of the vacation time awarded to Japanese workers is used. Employees are voluntarily working the other 40 percent, even without extra pay. Obviously time off is not foremost on the minds of the Japanese. The Leisure Development Center has its work cut out for it.

25. And at the Leisure Development Center itself, what percentage of vacation is used? "That's a problem," Miyano says. He pauses. "Earlier I said that Japanese use only 60 percent of the paid holidays." He pauses again. "Here, we use only 50 percent."

26. Miyano understands how comical it may seem, but he says he's neither proud nor ashamed of his organization's own record on leisure time. Part of him likes the fact that his people labor so hard. "People here actually enjoy what they do," he explains. "The work they do here can be included as leisure."

1998 words

Reading Times	Reading Speed
1st reading _____ minutes	9 minutes = 222 wpm
3rd reading _____ minutes	8 minutes = 250 wpm
	7 minutes = 285 wpm
	6 minutes = 333 wpm

1.2
SECOND READING

Go back and read the selection again. Take as much time as you need this time. Look up some of the unfamiliar words in the glossary at the end of the book or in your dictionary if you wish.

1.3
THIRD READING

Read the selection quickly a third time. Concentrate on understanding the main ideas of the selection and the meanings of new vocabulary words in the context in which they appear.

1.4
READER RESPONSE

In order to explore your response to this reading, write for 15 minutes about anything that interested you in this selection. You may wish to write about a personal experience this selection reminded you of — or you may wish to disagree with something in the selection. Try to explore *your own thoughts and feelings* as much as possible. Do *not* merely summarize or restate the ideas in this selection.

1.5
RESPONSE SHARING

Read your response to two or three other people in your class. Listen carefully to what the others have written. After you have discussed each other's responses, talk about other points of interest in the selection.

1.6
IDENTIFYING MAIN IDEAS

Working with the same small group, make a list of the main ideas in this selection. Be sure to state the main ideas in your own words. Don't just copy sentences directly from the text. Think carefully about what the writer is trying to tell you.

1.7
ANALYZING THE TEXT

Work with your group members on this exercise. Discuss the answers carefully, particularly if there are disagreements among members of your group. In some cases, there may be more than one possible interpretation.

1. Which statement best describes the main idea of this entire reading?
   a. "People here actually enjoy what they do. The work they do here can be included as leisure." (paragraph 26)
   b. Dedication to the task at hand is its own reward. This determination is reflected in leisure activities and in the flip side of leisure — work. (paragraph 2)
   c. While America is a nation of consumers, Japan is a nation of savers. . . . (paragraph 4)
2. The question "How do you explain that you have more than one family in Japan?" (paragraph 3) refers to Mr. Bush's feeling that
   a. working men have a closer relationship to their office colleagues than to their wives and children.
   b. the Japanese don't go home at 5 o'clock because they don't like their wives and children.
   c. Japanese men prefer to work long hours.
3. Why is there such a long description of "gateball" in this reading?
   a. To explain how popular the game is among elderly Japanese.
   b. To give a vivid example of the "compulsion to perform" among Japanese.
   c. To show how a gentle Western game has been "Japanized."
   Why did you choose your answer?
4. However, it isn't uncommon for a man to have never met his best friend's wife, even after decades of friendship. (paragraph 14) This statement means that:
   a. a man will never meet his best friend's wife.
   b. a man has probably met his best friend's wife.
   c. a man has probably not met his best friend's wife.
5. According to the Leisure Development Center, nearly 16 percent of the nation's Gross National Product (GNP) is devoted to leisure pursuits. Fifty to 60 percent of the total is for after-work entertainment. This statement means that:
   a. after-work entertainment accounts for approximately half of the 16 percent of the GNP that is spent on leisure pursuits.

   b. 16 percent of the GNP is devoted to after-work entertainment.

   c. Fifty to 60 percent of the total population enjoy after-work enter-
      tainment.

1.8
VOCABULARY STUDY

Study the italicized words and phrases in their context and guess at their
meanings. Write your guess in the first blank. Then, look up the word or
phrase in your dictionary.

1. (paragraph 2) A *relentlessness* propels the typical Japanese. Dedication to
the task at hand is its own reward. This determination is reflected in
leisure activities and in the flip side of leisure — work.

   a. (guess) _____

   b. (dictionary) _____

2. (paragraph 7) Some might prefer not to spend their free time with the
people from the office, nor to tee off for golf on a rainy Sunday at 4:30
a.m. — after an hour-long ride by taxi from Tokyo. But these activities
are expected. . . . One must at least appear to work hard, and this
requires *sacrifice*.

   a. (guess) _____

   b. (dictionary) _____

3. (paragraph 7) Even if it isn't sincerely enjoyed, golf is *prestigious* because
it is expensive — a land-intensive game in a nation with little land to
spare.

   a. (guess) _____

   b. (dictionary) _____

4. (paragraph 18) Greater *affluence* means more time and individuality,
and spending figures already suggest a steady increase in interest in
leisure. . . . Nearly 16 percent of the nation's GNP is devoted to leisure
pursuits.

   a. (guess) _____

   b. (dictionary) _____

5. (paragraph 20) One doesn't need a poll or a study to *discern* the importance of after-work entertainment. Some city blocks have literally
hundreds of bars. . . .

a. (guess) ———————————————————————

b. (dictionary) ———————————————————

1.9
CONTEXT AND IMPLICATIONS

Sometimes, to understand a statement, you need to "read between the lines." That is, you must think about what the speaker *means* even if he or she doesn't say it directly in words. In the following exercise, analyze what the person really means — what the context is implying. You may want to reread the entire paragraph noted before answering the question.

1. Miyano says a U.S. diplomat he knew in Moscow couldn't wait to retire to a comfortable life in the American Southwest. "Honestly speaking," Miyano says, "I, as a Japanese, could not understand why he would want to quit his life's work and move to the Southwest." (paragraph 6) In this statement, Mr. Miyano implies, but does not directly say, that:
   a. he does not like the idea of retirement for himself.
   b. he thinks the American Southwest is an unpleasant place to live.
   c. the U.S. diplomat probably disliked living in Moscow.

2. Some might prefer not to spend their free time with the people from the office, nor to tee off for golf on a rainy Sunday morning at 4:30 a.m. But these activities are expected, and Japan is a land where people perform to expectations (paragraph 7). From this statement, you can infer that:
   a. the Japanese really don't like to take vacations or play golf. They only like to work.
   b. people in Japan are probably very concerned about what other Japanese think of them.
   c. people in Japan are comfortable doing whatever they want and don't worry about what other people think.

3. "You don't have to commit suicide over gateball," chides Moroi Suzuki. But Suzuki understands how it could happen. "In any sport, you need intensity," he explains (paragraph 10). Would Mr. Suzuki probably think the following statements are true *(T)* or false *(F)*? Explain your answers.

   a. ——— In sport, as in any other accomplishment, you must constantly try to improve.

   b. ——— It's all right to commit suicide if you do poorly in a sport.

   c. ——— When you are doing some sport as a hobby, you should take it easy and relax.

   d. ——— It really matters who wins and who loses.

   e. _____ Mr. Suzuki is terribly upset about the fact that an elderly gate-
        ball player committed suicide because of his poor score.
4. "When I go fishing, what I care about is how many fish I catch," Hamada says. "But in the U.S. they enjoy nature or talk with friends or take
   a nap." Reread paragraph 11. What is Mr. Hamada implying in his
   statement?
   a. Western products and services are as good as those in Japan.
   b. The Western concept of relaxation should be adopted by the Japa-
      nese.
   c. Westerners aren't serious enough about what they do.
5. By day women may be taking classes. The students come "just to kill
   time," in the opinion of Tamio Okada (paragraph 22). Mr. Okada is
   saying that the women:
   a. enjoy taking classes.
   b. have nothing else to do.
   c. now have leisure time.
6. As in many other things, in the pursuit of relaxation the Japanese husband and wife are not together (paragraph 13). From this statement, you
   can guess that:
   a. Japanese families share many interests and activities.
   b. Japanese husbands and wives do many other things together even
      though they don't share leisure activities.
   c. Japanese husbands and wives share very few activities.

1.10
APPLICATION, CRITICAL EVALUATION, AND SYNTHESIS

In this reading, the people interviewed describe the Japanese attitudes
towards leisure and compare it to Western (especially U.S.) attitudes.
Think about each of the following quotes and write your reaction to it.
Agree or disagree. What does the quote tell you about the Japanese attitude,
and how does that compare to general attitudes in your country? You may
also want to compare your own attitude to that in the United States.

1. "When I go fishing, what I care about is how many fish I catch. In the
   U.S. they enjoy nature or talk with friends or take a nap." Hamada never
   takes a nap when he fishes, so how does he relax? "I go drinking and
   singing at karaoke bars every night. I go out with my friends."
2. "People say Japanese society is wealthy, but that happened recently. To
   avoid feeling guilty, we work hard." (Would people in your country feel
   guilty if they suddenly became wealthy? Why?)
3. "Here we use only fifty percent [of the paid holidays]. People here
   actually enjoy what they do," [Mr. Miyano] explains. "The work they do

here can be included as leisure." (Do you think work can be considered as leisure?)

4. "In any sport, you need intensity."

5. Concerning married women, "their life is likely to be limited to husband, children, a few close relatives, some old schoolday girl friends, and possibly the activities of the PTA. It isn't uncommon for a man to have never met his best friend's wife, even after decades of friendship."

2
Two Views of Leisure

This section is made up of two short readings. One is a survey of how people in 11 countries spend their free time. The second is an excerpt from a book on Australia. Read them both before doing the exercises.

2.1
FIRST READING

Read these two short selections quickly for the main ideas. Pay attention to the title and the general ideas as you read. Do *not* stop to look up words in your dictionary.

Leisure Time Measured in New Survey: Americans Fall Short, Sociologist Finds

Research studies sometimes have surprising results. This newspaper article describes a survey that compared leisure time in Europe, Japan, and the United States. (*Los Angeles Times,* January 13, 1986) Reprinted by permission.

1. Is it true that Americans have more fun? As a matter of fact, they do not. But blonds apparently do.
2. Compared with their Western neighbors, Americans rank right about in the middle in hours of free time, and they are no leisure-time match for the fair-haired Dutch. So says University of Maryland sociology professor John Robinson, who has been studying free time for more than 20 years. Recently Robinson has come up with some preliminary findings on a free-time survey of 11 Western nations, suggesting that Americans, long portrayed by themselves and others as fun-worshipers, actually lag behind the Dutch, Danish, Canadians and British.

3. Leisure activities were roughly defined as: watching television, socializing, reading; recreational, sports and cultural activities; and participation in clubs and organizations. With more than 2,000 people in each country keeping diaries of their daily activities, those in the Netherlands averaged 31 hours of free time per week; Denmark, 28; Canada, 27; the United Kingdom, 25; Finland and the United States, 24; Austria, Japan and Switzerland, 23; Norway 22; and France 20.

4. Robinson theorizes that, among other factors, the Dutch may spend less time than other nations at jobs. "It's a more stable, more predictable economy," Robinson said, "just a more organized and better ordered life."

5. In defining free time, what Robinson really had to do was define and categorize non-free time. He decided that other than free time there is necessary time (mainly sleeping, eating and other personal care), committed time (mainly housework, family care and shopping) and contracted time (mainly paid work and commuting time).

6. Of these, Robinson found that across the board the most time was spent with the "necessary" activities, ranging from 44 percent of the time in Finland to 50 percent in France. Men tended to have more free time than women, and employed women had the least free time of all: 19 hours a week in the United States, compared to 22 hours a week for employed American men. But Robinson said this should not be considered evidence of a universal "woman's burden."

7. "It's the *working* woman's burden," Robinson said, getting right to the point. "When you factor in employed women and housewives together as just women, across the whole life span free time of men and women averages out to be pretty equivalent."

Leisure Hours per Week

Nation	Hours
Netherlands	31
Denmark	28
Canada	27
United Kingdom	25
Finland	24
United States	24
Austria	23
Japan	23
Switzerland	23
Norway	22
France	20

The Australians

This excerpt describes how Australians spend their leisure time. It is taken from a book called *The Australians,* by Ross Terrill, a writer born and raised in Australia, who now lives in the United States. (Simon and Schuster, 1987)

1. The weekend is sacred from the profane intrusion of toil. Saturday arvo (afternoon) in particular is a time of migration from responsibility. Post office service and delivery do not exist on Saturday, and by noon nearly all shops, even news agents, are closed; Australia has entered the magic cave of leisure and will emerge with grumpy reluctance only at breakfast time on Monday. Even the counting of votes after a Saturday national election cannot conquer the Australian Sunday; from Saturday evening the explosive ballots lie around until Monday morning.

2. Students, bellwether of any culture, take off for the weekend as if books no longer existed and urban life were a dream. Even in sophisticated Melbourne, campus tension evaporates on a Friday night as the great outdoors claims the weekend. Sydney and other cities are remote; nature-oriented pursuits hold sway by default. Students go bushwalking and bird-watching. They drive to the ski slopes in northeastern Victoria. They play tennis or cricket under leafy trees. They put their heads down to the serious business of gardening. Year-round, their weekend has the laid-back feel of midsummer weekends for youth in Boston or Paris or Tokyo.

3. In midsummer at Christmas and New Year's the nation virtually stops functioning. Not only do politicians disappear, and newspapers devote their columns to food and drink and the odd report of a bushfire or a shark attacking a swimmer at the beach, but basic services close down for days at a stretch.

4. Australia's heart is not at its center — a swath of the Northern Territory, Western Australia, Queensland, and South Australia that is, except for the charming town of Alice Springs, virtually a void — but on the beach. The most Australian thing you can do is lie on a clean, wide, beautiful beach. Here Australian indifference reaches its peak. Here the Australian declares himself as much outside of history as a patient under anesthesia is beyond the conscious world. Even the ugly gray sharks, with their cold eyes and mouths that never close, do not break the torpor. They kill nearly every season, but they are unable to make the Australian beach lover anxious. The beach possesses the Australian soul because it is an unanswerably Australian asset for a people often dismissed — even by themselves — as mere derivatives from cold and distant Europe.

5. The Australian will often cheerfully admit to being a bludger (a lazy one). He prefers a slow pace and is easygoing except when someone seeks to set a faster pace or behaves self-importantly. His hedonism is seldom loud or violent.

925 words

Reading Times	Reading Speed
1st reading ____ minutes	7 minutes = 132 wpm
3rd reading ____ minutes	6 minutes = 154 wpm
	5 minutes = 185 wpm
	4 minutes = 231 wpm

2.2
SECOND READING

Go back and read the selections again. Take as much time as you need this time. Look up some of the unfamiliar words in the glossary at the end of the book or in your dictionary if you wish.

2.3
THIRD READING

Read the selections quickly a third time. Concentrate on understanding the main ideas and the meanings of new vocabulary words in the context in which they appear.

2.4
READER RESPONSE

In order to explore your response to these readings, write for 15 minutes about anything that interests you in these readings. You may wish to write about a personal experience these readings reminded you of—or you may wish to disagree with something. Try to explore *your own thoughts and feelings* as much as possible. Do *not* merely summarize or restate the ideas in these readings.

2.5
RESPONSE SHARING

Read your response to two or three other people in your class. Listen carefully to what the others have written. After you have discussed each other's responses, talk about other points of interest in the readings.

2.6
IDENTIFYING MAIN IDEAS

Working with the same small group, make a list of the main ideas in these readings. Be sure to state the main ideas in your own words. Don't just copy sentences directly from the text. Think carefully about what the writer is trying to tell you.

2.7
ANALYZING THE TEXTS

Work with your group members on this exercise. Discuss the answers carefully, particularly if there are disagreements among members of your group. In some cases, there may be more than one possible interpretation.

1. Write whether these statements are true *(T)* or false *(F)* according to the free time survey.

   a. _____ These are initial results of Professor Robinson's research.

   b. _____ Americans are unhappy because they lag behind other countries.

   c. _____ Leisure activities really cannot be defined.

2. Professor Robinson concludes that:
   a. stable societies are likely to have more free time.
   b. working women have the same amount of free time as housewives.
   c. non-free time is more important than free time.

3. In the Australia selection, "the weekend" is the main topic of:
   a. paragraph 1.
   b. paragraph 2.
   c. paragraph 3.
   d. paragraphs 1 and 2.
   e. paragraphs 2 and 3.

4. Mr. Terrill describes the sharks on the beach as an example of Australian:
   a. indifference.
   b. anxiety.
   c. derivatives.

5. Which of the words below describe the free-time survey, and which describe the Australia excerpt?

descriptive	lyrical	rational
emotional	objective	reporting
factual	personal	subjective
interpretive		

2.8
VOCABULARY STUDY

Study the italicized words and phrases in their context and guess at their meanings. Write your guess in the first blank. Then, look up the word or phrase in your dictionary.

1. (paragraph 2) Americans . . . *lag* behind the Dutch, Danish, Canadians and British. . . . those in the Netherlands averaged 31 hours of

free time per week; Denmark, 28; Canada, 27; the United Kingdom, 25; Finland and the United States, 24. . . .

   a. (guess) _____

   b. (dictionary) _____

2. (paragraph 5) In defining free time, what Robinson really had to do was define and categorize non-free time. He decided . . . there is necessary time . . . committed time . . . and contracted time. . . . Of these, Robinson found that *across the board* the most time was spent with the "necessary" activities. . . .

   a. (guess) _____

   b. (dictionary) _____

3. (paragraph 1 in "The Australians") The weekend is sacred from the profane *intrusion* of toil. . . . Post office service and delivery do not exist on Saturday, and by noon nearly all shops, even news agents, are closed. . . .

   a. (guess) _____

   b. (dictionary) _____

4. (paragraph 2) . . . nature-oriented *pursuits* hold sway by default. Students go bushwalking and bird-watching. They drive to the ski slopes in northeastern Victoria.

   a. (guess) _____

   b. (dictionary) _____

5. (paragraph 4) Here Australian *indifference* reaches its peak. Here the Australian declares himself as much outside of history as a patient under anesthesia is beyond the conscious world.

   a. (guess) _____

   b. (dictionary) _____

2.9
DESCRIPTIVE WRITING

The Australia selection is filled with word images. What do these sentences make you think of? Discuss your ideas with your group members.

1. The weekend is sacred from the profane intrusion of toil. (What kind of words are *sacred* and *profane*?)
2. By noon Australia has entered the magic cave of leisure and will emerge

with grumpy reluctance only at breakfast time on Monday. (What do *cave* and *emerge with grumpy reluctance* make you think of?)

3. Even the counting of votes after a Saturday national election cannot conquer the Australian Sunday; from Saturday evening the explosive ballots lie around until Monday morning. (What does *conquer* imply? Why are the votes *explosive?*)

4. Students take off for the weekend as if books no longer existed. Campus tension evaporates. They put their heads down to the serious business of gardening. (Is gardening really more serious than school? Why is it described that way?)

5. The most Australian thing you can do is lie on a clean, wide, beautiful beach. Here the Australian declares himself as much outside of history as a patient under anesthesia is beyond the conscious world. (What might Australians do or be like on the beach? Can you imagine a typical Australian beach scene? Describe.)

6. The Australian will often cheerfully admit to being lazy. He prefers a slow pace and is easygoing except when someone seeks to set a faster pace or behaves self-importantly. (What might an Australian do or be like when someone behaves self-importantly? What can you guess about the Australian personality from this statement?)

2.10
APPLICATION, CRITICAL EVALUATION, AND SYNTHESIS

1. If your country isn't shown on the survey chart, how many hours a week would you guess people in your country spend on leisure? How do people spend their leisure time? If your country is on the chart, do you think it is accurate? Why or why not? Where do you think the Australians would rank on this chart? Give some reasons and examples.

2. How do life and leisure in Australia compare to life and leisure in Japan? Do you think an Australian would be comfortable in Japan? Why or why not? What kind of "culture shock" would a Japanese probably have if he or she went to Australia? Think of a few examples of what might happen.

3. Take the above comparison further. Compare Australia and Japan with your country or with the United States. Where are the similarities? The differences? How would *you* survive in Japan or Australia? Which country would you prefer to live in? Which would be harder to live in? Give some examples.

3
Conquest of Aconcagua

William Broyles, Jr., former editor-in-chief of *Newsweek* magazine, needed a challenge. He found it climbing a mountain in the Andes in South America. This magazine selection tells the story of his adventure. Some people get great personal satisfaction from mountain climbing; others just call it hard work. And still others say that endangering one's life in such an activity is not "leisure." (*Esquire,* June 1987) Reprinted by permission.

3.1
FIRST READING

Read this selection quickly to understand the story. Pay attention to the title and the section headings as you read. Do *not* stop to look up words in your dictionary.

1. I am hanging by my fingertips from a rock ledge 23,000 feet above sea level. My foot, searching for a dimple* in the rock to push from, finally catches on a tiny protrusion. I take eight breaths, then push. My hand goes up to another rock, finds a hold.

2. Somewhere above me is the summit of Aconcagua, at 23,036 feet the tallest mountain in the Western Hemisphere. Storm clouds are gathering. It is past five in the afternoon, and soon the temperature will fall to 20 degrees below zero. For three days I have been unable to eat. I am dehydrated. My brain, starved for oxygen, has all but ceased to function. In the snow on the summit is the body of an Argentine who froze to death after reaching the top a few days before. Four other climbers have died on the mountain in the past month.

---

* *dimple:* a small indentation or groove

3. I have never climbed a mountain in my life. In fact, I am afraid of heights. *What am I doing here?*

4. In the year prior to this undertaking, I had begun to realize that determination and ambition do not always lead up the right ladder. Each morning I struggled into my suit, picked up my briefcase, went to my glamorous job, and died a little. I was the editor-in-chief of *Newsweek,* a position that in the eyes of others had everything; only it had nothing to do with me. I took little pleasure in running a large institution. I had been a Marine in Vietnam, and Marines are trained to keep on charging up the hill, no matter what. But I had climbed the wrong mountain, and the only thing to do was go down and climb another one.

5. I wanted to be tested, mentally and physically; to succeed, but by standards that were clear and concrete, not dependent on the opinion of others. In an earlier time, I might have gone west or to sea. But I had two children and responsibilities. Taking a month out to climb this mountain was the perfect thing.

6. Aconcagua (the name means "stone sentinel") is in the southern Andes about 650 miles northwest of Buenos Aires. For serious climbers it is more a test of endurance than skill. But the lack of dramatic technical problems tends to mask the danger of Aconcagua's extreme altitude and unpredictable weather. In a graveyard near the mountain are some 60 markers in memory of climbers who have died there, and the actual number may exceed 100 — about as many as have died on Mount Everest and K2 put together.

7. Our expedition, 12 climbers and four guides, met last February in Mendoza, a town just east of the Andes, then traveled by bus to Puente del Inca, at the foot of the mountain. Members of the group included Ralph Gorton, 31 and a mountain climber since 1979; Mike Larrabee, 53, who won two gold medals in track at the 1964 Tokyo Olympics; Mitch Flores, 35, an enthusiastic triathelete*; Gabe Papp, 33, a mountaineering instructor. Expedition leader Harry Johnson had recently competed in the Pikes Peak Marathon.

8. At least, I thought, I could keep up with gray-haired Art Schultz and delicate Kim Baldwin. At 60, Art was the oldest member of the expedition; it turned out he had raced in cross-country ski marathons around the world. And Kim? She'd set a record in California's Seal Beach Triathlon. Was this the place for a 42-year-old jogger? I was beginning to wonder.

9. That night I loaded my pack. It weighed 46 pounds without the tents, food, stoves and other community gear I'd carry. The straps bit down into my shoulders. I could barely keep my balance. The next morning a truck let us out in a high mountain meadow dotted with wildflowers

---

* *triathlete:* a person who competes in a race which consists of a 2-mile swim, a 100-mile bicycle race, and a 25-mile run all in one day

and grazing horses. I struggled to put on my pack, then followed the others up the trail—one step at a time.

10. High above us were striated* ledges, massive rock cathedrals perched atop ridge lines 14,000 feet high. Buttes† bathed in iron and copper ore rose out of great fields of scree.‡ We could walk only by leaning into the wind that howled down the valley. A sudden hail storm pelted us with ice. In 15 minutes the temperature dropped 40 degrees. Finally we reached a valley carpeted with the last hardy remnants of grass. We sat in the shelter of some rocks—former strangers, holding each other tight for warmth.

11. **Quitting Time.** The following day the wind was worse, blowing down from the mountain like a message: stay away. With the wind came dust, clouds of it, choking and blinding us. We climbed up narrow rock trails, clinging to cliffs. Through gaps in the wall of peaks I could catch glimpses of something massive and mysterious. That afternoon we emerged at Plaza de Mulas, our base camp—two small ledges more than 14,000 feet above sea level. We had come 5000 vertical feet from Puente del Inca; we had 9000 to go.

12. "Where's the mountain?" I asked Harry.

13. "You're under it," he said, gesturing behind him. I looked and there it was, rising up above me in tier after tier of cliffs and rock. I had to lean backward to see the top.

14. We had spaghetti for dinner, but I had a hard time eating. I was in the first stages of altitude sickness. Above 14,000 feet, the air contains less than half the oxygen present at sea level, and the body's ability to absorb that oxygen is dramatically reduced. Severe headaches, shortness of breath, disorientation, loss of appetite, palpitations, nausea, insomnia, dehydration, clumsiness, and impairment of short-term memory are common symptoms. I had them all.

15. Given time, most climbers begin to adapt to high altitude, which is why high-altitude climbs are slow, careful projects. But altitude can quickly kill climbers who adapt poorly. The combination of higher blood pressure, lower oxygen content and higher heart rate can force plasma through the walls of the capillaries in the lungs and brain. With pulmonary edema, the lungs fill with fluid; if the victim does not go down at once, he literally drowns.

16. That night, the wind blew even harder. Dizzy, nauseated and, I had to confess, scared, I resolved to go back down first thing in the morning. It was a wonderfully soothing idea. Then I became angry with myself. I wasn't a quitter. I fell asleep at dawn; when I woke the sun had begun to warm my tent.

* *striated:* marked with narrow lines
† *butte:* a small mountain with steep sides
‡ *scree:* small stones

17. **Beethoven for the Summit.** On the fourth day after leaving Puente del Inca we began to move up to Nido de Condores ("Condor's Nest") at 18,000 feet, our next camp. We would cache our supplies at Nido and return to base camp to rest and acclimatize before we climbed up for good. The trail went all but straight up. I settled into a pace: step, breathe, step, breathe. Because of my frequent stops, the strongest climbers got ahead of me. I wanted to keep up, so I pushed myself— which was a mistake. You don't compete with other climbers, only with yourself and with the mountain.

18. I caught up with the others, and together we climbed 2000 feet to a snowfield. I was already exhausted when the altitude hit me. Each step took tremendous effort. I had to breathe once, twice, three times, then concentrate as hard as I could, lift my foot and set it down. At last I reached Nido de Condores — and collapsed. Harry took one look at me and told me to get back to base camp. I had to go lower, to find more oxygen to feed my starving mind and body.

19. In fact my mind had already shut down. That night, back at Plaza de Mulas, I tried to tell a story at dinner, but couldn't remember the punch line.* My mind had become a stranger. I walked out under the stars, vomited up everything I had eaten that day, and then slept well, without dreams. The wind had died. Perhaps the mountain would let us climb it after all.

20. The next day three members of our group abandoned the mountain, and several others were sick. For two days we stayed in camp. On the seventh day we were to move camp up to Nido. From there we would climb to Berlin camp, and from Berlin we would try for the summit. The morning was clear and cold as we loaded our packs. In addition to extra clothing, some food and the tent poles, I had tapes for the Walk-man I carried on my belt: Bruce Springsteen and Buddy Holly for the tough going; Mozart and Handel for the more contemplative stages; Wagner for drama; Beethoven for the summit.

21. **"I'm Going to Make It."** An hour into the climb I resented every-thing in my pack, every ounce of weight. By the time I emerged on a barren, snow-filled basin in the shadow of the summit, the first climbers of our group were already putting up tents. When we crawled into our sleeping bags, the temperature was well below zero. I could feel the mountain outside my tent, painfully close, like someone standing with his face next to mine, staring.

22. The next day after a steep but uneventful climb, we reached Berlin camp, a squalid† collection of old huts. I forced myself to eat some instant split-pea soup, then lay down. Nausea came over me.

---

* *punch line:* the funny ending of a joke
† *squalid:* dirty and rundown

23. "Are you going to make it?" Harry asked me, meaning, *Should I send you down?*

24. "I don't know," I said. "But if I can eat some oatmeal in the morning I'm going." That night, sandwiched in a tent between Kim and Mitch, I told myself over and over, *I'm going to make it.*

25. We woke at 4 a.m. The air was bitterly cold. I tried to eat some oatmeal, but had to chew each bit eight or nine times in order to swallow. I could feel my stomach gathering its protest.

26. **Lost!** As the light dawned we were climbing the switchbacks to the Independencia hut at 21,000 feet, and I was falling behind. At 9 a.m. I reached Independencia, a tiny A-frame with a hole in its roof. I fell onto the rocks and began to retch; so much for keeping the oatmeal down. My pack was intolerably heavy. I stashed the Walkman and the tapes under some rocks. I couldn't listen to music anyway; my mind wouldn't have tolerated the noise. All my life I had been accumulating things. Now I had embarked on a venture where nothing I had accumulated would do me the slightest good.

27. Above Independencia I crossed a snowfield. The trail stopped. I was at the foot of the Canaleta. Here was the last barrier; a river of loose scree and boulders stretching up more than 1000 feet. Up the middle went the faint hint of a trail. I kicked my toe into it, hoping for a foothold. Three feet above me, the rock started to slide. As I watched, the toe I had kicked in slid past my other foot, and I began to slip backward. I was already taking six breaths a step. The summit was lost in clouds. Panic came over me.

28. "Help!" I yelled. "I'm lost!"

29. But my voice was weak from fatigue and dehydration, and the wind snatched it away. No one was going to help me. I was responsible for myself. My will, however, was eroding. I wanted to go down. Down was hot food and showers and my sleeping bag. But I couldn't turn back. The idea of "up" was so powerful it kept my feet moving and my hands reaching.

30. I kept pulling myself up the cliffs, lying gasping on the ledges. At 22,800 feet, two boots suddenly appeared in front of my face. It was Harry.

31. "I thought you'd gone down," he said.

32. I shook my head. Harry took a minute to survey the situation. It was getting late, the clouds were building, we should go down. But I was so close, so very close.

33. "Let's go," Harry said, and headed back up. I breathed carefully, eight times, located a handhold, pulled. Then I did it again. An hour passed. Finally I stood beside him. Above my head was a ledge.

34. "Up there," Harry said.

35. I pulled myself up onto yet another ledge, and lay gasping. I looked around for the next place to go up. But there was no more up.
36. I was on the summit!
37. The clouds had blown away and the sky was blue. I was on top of the Western Hemisphere, quite probably higher at that moment than any other human being on solid ground in the world. I had expected some epiphany, some magic moment filled with insight into man and nature, into ambition, success, and the fruits of human endeavor. I thought none of those things. In fact, I thought nothing.
38. I had begun my climb in green pastures, surrounded by life. My step was springy, my head clear. I was ending it weak and bent, lungs gasping for breath, my mind senile. I thought to recover my youth; instead I became an old man. I didn't want to linger; I wanted *down.*
39. "Let's go," I said. I had been on the summit less than ten minutes. Down was easy. I made my way to Independencia, then proceeded to the camp at Berlin. I woke up the next morning feeling clearheaded, stronger, and hungry. I was tired but exhilarated. Mitch and Kim were lying in their sleeping bags, also awake.
40. "We made it," Mitch said.
41. We smiled at each other. There were no other words to say.
42. Why had I done it? George Mallory, who became famous for climbing Everest "because it was there," wrote about the experience: "Something in man responds to the challenge of this mountain and goes to meet it: the struggle is the struggle of life itself upward and forever upward. . . . What we get from this adventure is sheer joy."
43. For the ordeal I had just undergone, joy might seem an odd description. But that is what I felt: the joy of accomplishment, of having been tested — the joy of being alive. The cares and complications of my life had receded into the valley.
44. I had been to the mountaintop.

2318

Reading Times
1st reading ___ minutes
3rd reading ___ minutes

Reading Speed
11 minutes = 211 wpm
10 minutes = 232 wpm
9 minutes = 258 wpm
8 minutes = 280 wpm
7 minutes = 331 wpm

3.2
SECOND READING

Go back and read the selection again. Take as much time as you need this time. Look up some of the unfamiliar words in the glossary at the end of the book or in your dictionary if you wish.

3.3
THIRD READING

Read the selection quickly a third time. Concentrate on understanding the main ideas of the selection and the meanings of new vocabulary words in the context in which they appear.

3.4
READER RESPONSE

In order to explore your response to this reading, write for 15 minutes about anything that interested you in this story. You may wish to write about a personal experience this story reminded you of—or you may wish to comment on some aspect that interested you. Try to explore *your own thoughts and feelings* as much as possible. Do *not* merely summarize or restate the ideas in this selection.

3.5
RESPONSE SHARING

Read your response to two or three other people in your class. Listen carefully to what the others have written. After you have discussed each other's responses, talk about other points of interest in the selection.

3.6
IDENTIFYING MAIN IDEAS

Working with the same small group, make a list of the main ideas in this selection. Be sure to state the main ideas in your own words. Don't just copy sentences directly from the text. Think carefully about what the writer is trying to tell you.

3.7
ANALYZING THE TEXT

Work with your group members on this exercise. Discuss the answers carefully, particularly if there are disagreements among members of your group. In some cases, there may be more than one possible interpretation.

1. The subject of this story is:
   a. meeting a personal challenge.

    b. how to climb a mountain.

    c. the dangers at high altitude.

2. In paragraphs 3, 23, and 24, some sentences are printed in italics because they represent:

    a. something Mr. Broyles said to the others in the group.

    b. Mr. Broyles' thoughts to himself.

    c. words that others said to him.

3. Paragraph 5 states, "I wanted to be tested, mentally and physically; to succeed, but by standards that were clear and concrete, not dependent on the opinion of others." The reason Mr. Broyles feels this way is explained in:

    a. paragraph 1.

    b. paragraph 4.

    c. paragraph 6.

4. "You don't compete with other climbers, only with yourself and with the mountain." (paragraph 17). This means that:

    a. you are testing your own capabilities, not comparing yourself to others.

    b. everyone tries to be the first to reach the peak (the top of the mountain).

    c. you shouldn't try mountain climbing unless you are in good physical condition.

5. In paragraph 19, Mr. Broyles says, "My mind had become a stranger." What does he mean?

    a. He thought he was going crazy.

    b. He couldn't remember the last line of a funny story.

    c. His mind was not functioning the way he knew it should.

6. From the tone of paragraphs 37 and 38, Mr. Broyles probably:

    a. felt he had not accomplished anything valuable by climbing Aconcagua.

    b. gained some important insights about himself.

    c. became older during the process of the climb.

Explain your answer.

7. Which paragraphs best sum up the conclusion of this article?

    a. paragraphs 35 and 36

    b. paragraphs 40 and 41

    c. paragraphs 43 and 44

8. Mr. Broyles was _____ to climb Aconcagua.

    a. brave

    b. foolish

    c. selfish

Please explain your answer.

3.8
VOCABULARY STUDY

Study these words and phrases in their contexts and guess at their meanings. Write your guess in the first blank. Then, look up the word or phrase in your dictionary.

1. (paragraph 4) Each morning I . . . went to my *glamorous* job. . . . I was the editor-in-chief of *Newsweek,* a position that in the eyes of others had everything. . . .

   a. (guess) _____

   b. (dictionary) _____

2. (paragraph 6) For serious climbers it is more a test of *endurance* than skill. But the lack of dramatic technical problems tends to mask the danger of Aconcagua's extreme altitude and unpredictable weather.

   a. (guess) _____

   b. (dictionary) _____

3. (paragraph 17) . . . we began to move up to . . . our next camp. We would cache our supplies . . . and return to base camp to rest and acclimatize before we climbed up *for good.*

   a. (guess) _____

   b. (dictionary) _____

4. (paragraph 26) My pack was *intolerably* heavy. I stashed the Walkman and tapes under some rocks. I couldn't listen to music anyway; my mind wouldn't have tolerated the noise.

   a. (guess) _____

   b. (dictionary) _____

5. (paragraph 38) I didn't want to *linger*; I wanted down. "Let's go," I said. I had been on the summit less than ten minutes.

   a. (guess) _____

   b. (dictionary) _____

3.9
DRAWING CONCLUSIONS

This story describes many things about Mr. Broyles' experience in an indirect way. You are given clues (examples), and then you have to decide things for yourself. For example, even though Mr. Broyles never actually says you need a high level of fitness to climb Aconcagua, he gives many examples of how fit the climbers are. By the end of the story, you realize this without thinking about how you gained the information. For each of the items below, find several clues *in the reading* that would lead you to the conclusion that is given.

1. *Conclusion:* Mountain climbing is a dangerous sport.
2. *Conclusion:* There are problems and dangers at high altitude.
3. *Conclusion:* A high level of fitness is required.
4. *Conclusion:* Harry Johnson is a very experienced leader and is in excellent physical condition.
5. *Conclusion:* Mr. Broyles had great determination.

3.10
APPLICATION, CRITICAL EVALUATION, AND SYNTHESIS

1. Mr. Broyles explains that he climbed Aconcagua as a challenge to himself, as a test of his endurance. Have you ever tested yourself in a special way — or known of someone else who has? Please describe the challenge. What was it? Why was it undertaken?
2. Some people regularly climb mountains as part of their leisure activities. Do you consider mountain climbing "leisure," or would you categorize it another way? Please explain.
3. You have read about both the Japanese and Australian attitudes towards leisure. Do you think mountain climbing would appeal more to the Japanese or to the Australians (or to both or neither)? Explain why you think so. What do you think most people in your country would say about mountain climbing as a leisure pursuit?

TURN TO THE EXPANSION SECTION ON PAGE 187 FOR PRACTICE IN DOING LIBRARY RESEARCH AND REPORT WRITING.

Unit 5
What Is Art?

DISCUSSION

Throughout history, people have used art as a means of recording their experience and expressing their thoughts and feelings. Yet a lot of people, perhaps even most people, feel that they don't understand art, and they are not sure what the purposes of art are. All of us seem to know something about art when we are children; at least we know we like to draw and make pictures of ourselves and others. But later on we are not so sure about how art fits into life. Many of us are quick to say, "I don't know anything about art. I just know what I like and what I don't like." In this unit, you will read about art and some of its purposes. Before you begin reading, think about the following statements and questions and discuss your answers.

1. "Art is something I can hang on my living room wall. It is something beautiful that I like to look at. If I can't hang it on my living room wall, it's not art." Do you agree with this definition of art? Why? Why not? Give examples and discuss in detail.
2. "A picture is worth a thousand words." What does this mean? Explain and give examples. Do you think it is true? Why? Why not?
3. What is the difference between being an artist and being a craftsperson? Is there a difference? Explain and give examples.
4. "Graffiti [writings and drawings on public property] is a type of art." Do you agree or disagree? Why? Please explain your answer in detail.
5. "Art is not always beautiful. In fact, sometimes it can be violent and gruesome and shocking. It can horrify us." Do you agree or disagree? Why? Please give examples and explain your answer in detail.

ESM Documentations/Art Resource, Duchamp, *Bicycle Wheel,* 1913, © 1990
ARS N.Y./ADAGP

1
The Artist and His Public

What is art and why is it art? These are questions that are discussed in some detail in the following passage. This selection comes from a highly respected and widely used college textbook on art history entitled *The History of Art: A Survey of the Major Visual Arts from the Dawn of History to the Present Day,* which was written by H. W. Janson of New York University. Reprinted by permission of Henry N. Abrams, Inc. The selection that follows comes from the 1985 edition.

1.1
FIRST READING

Read this selection quickly for the main ideas. Pay attention to the title and the text headings as you read. Do *not* stop to look up words in your dictionary.

1. "Why is this supposed to be art?" How often have we heard this question asked — or asked it ourselves, perhaps — in front of one of the strange, disquieting works that we are likely to find nowadays in museums or art exhibitions. There usually is an undertone of exasperation, for the question implies that *we* don't think we are looking at a work of art, but that the experts — the critics, museum curators, art historians — must suppose it to be one. Why else would they put it on public display? Clearly, their standards are different from ours; we are at a loss to understand them and we wish they'd give us a few simple, clear-cut rules to go by. Then maybe we would learn to like what we see, we would know "why it is art." But the experts do not post exact rules, and the layman is apt to fall back upon his final line of defense: "Well, I don't know anything about art but I know what I like." . . .
2. Deciding what is art and evaluating a work of art are separate problems; if we had an absolute method for distinguishing art from non-art, this

method would not necessarily enable us to measure quality. People have long been in the habit of compounding the two problems into one; quite often when they ask, "Why is it art?" they mean, "Why is it *good* art?" Yet, all systems for rating art so far proposed fall short of being completely satisfactory; we tend to agree with their authors only if they like the same things we do. If we do not share their taste, their system seems like a strait jacket to us. This brings us to another, more basic difficulty. In order to have any rating scale at all, we must be willing to assume that there are fixed timeless values in art, that the true worth of a given work is a stable thing, independent of time and circumstance. Perhaps such values exist; we cannot be sure that they do not. We do know, however, that opinions about works of art keep changing, not only today but throughout the known course of history. Even the greatest classics have had their ups and downs, and the history of taste — which is part of the history of art — is a continuous process of discarding established values and rediscovering neglected ones. It would seem, therefore, that absolute qualities in art elude us, that we cannot escape viewing works of art in the context of time and circumstance, whether past or present. How indeed could it be otherwise, so long as art is still being created all around us, opening our eyes almost daily to new experiences and thus forcing us to adjust our sights? . . .

3. Defining art is about as troublesome as defining a human being. Plato, it is said, tried to solve the latter problem by calling man "a featherless biped," whereupon Diogenes introduced a plucked rooster as "Plato's Man." Generalizations about art are, on the whole, equally easy to disprove. Even the most elementary statements turn out to have their pitfalls. Let us test, for instance, the simple claim that a work of art must be made by man, rather than by nature. This definition at least eliminates the confusion of treating as works of art phenomena such as flowers, sea shells, or sunsets. It is a far from sufficient definition, to be sure, since man makes many things other than works of art. Still, it might serve as a starting point. Our difficulties begin as soon as we ask, "What do we mean by making?" If, in order to simplify our problem, we concentrate on the visual arts, we might say that a work of art must be a tangible thing shaped by human hands. Now let us look at the striking *Bull's Head* by Picasso, which consists of nothing but the seat and the handlebars of an old bicycle.

4. How meaningful is our formula here? Of course the materials used by Picasso are man-made, but it would be absurd to insist that Picasso must share the credit with the manufacturer, since the seat and handlebars in themselves are not works of art. While we feel a certain jolt when we first recognize the ingredients of this visual pun, we also sense that it was a stroke of genius to put them together in this unique way, and we cannot very well deny that it is a work of art. Yet the handiwork — the

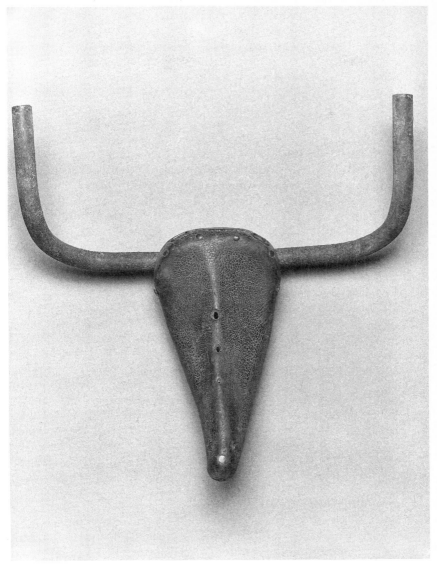

Cliché des Musées Nationaux, Picasso, *Bull's Head,* 1943, © 1990 ARS
N.Y./SPADEM

mounting of the seat on the handlebars — is ridiculously simple. What is far from simple is the leap of the imagination by which Picasso recognized a bull's head in these unlikely objects; that, we feel, only he could have done. Clearly, then, we must be careful not to confuse the making of a work of art with manual skill or craftsmanship. Some works of art may demand a great deal of technical discipline; others do not. And even the most painstaking piece of craft does not deserve to be called a work of art unless it involves a leap of the imagination. But if this is true, are we not forced to conclude that the real making of the *Bull's Head* took place in the artist's mind? No, that is not so, either. Suppose that, instead of actually putting the two pieces together and showing them to us, Picasso merely told us, "You know, today I saw a bicycle seat and handlebars that looked just like a bull's head to me." Then there would be no work of art and his remark would not even strike us as an interesting bit of conversation. Moreover, Picasso himself would not feel the satisfaction of having created something on the basis of his leap of the imagination alone. Once he had conceived his visual pun, he could never be sure that it would really work unless he put it into effect.

CREATIVITY

5. Thus the artist's hands, however modest the task they may have to perform, play an essential part in the creative process. Our *Bull's Head* is, of course, an ideally simple case, involving only one leap of the imagination and a single manual act in response to it — once the seat had been properly placed on the handlebars, the job was done. Ordinarily, artists do not work with ready-made parts but with materials that have little or no shape of their own; the creative process consists of a long series of leaps of the imagination and the artist's attempts to give them form by shaping the material accordingly. The hand tries to carry out the commands of the imagination and hopefully puts down a brush stroke, but the result may not be quite what had been expected, partly because all matter resists the human will, partly because the image in the artist's mind is constantly shifting and changing, so that the commands of the imagination cannot be very precise. In fact, the mental image begins to come into focus only as the artist "draws the line somewhere." That line then becomes part — the only fixed part — of the image; the rest of the image, as yet unborn, remains fluid. And each time the artist adds another line, a new leap of the imagination is needed to incorporate that line into his ever-growing mental image. If the line cannot be incorporated, he discards it and puts down a new one. In this way, by a constant flow of impulses back and forth between his mind and the partly shaped material before him, he gradually de-

fines more and more of the image, until at last all of it has been given
visible form. Needless to say, artistic creation is too subtle and intimate
an experience to permit an exact step-by-step description; only the
artist himself can observe it fully, but he is so absorbed by it that he has
great difficulty explaining it to us. Still, our metaphor of birth comes
closer to the truth than would a description of the process in terms of a
transfer or projection of the image from the artist's mind, for the
making of a work of art is both joyous and painful, replete with surprises, and in no sense mechanical. . . .

6. Clearly, then, the making of a work of art has little in common with
what we ordinarily mean by "making." It is a strange and risky business
in which the maker never quite knows what he is making until he has
actually made it; or, to put it another way, it is a game of find-and-seek
in which the seeker is not sure what he is looking for until he has found
it. (In the *Bull's Head,* it is the bold "finding" that impresses us
most. . . .) To the non-artist, it seems hard to believe that this uncertainty, this need-to-take-a-chance, should be the essence of the artist's
work. For we all tend to think of "making" in terms of the craftsman
or manufacturer who knows exactly what he wants to produce from the
very outset, picks the tools best fitted to his task, and is sure of what he
is doing at every step. Such "making" is a two-phase affair: first the
craftsman makes a plan, then he acts on it. And because he — or his
customer — has made all the important decisions in advance, he has to
worry only about means, rather than ends, while he carries out his plan.
There is thus little risk, but also little adventure, in his handiwork,
which as a consequence tends to become routine. It may even be
replaced by the mechanical labor of a machine. No machine, on the
other hand, can replace the artist, for with him conception and execution go hand in hand and are so completely interdependent that he
cannot separate the one from the other. Whereas the craftsman only
attempts what he knows to be possible, the artist is always driven to
attempt the impossible — or at least the improbable or unimaginable.
Who, after all, would have imagined that a bull's head was hidden in
the seat and handlebars of a bicycle until Picasso discovered it for us;
did he not, almost literally, "make a silk purse out of a sow's ear"? No
wonder the artist's way of working is so resistant to any set rules, while
the craftsman's encourages standardization and regularity. We acknowledge this difference when we speak of the artist as *creating* instead of merely *making* something, although the word is being done to
death by overuse nowadays, when every child and every lipstick manufacturer is labeled "creative."

7. Needless to say, there have always been many more craftsmen than
artists among us, since our need for the familiar and expected far
exceeds our capacity to absorb the original but often deeply unsettling

experiences we get from works of art. The urge to penetrate unknown realms, to achieve something original, may be felt by every one of us now and then; to that extent, we can all fancy ourselves potential artists. . . . What sets the real artist apart is not so much the desire to *seek,* but that mysterious ability to *find* which we call talent. We also speak of it as a "gift," implying that it is a sort of present from some higher power; or as "genius," a term which originally meant a higher power — a kind of "good demon" — that inhabits the artist's body and acts through him. All we can really say about talent is that it must not be confused with aptitude. Aptitude is what the craftsman needs; it means a better-than-average knack for doing something that any ordinary person can do. An aptitude is fairly constant and specific; it can be measured with some success by means of tests which permit us to predict future performance. Creative talent, on the other hand, seems utterly unpredictable; we can spot it only on the basis of *past* performance. And even past performance is not enough to assure us that a given artist will continue to produce on the same level: some artists reach a creative peak quite early in their careers and then "go dry," while others, after a slow and unpromising start, may achieve astonishingly original work in middle age or even later.

ORIGINALITY

8. Originality, then, is what distinguishes art from craft. We may say, therefore, that it is the yardstick of artistic greatness or importance. Unfortunately, it is also very hard to define; the usual synonyms — uniqueness, novelty, freshness — do not help us very much, and the dictionaries tell us only that an original work must not be a copy, reproduction, imitation, or translation. What they fail to point out is that originality is always relative: There is no such thing as a completely original work of art. Thus, if we want to rate works of art on an "originality scale" our problem does not lie in deciding whether or not a given work is original (the obvious copies and reproductions are for the most part easy enough to eliminate) but in establishing just exactly *how* original it is. To do that is not impossible. However, the difficulties besetting our task are so great that we cannot hope for more than tentative and incomplete answers. Which does not mean, of course, that we should not try; quite the contrary. For whatever the outcome of our labors in any particular case, we shall certainly learn a great deal about works of art in the process. . . .

9. If originality is what distinguishes art from craft, tradition serves as the common meeting ground of the two. Every budding artist starts out on the level of craft, by imitating other works of art. In this way, he gradually absorbs the artistic tradition of his time and place until he has

gained a firm footing in it. But only the truly gifted ever leave that stage of traditional competence and become creators in their own right. No one, after all, can be taught how to create; he can only be taught how to go through the motions of creating. If he has talent, he will eventually achieve the real thing. What the apprentice or art student learns are skills and techniques — established ways of drawing, painting, carving, designing; established ways of *seeing*. . . .

LIKES AND DISLIKES

10. It is now time to return to our troubled layman and his assumptions about art. He may be willing to grant, on the basis of our discussion so far, that art is indeed a complex and in many ways mysterious human activity about which even the experts can hope to offer only tentative and partial conclusions; but he is also likely to take this as confirming his own belief that "I don't know anything about art." Are there really people who know nothing about art? . . . Our answer must be no, for we cannot help knowing *something* about it, just as we all know something about politics and economics no matter how indifferent we may be to the issues of the day. Art is so much a part of the fabric of human living that we encounter it all the time, even if our contacts with it are limited to magazine covers, advertising posters, war memorials, and the buildings where we live, work, and worship. Much of this art, to be sure, is pretty shoddy — art at third- and fourth-hand, worn out by endless repetition, representing the lowest common denominator of popular taste. Still, it is art of a sort; and since it is the only art most people ever experience, it molds their ideas on art in general. When they say, "I know what I like," they really mean, "I like what I know (and I reject whatever fails to match the things I am familiar with)"; such likes are not in truth theirs at all, for they have been imposed upon them by habit and circumstance, without any personal choice. To like what we know and to distrust what we do not know is an age-old human trait. . . .

THE ARTIST'S AUDIENCE

11. The artist does not create merely for his own satisfaction, but wants his work approved by others. In fact, the hope for approval is what makes him want to create in the first place, and the creative process is not completed until the work has found an audience. Here we have another paradox: The birth of a work of art is an intensely private experience (so much so that many artists can work only when completely alone and refuse to show their unfinished pieces to anyone); yet it must, as a final step, be shared by the public, in order for the birth to be successful. . . . At a minimum, this audience need consist of no more than

one or two people whose opinion he values. If he can win them over by his work, he feels encouraged to go on; without them, he despairs of his calling. There have been some very great artists who had only such a minimum audience. They hardly ever sold any of their work or had an opportunity to display it in public, but they continued to create because of the moral support of a few faithful friends. . . . The audience whose approval looms so large in the artist's mind is a limited and special one, not the general public: The merits of the artist's work can never be determined by a popularity contest. . . .

1672 words

Reading Times	Reading Speed
1st reading ____ minutes	10 minutes = 167 wpm
3rd reading ____ minutes	9 minutes = 186 wpm
	8 minutes = 209 wpm
	7 minutes = 239 wpm
	6 minutes = 279 wpm

1.2
SECOND READING

Go back and read this passage again. Take as much time as you need this time. Look up some of the unfamiliar words in the glossary at the end of the book or in your dictionary if you wish.

1.3
THIRD READING

Read the passage quickly a third time. Concentrate on understanding the main ideas of each paragraph. Figure out how the title and the headings relate to the text. Since this passage is very densely written (it is tightly packed with ideas), do not hesitate to read it over a fourth and even a fifth time.

1.4
READER RESPONSE

In order to explore your response to this reading, write for 15 minutes about anything that interested you in this passage. You may wish to write about a point that you strongly agreed — or disagreed — with, or you may wish to write about an idea in the text that you had never thought of before. Try to explore *your own thoughts and feelings* as much as possible. Do *not* merely summarize or restate the ideas in this passage.

1.5
RESPONSE SHARING

Read your response to two or three other people in your class. Listen carefully to what the others have written. After you have discussed each other's responses, talk about other points of interest in the passage.

1.6
IDENTIFYING MAIN IDEAS

Working with the same small group, make a list of the main ideas in this passage. Go through the passage paragraph by paragraph; pick out the main ideas in each paragraph. *Note:* In this text, there are several important ideas in each paragraph. Try to express these ideas in your own words wherever possible.

1.7
ANALYZING THE TEXT

Work with your group members on this exercise. Discuss the answers carefully, particularly if there are disagreements among members of your group. In some cases, there may be more than one possible interpretation.

1. Write whether these statements are true *(T)* or false *(F)*.

   a. _____ There are absolute, clear-cut standards for evaluating a work of art.

   b. _____ A work of art does not necessarily depend upon the manual skill or craftsmanship of the artist.

   c. _____ An artist takes more risks than a craftsman does.

   d. _____ An artist makes a plan before he or she begins creating and sticks to that plan faithfully. All decisions are made in advance.

   e. _____ Most artists create for their own satisfaction; they do not care about the approval of anyone else.

2. What are some of the main differences between art and craft? List some of these differences below.

Art	Craft
_____	_____
_____	_____
_____	_____
_____	_____

Explain the points you listed to others in your class.

3. Explain what each statement means in the context in which it was used.
   a. Thus the artist's hands, however modest the task they may have to perform, play an essential part in the creative process. (paragraph 5)
   b. [Making a work of art] is a game of find-and-seek in which the seeker is not sure what he is looking for until he has found it. (paragraph 6)
   c. Did [Picasso] not, almost literally, "make a silk purse out of a sow's ear"? (paragraph 6)
   d. Originality, then, is what distinguishes art from craft. (paragraph 8)
   e. No one, after all, can be taught how to create; he can only be taught how to go through the motions of creating. (paragraph 9)

4. According to Janson, the author of this passage, art (visual art, in this case):
   a. can exist only in the author's imagination; it does not have to be realized in any external form.
   b. must be made by man, rather than by nature.
   c. cannot be made up of man-made or ready-made parts.
   d. is higher up on the originality scale than is craft.
   e. must have an audience, however small that audience may be.
   f. All of the above.
   g. *a, b, d,* and *e*
   h. *b, d,* and *e*

5. The implication of the last paragraph (paragraph 11) is that:
   a. the best artists are immediately recognized by the public, and they are very popular.
   b. many good artists have a very small number of people who really appreciate and understand their work.
   c. an artist's popularity is an accurate measure of his or her worth.

1.8
VOCABULARY STUDY

Study the italicized words and phrases in their contexts. Guess at their meanings. Write your guess in the first blank. Then, look up the word or phrase in your dictionary.

1. (paragraph 1) But the experts do not post exact rules [about art], and the *layman* is apt to fall back upon his final line of defense: "Well, I don't know anything about art but I know what I like."

   a. (guess) _____

   b. (dictionary) _____

2. (paragraph 3) Even the most elementary statements turn out to have their *pitfalls.* Let us test, for instance, the simple claim that a work of art must be made by man, rather than by nature.

a. (guess) _____

b. (dictionary) _____

3. (paragraph 4) Some works of art may demand a great deal of technical discipline; others do not. And even the most *painstaking* piece of craft does not deserve to be called a work of art unless it involves a leap of the imagination.

   a. (guess) _____

   b. (dictionary) _____

4. (paragraph 5) . . . the making of a work of art is both joyous and painful, *replete* with surprises, and in no sense mechanical.

   a. (guess) _____

   b. (dictionary) _____

5. (paragraph 11) Here we have another *paradox:* The birth of a work of art is an intensely private experience (so much so that many artists can work only when completely alone and refuse to show their unfinished pieces to anyone); yet it must, as a final step, be shared by the public, in order for the birth to be successful.

   a. (guess) _____

   b. (dictionary) _____

1.9
CLOZE EXERCISE

Write an appropriate word in each blank. Discuss your word choice with your group. *Note:* In some cases, more than one word may be appropriate, or no word may be needed.

There are no exact _____(1)_____ for telling what is _____(2)_____ and what is not art. _____(3)_____ fact is very troubling to _____(4)_____ people who are not _____(5)_____ in art. These people _____(6)_____ assistance in deciding whether _____(7)_____ piece of art is good — _____(8)_____ even if it is really art. _____(9)_____ art is like understanding _____(10)_____ other field: music, literature, science, mathematics, for example. _____(11)_____ more you study, the _____(12)_____ you understand. To be _____(13)_____

expert in art, it is _____ to know something about _____
                        (14)   (15)
history of art and the period _____ which the piece was created.
                                          (16)

1.10
APPLICATION, CRITICAL EVALUATION, AND SYNTHESIS

1. Many people have looked at Pablo Picasso's famous *Bull's Head,* and they have wondered to themselves, "Is this *really* art?" What do you think? Why? Are you bothered by the commonplace materials — the bicycle parts? Do they seem unartistic to you? Are you familiar with other works of art that use commonplace materials? If so, explain and describe.
2. Why do you think many, if not most, great artists and writers are not recognized and appreciated in their lifetime? Can you give an example of an artist or writer who became well known only after his or her death?
3. Discuss a famous artist from your country. It this person still living? If not, when did he or she live? What kind of art did the person do? What was original or important about this person's work? Describe a work by this person.
4. Discuss your favorite work of art. What is it? Who was the artist? Why is it your favorite work? What does it mean to you?
5. How important do you think art is in society? Is it as important as science, for example? Business? Give reasons and examples to support your point of view. Do you think art is as important today as it was in the past? Why? Why not?

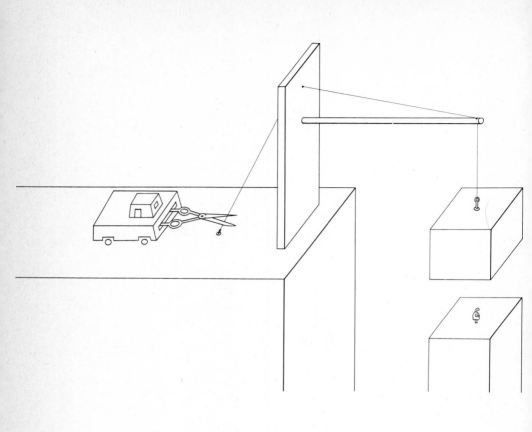

2
What Does It Mean?

Art has many purposes, and one of these purposes is social comment and criticism. Some artists use their drawings to ask questions and make statements about society. An example of this kind of social criticism would be political cartoons that appear in newspapers. In this chapter, you will be introduced to some drawings by Máris Bishofs, a Latvian artist who has lived in the Soviet Union, Israel, and France and now is living in the United States. Bishofs is a world-renowned illustrator, and his drawings have appeared in newspapers and magazines around the world. He is the author of several books, including *Feisty Virginia Wolf* (1985), *The Alien Diaries* (1986), and *Soho* (1988), all published by Adama Books in New York City. We are grateful to Máris Bishofs and to Adama Books for permission to use the following drawings.

WHAT DOES IT MEAN? is a transcript of a discussion that took place in April, 1988, in New York City. The four participants — Carlos, David, Liz, and Sandy — volunteered to take part in this discussion. Carlos and Sandy were students at the City University of New York at the time. Carlos, 20, was majoring in English literature, and Sandy, 21, in biology. David, 34, was a businessman. Liz, 16, was a high school student. All four participants said that they had limited backgrounds in art, that they wished sometimes that they knew more about art, and that they occasionally went to art museums. They all said that they didn't always understand what they saw there. Finally, it should be noted that this is a transcript of spoken English and that the specific characteristics and markers of spoken English have been deliberately retained.

2.1
FIRST READING

Read this passage quickly for the main ideas. Pay particular attention to the process used to develop understanding of the drawings. *Note: M =* Moderator, *C =* Carlos, *D =* David, *L =* Liz, and *S =* Sandy. Before you begin, study the first drawing carefully. Think about what it could mean.

When you come to the second drawing, take the time to study it carefully too.

M: Now that you have had a chance to look at this first drawing [see page 166], I want you to tell me what you think it means. Let's start off first with a basic description. Would one of you just start by telling us what you see, exactly what you see? Don't try to figure it out, to interpret it. Just describe what you see.

C: All right. I'll start. A person — a man or it could be a woman, I think — is standing on a block of some sort.

L: I think the person is standing on top of a building, on the roof of a building.

C: Perhaps. And a weight — a heavy weight — is hanging over the person. It's a large cube.

L: It — the weight — is attached to a cable, and the cable is attached to another building.

C: There is a wall on the second building. The cable runs through the wall, and it is extended out over the second building by a long pole. It looks like a flag pole — a sort of horizontal flag pole.

D: On the second building, the taller building, there is a machine, a large machine of some sort. It's not a tractor. I don't know what it is. It's a kind of tank-like machine. Yet, it looks sort of like a tank.

S: This tank-like machine — let's just call it a tank — has a pair of scissors, very large scissors, sticking out of it. The scissors are evidently operated by the machine. The scissors are poised to cut the cable.

M: What will happen if the cable is cut?

S: What will happen? It'll be all over for the little guy, the little person. That person will be crushed, smashed to smithereens. That's what will happen.

M: Okay, now we have a basic description. Let's interpret it. What do you think this could mean? Start off with something obvious, the first thing that comes to mind.

S: Well — hmmmm — this part is obvious, very obvious. This person is facing disaster. It's hanging over him — impending disaster. If that thing — that weight — falls on him or her, it's certain death, complete annihilation.

L: And the person is not aware of the danger, the potential disaster. The person is looking straight ahead and doesn't see it.

M: Could you talk more about the disaster?

C: Well, the first thing that comes to mind is that it's a man-made disaster. It's not a natural disaster like an earthquake or lightning or something of that sort. This cube is something man has made.

D: That's a good point. Man has created this disaster, this potential disaster. We see the man-made technology — the tank, the scissors.

M: What about the wall?

C: Hmmmm. I'm not sure. It cuts off vision.

M: Go on.

C: You can't see through the wall.

D: Here's an idea. I don't know if you'll agree.

M: Go on.

D: The operator of the machine — the person operating the machine — can't see through the wall.

M: What can't the person see?

D: The person can't see what will happen if the cable is cut.

L: The potential destroyer and the person about to be destroyed (the destroyee?) — they can't see what is going to happen. Neither one of them can see the potential disaster.

M: Does this make you think of anything? Can you relate this to anything, any situation, in the world today?

L: Well, this is what came to mind as we were talking. Nuclear war. The threat of nuclear war hangs over us all the time, and yet, like the person in the picture, we're not really aware of it. But somewhere, some place, there is a person who could push a button, and we'd be destroyed. Or we could push the button. We could be the destroyer.

C: Oh, that's interesting, really interesting, Liz. Also the machine operator is not aware of the disaster he or she could cause just by pushing the button or pulling the lever or whatever.

S: That wall could be self-imposed, of course.

M: What do you mean?

S: It could be a block — a mental block, like a wall — that keeps us from seeing the full extent of the devastation we could cause if we pushed the button or pulled the lever. We block that out — we wall that out — because, I guess, because it would be too terrible, too horrible, for us to face. So, we don't face it.

C: We don't take responsibility for our actions, what we could do.

D: The big building and the smaller one — I think this is about power. A powerful country could wipe out people in a less powerful country.

C: Right. And that flag pole. That makes me think of patriotism, of nationalism. One country could destroy a less powerful one in the name of patriotism and nationalism.

M: Could one of you sum up now?

S: I'll try. We could all be destroyed — completely annihilated — by modern technology, the technology that we have created. And we ignore this fact. We are oblivious to it. At any moment, we could destroy or be destroyed. The world is a very dangerous place. People have made it dangerous.

C: And there is no responsibility, no moral responsibility. The destroyers refuse to look at the destruction — the innocent lives that will be lost. That's the worst part, I think — the refusal to accept moral responsibility for our actions.

M: Why doesn't Máris Bishofs, the artist, just draw a picture, a realistic picture, of a nuclear bomb being dropped?

C: I think we have seen so many realistic pictures of war and destruction that we just block them out. We are immune to them. Like a war movie on TV. We don't take it seriously. We've seen too many war movies. We can't be shocked that way any more.

D: This drawing is so powerful because you have to think. You have to figure it out. Then it dawns on you. You get the meaning, and you don't forget it. I won't forget this.

S: I have to admit that I didn't understand this drawing at all at first. It was a mystery to me. I was thinking, "Oh, great. You're the only one who doesn't get it."

C: I didn't get it at first either. I was in a panic. I kept thinking, "What does this *mean*?"

M: How did you come to understand it?

S: Discussing it together — that helped me a lot. Other people saw things I didn't see. And then I got ideas from what they said.

D: I thought it was helpful to start with a description — just to talk about exactly what we saw in the picture and not to worry about what it could mean.

C: Yes, doing the description was helpful. It led right into meaning.

M: All right. Let's look at the second drawing. First, let me give you a little background. This drawing comes from a book by Máris Bishofs called *The Alien Diaries.* An alien comes to Earth for a short visit, to New York City, as a matter of fact. The Alien records her impressions visually of interesting and mystifying features of life on this strange planet Earth. The Alien is fascinated by sports, among other things, and this drawing comes from the section on sports.

M: So — how do we begin?

D: With a basic description. Hmmmm — here we see a stadium, like a baseball or football stadium.

L: There are a lot of people sitting in the grandstand, and they are watching a sporting event.

M: And the sporting event?

S: I never saw anything like this before in my life.

M: Who is looking at this, recording this impression?

S: An alien — someone from outer space, from another planet or whatever.

M: What does the Alien see? Just describe that sporting event.

S: Well, there are cars, several cars, and they are — pulling people through the air. The people are attached to the cars by cables.

L: This is a race. Time is an important factor. See the clock? That means time is important. The car with the fastest time wins, you know, like in a horse race. The one that crosses the finish line first wins.

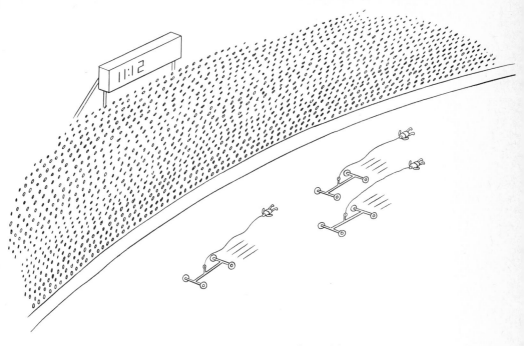

C: So many people are watching this — this — this —

M: Go on.

C: This bizarre sport. I have never heard of such a sport. Of course, I'm not an alien. Oh, I get it!

M: Get what?

C: Earth sports seem strange and bizarre to the Alien. She can't understand what in the world is going on.

D: This so-called sport is just full of danger and violence.

L: Yeah, like football.

D: Those guys being dragged through the air on the cables — I wouldn't like to be one of them. No, thanks.

L: This reminds me of football — the senseless violence. When I watch football, I feel like an alien.

M: Why?

L: I don't get the point of it. What's so great about smashing into people at top speed and tackling them? All for a ball, a funny-shaped ball? This sport is no more ludicrous than football.

C: That's unfair, Liz. Football is not as ludicrous — as bizarre — as weird — as this sport.

L: To me, it is. I'm like the Alien when it comes to football.

D: I feel that way about boxing. I have to admit it.

S: I guess many sports are shocking and violent and senseless unless you are a fan of that sport. Fans see some point to that violence. Non-fans, aliens, don't.

C: People have always loved to watch horrible things. The Romans used to love watching lions chase Christians around the arena — and not just chase either. They — the lions — ate them. People — fans — are pretty bloodthirsty. That's part of the thrill. Gruesome, isn't it?

D: You know, once again this drawing has the power it does because it is *not* a realistic portrait of something we recognize. I mean, if this were a football game, we would say, "Oh, football. So what?" It wouldn't mean anything to us. We're too used to football. It has no power to surprise us, to shock us.

C: That's right. But this sport — because we've never seen it before — it has the power to shock us. This sport is alien to us, so it has the power to shock and horrify us.

1672 words

Reading Times
1st reading ＿＿ minutes
3rd reading ＿＿ minutes

Reading Speed
10 minutes = 167 wpm
 9 minutes = 186 wpm
 8 minutes = 209 wpm
 7 minutes = 239 wpm
 6 minutes = 279 wpm

2.2
SECOND READING

Go back and read the passage again. Before you begin, study the drawings carefully. Take as much time as you need this time. Look up some of the unfamiliar words in the glossary at the end of the book or in your dictionary if you wish.

2.3
THIRD READING

Read the passage quickly a third time. Concentrate on understanding the main ideas of the passage and the meanings of new vocabulary words in the context in which they appear. Note again the process for developing an understanding of the drawings.

2.4
READER RESPONSE

In order to explore your response to this reading, write for 15 minutes about anything that interested you in this passage. You may wish to write about a personal experience this passage reminded you of — or you may wish to agree or disagree with something in the passage. Try to explore *your own thoughts and feelings* as much as possible. Do *not* merely summarize or restate the ideas in this passage.

2.5
RESPONSE SHARING

Read your response to two or three other people in your class. Listen carefully to what the others have written. After you have discussed each other's responses, talk about other points of interest in the passage.

2.6
IDENTIFYING MAIN IDEAS

Working with the same small group, make a list of the main ideas or main points in this passage. Be sure to state the main ideas in your own words. Don't just copy sentences directly from the text. Think carefully about what the writer (the moderator, in this case) is trying to tell you.

2.7
ANALYZING DRAWINGS

Look at the Máris Bishofs' drawing below, another drawing by the Alien from the book entitled *The Alien Diaries*. After you have had a chance to

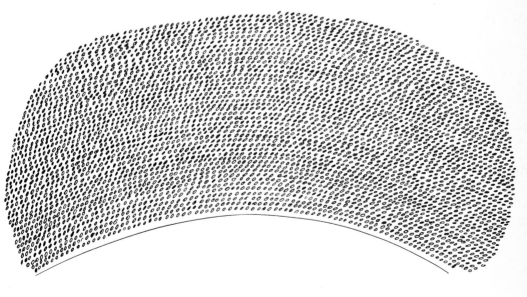

study the drawing carefully, talk with your groupmates about this drawing and what you think it means. Remember to start with a basic description of exactly what you see. Then, talk about meaning. Finally, what does this drawing say about society?

Study this last drawing. It is also from *The Alien Diaries*. Follow the same procedure with your groupmates for figuring out what the drawing means. What does this drawing say about society?

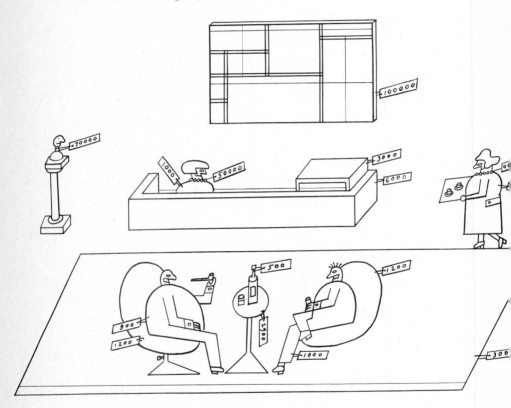

2.8
VOCABULARY STUDY

Study the italicized words and phrases in their contexts. Guess at their meanings. Write your guess in the first blank. Then, look up the word or phrase in your dictionary.

1. This tank-like machine . . . has a pair of scissors, very large scissors, sticking out of it. The scissors are evidently operated by the machine. The scissors are *poised* to cut the cable.

a. (guess) _____

b. (dictionary) _____

2. This person is facing disaster. It's hanging over him — *impending* disaster.

   a. (guess) _____

   b. (dictionary) _____

3. If that thing — that weight — falls on him or her it's certain death, complete *annihilation.*

   a. (guess) _____

   b. (dictionary) _____

4. Man has created this disaster, this *potential* disaster.

   a. (guess) _____

   b. (dictionary) _____

5. That wall could be *self-imposed,* of course. . . . It could be a block — a mental block, like a wall — that keeps us from seeing the full extent of the devastation we could cause if we pushed the button or pulled the lever.

   a. (guess) _____

   b. (dictionary) _____

2.9
CLOZE EXERCISE

Write an appropriate word in each blank. Discuss your word choice with your group. *Note:* In some cases, more than one word may be appropriate, or no word may be needed.

There are many _____(1)_____ kinds of art, and _____(2)_____ different kinds of art _____(3)_____ not all have the same purposes. _____(4)_____ is important to understand _____(5)_____ piece of art on _____(6)_____ own terms and not _____(7)_____ try to compare pieces _____(8)_____ art that really aren't _____(9)_____. It is helpful to _____(10)_____ something about the society _____(11)_____ the time in which _____(12)_____ artwork was created. Art _____(13)_____ contemporary, and a good _____(14)_____ can

look at society _____ see what is really remarkable _____
                    (15)   (16)
that society, that time and _____, long before non-artists
                                       (17)
_____. Consequently, most non-artists are _____ comfort-
     (18)   (19)
able with artwork from _____ past because they feel they under-
                              (20)
stand the past better than they understand the present.

2.10
APPLICATION, CRITICAL EVALUATION, AND SYNTHESIS

1. Gertrude Stein was a writer who had a great influence on other writers and artists. Born in Pennsylvania in 1874, she lived in Paris from 1903 until she died in 1946. Her apartment in Paris became famous as a meeting place for writers and artists who came to discuss art and literature with her and to see her large collection of contemporary paintings. The following are some of her statements about art and writing. What do you think they mean? Why? Relate these statements to the two passages you have read so far in this unit.
   a. The business of Art . . . is to live in the actual present, that is the complete actual present, and to completely express that complete actual present. (from *Lectures in America,* 1934)
   b. If every one were not so indolent they would realize that beauty is beauty even when it is irritating and stimulating not only when it is accepted and classic. Of course it is extremely difficult nothing more so than to remember back to its not being beautiful once it has become beautiful. (from "Composition As Explanation," 1926)
   c. . . . certainly I said I do want to get rich [from my writing] but I never want to do what there is to do to get rich. (from *Everybody's Autobiography,* 1936)
   d. Picasso used to be fond of saying that when everybody knew about you and admired your work there were just about the same two or three who were really interested as when nobody knew about you, but does it make any difference. (from *Everybody's Autobiography,* 1936)
   e. I do not consider that any creative artist is anything but contemporary. Only he is sensitive to what is contemporary long before the average human being is. He puts down what is contemporary and it is exactly that. Sooner or later people realize it. (from "A Transatlantic Interview," 1946)
2. The last passage you read, the discussion of Bishofs' drawings, is a transcription of oral English, and it contains the markers and general characteristics of spoken rather than written language. Go back and look

at the passage again and pick out some of the ways that oral English differs from written English, e.g., beginning a sentence with "Well" or saying "hmmmm." Pick out as many markers of oral English as you can find.

3. Bring some cartoons to class and explain what they mean. What do these cartoons say about society? *Note:* You can find cartoons in most newspapers and in many magazines, particularly news magazines. If possible, bring some cartoons from your country to class and explain their significance to your classmates.

Translation: "Never give in or stray from the road."

3
All This We Have Seen

Art is sometimes used for political purposes to comment upon and criticize political events affecting people's lives. "All This We Have Seen" comes from a book by Guy Brett entitled *Through Our Own Eyes: Popular Art and Modern History* published in 1987 by New Society Publishers of Philadelphia, PA. As Brett states, "In periods of overwhelming historical change, groups of 'ordinary' people have sometimes reached for art as a means to express the experiences they are going through. Without artistic training, and using whatever materials are to hand, they have nevertheless produced intensely moving images. [These images] often give a deeper insight into the contemporary world than the major established forms of art, or than the mass media."

"All This We Have Seen" is about the wall hangings created by women in Chile. These wall hangings, in addition to being colorful and visually striking, reflect the women's feelings towards political and social events affecting their lives and the lives of their families. Reprinted by permission.

3.1
FIRST READING

Read this chapter quickly to understand the main ideas. Do *not* stop to look up words in your dictionary.

1. They gather in the church hall, or another building which is more solid and spacious than the shacks of the shanty-town. There are ten or twelve women. They sit around a table heaped with off-cuts and scraps of material collected from textile factories, balls of wool, and square pieces cut from flour sacks. A stray dog wanders in and out. Children kick a ball in the dust outside; younger ones sit with their mothers on the bench. A kettle is boiling on a camping-gas ring in the corner. As they sew the talk ebbs and flows: about everyday problems of getting by in conditions of

near total unemployment, about the latest gesture by the government. . . . The talk is laced with humour, but faces darken as somebody mentions a woman they all know well who was found drowned in a water-filled ditch, unable to endure her hardships any longer.

2. After a while, one woman finishes stitching onto her patchwork a long loop of black wool which stands for an electricity cable, and holds up for the others to see her version of the theme all have agreed to embroider that week: a local meeting to inform the authorities of their refusal for reasons of poverty to pay for water and electricity.

3. Groups like this in the poor areas of Chile's capital Santiago have produced thousands of patchwork pictures *(arpilleras)* in the last ten years. All are based on the startling dichotomy of a childlike, innocuous, 'toy town' form used to give expression to the direst realities which face the mass of people every day in most countries of the Third World. From these thousands of images a complete and detailed chronicle could be made of the experiences of the Chilean working class since the . . . military coup of 1973.

4. How did such an artistic phenomenon come into being? Conditions after the coup were hardly auspicious for any kind of creative activity. But the remarkable thing about the *arpillera* movement is how closely connected with recent events in Chile it has been, and how near the pulse of popular feelings both of despair and of resistance.

5. Chile is not a country of great strategic importance in terms of its geopolitical position and natural resources. But, as has been pointed out many times, it has aroused world-wide interest in the last fifteen years for the intensity of the political/social/economic experiments it has undergone. On the one hand Chile has the typical characteristics of a Third World country: an economy at the mercy of the market fluctuations of one commodity (copper), indigenous industries stifled by foreign multinationals, a small privileged elite and a mass of oppressed people many of whom have moved to the cities in search of work and live in shanty-towns on their fringes. But Chile also has (or had) many characteristics of a developed country: a large middle class, long-standing civic and parliamentary traditions, educational and welfare programmes, high literacy, and a conscious and organized working class. . . .

6. The ordinary people of Chile faced after the coup [in 1973] an overwhelmingly adverse situation. Many had lost friends or relatives — killed, or vanished in the even worse trauma of the 'disappeared people.' Censorship was omnipresent, political activity of all kinds was banned. The junta's economic policies led to mass unemployment, cut off public funding for health care, housing, education and so on. Hunger faced the families of workers and shanty-town dwellers. Against this, on the positive side, there were really two factors: the considerable level of political consciousness and cultural aspiration of the people which had been growing over a long period, and the position of the Roman Catholic

church which did not identify completely with the new regime and become a centre for emergency assistance of every kind.

7. The emergence of the *arpilleras* is intimately tied in with all these events. Some precedents existed in local folk art. There was a tradition of decorating bags and baskets, and of pictures made of coloured wool by a community on Isla Negra, whose work was admired by the poet Pablo Neruda and the folk-singer Violeta Parra. But there was no direct connection. Although it is hard to be absolutely precise, *arpillera*-making probably had two separate points of origin. One was among the mothers and grandmothers of the (mostly young) people secretly seized by the DINA (secret police) and rarely heard of again. These relatives used to go frequently to the church office of the Vicaria in downtown Santiago, the only place which would offer help and legal assistance in their frustrating search for information, and by regularly meeting others in the same situation they gradually formed themselves into a protest group, the Families of the Disappeared. The other point of origin was among the women of the shanty-towns whose husbands were unemployed and whose families faced starvation. The church assisted them in setting up laundries, simple workshops and soup kitchens. For both these anguished groups *arpillera*-making was a kind of therapy. They have often spoken of the relief of finding this means of expression. For the second group it was also from the beginning an absolute necessity for survival. The church bought the *arpilleras* for small sums, distributed and sold them first in Chile and later abroad.

8. [As one Chilean woman said,]

> There's one *arpillera* I'll never forget. I made it at the end of 1975. 'El Gordo' [her husband] had lung trouble, in fact he had cancer and he had to go to hospital. I was left with the kids. My boy, who was about ten then, asked for something to eat and we just had nothing to give him.
>
> It was such a big problem for me, I felt impotent, I didn't know what to do. I decided to vent my feelings by making an *arpillera*. I made a road which went up into the mountains and had no end, then I made a sun which I gazed at and it gave me strength. This sun I made from pure red wool . . .

9. For most of the women patchwork-making is valued for two essential reasons: It can bring some money to their homes, and it can carry a message to other parts of the world. The women cannot afford to keep any patchworks for themselves, or to give them to friends; their sale is a life and death matter. Nor can the women themselves afford to move, barely even to the city centre. They are rooted to the spot, but their message can travel. For these reasons the workshops are carefully organized and production is controlled. Usually the women in a group make one patchwork each a week. An intermediary, either from the Vicaria or

some independent organization, brings plastic bags full of jumble and rags and takes away the finished work. The money from sales is distributed by a treasurer and a proportion kept back for buying materials and for emergencies. The themes for the patchworks are decided by discussion and the finished pictures are also looked over and analysed, to see that they are well made and that they really 'say something.'

[Another *arpillera*-maker sums up the importance of the *arpillera*-making experience,]

> Apart from all this it's a great joy that people consider that we are making art, that we are artists in this. For us, as housewives, we've never been, or dreamt of being, artists or working in that sort of thing. In this there's some compensation for all that's happened. It gives us more strength to go on, to go on struggling to live. God willing, we'll be able to make them better every day.

1342 words

Reading Times	Reading Speed
1st reading ____ minutes	8 minutes = 168 wpm
3rd reading ____ minutes	7 minutes = 192 wpm
	6 minutes = 224 wpm
	5 minutes = 268 wpm
	4 minutes = 335 wpm

3.2
SECOND READING

Go back and read the selection again. Take as much time as you need this time. Look up some of the unfamiliar words in the glossary at the end of the book or in your dictionary if you wish.

3.3
THIRD READING

Read the selection quickly a third time. Concentrate on understanding the main ideas of the selection and the meanings of new vocabulary words in the context in which they appear.

3.4
READER RESPONSE

In order to explore your response to this reading, write for 15 minutes about anything that interested you in this selection. You may wish to write about something this passage reminded you of — or you may wish to disagree with something in the passage. Try to explore *your own thoughts and feelings* as much as possible. Do *not* merely summarize or restate the ideas in this passage.

The soup kitchen is a place to feed children and to meet people.

3.5
RESPONSE SHARING

Read your response to two or three other people in your class. Listen carefully to what the others have written. After you have discussed each other's responses, talk about other points of interest in the passage.

3.6
IDENTIFYING MAIN IDEAS

Working with the same small group, make a list of the main ideas in this article. Be sure to state the main ideas in your own words. Don't just copy sentences directly from the text. Think carefully about what the writer is trying to tell you.

3.7
ANALYZING ART

Chilean women express their feelings through *arpillera*-making. Look at one of the *arpillera* pictures in this chapter and discuss what you think the creator was trying to tell you through this *arpillera*. Start off with a clear, detailed description of the *arpillera*. After the description, discuss the meaning. Finally, talk about how successfully you think the *arpillera* conveys meaning. Why is it successful?

3.8
VOCABULARY STUDY

Study the italicized words and phrases in their contexts. Guess at their meanings. Write your guess in the first blank. Then, look up the word or phrase in your dictionary.

1. (paragraph 1) The talk is *laced* with humour, but faces darken as somebody mentions a woman they all know well who was found drowned in a water-filled ditch, unable to endure her hardships any longer.

   a. (guess) _____

   b. (dictionary) _____

2. (paragraph 3) Groups like this in the poor areas of Chile's capital Santiago have produced thousands of patchwork pictures . . . in the last ten years. All are based on the startling *dichotomy* of a childlike . . . 'toy town' form used to give expression to the direst realities which face the mass of people every day in most countries of the Third World.

   a. (guess) _____

b. (dictionary) _____

3. (paragraph 3) From these thousands of images a complete and detailed *chronicle* could be made of the experiences of the Chilean working class since the . . . military coup of 1973.

   a. (guess) _____

   b. (dictionary) _____

4. (paragraph 6) The ordinary people of Chile faced after the coup an overwhelmingly *adverse* situation. Many had lost friends or relatives. . . . The junta's economic policies led to mass unemployment, cut off public funding for health care, housing, education and so on. Hunger faced the families of workers and shanty-town dwellers.

   a. (guess) _____

   b. (dictionary) _____

5. (paragraph 7) The emergence of the arpilleras is intimately tied in with all these events. Some *precedents* existed in local folk art. There was a tradition of decorating bags and baskets, and of pictures made of coloured wool. . . .

   a. (guess) _____

   b. (dictionary) _____

3.9
CLOZE EXERCISE

Write an appropriate word in each blank. Discuss your word choice with your group. *Note:* In some cases, more than one word may be appropriate, or no word may be needed.

As Guy Brett, _____ author of *Popular Art, and Modern History,*
                    (1)

_____, "In periods of overwhelming historical change, groups
  (2)

_____ 'ordinary' people have sometimes reached _____ art
  (3)   (4)

as a means to _____ the experiences they are going _____.
                   (5)   (6)

Without artistic training, they have nevertheless _____ intensely
                                                         (7)

moving images." Chilean women _____ used *arpilleras* very effec-
                                      (8)

tively _____ express their feelings about their _____ and the
           (9)   (10)

harsh experiences they _____ endured. Chilean women have two
                            (11)

main _____ for their *arpillera*-making: to _____ sorely
            (12)   (13)

needed money for themselves and their _____ and, secondly, to
                                              (14)

send a message _____ into the world about social/political
                    (15)

_____ they would like to change _____ their society. The
    (16)   (17)

experience of _____ art has given the women a _____ of
                   (18)   (19)

pride in themselves and _____ that the future will be better than the
                              (20)

present.

3.10
APPLICATION, CRITICAL EVALUATION, AND SYNTHESIS

1. Think about these two famous quotations:
   "The pen is mightier than the sword."
   "A picture is worth a thousand words."
   What do they mean? How, for example, can a pen be mightier than a
   sword? And why is a picture worth a thousand words? Do you agree?
   Why? Why not? Can you give examples to support your statements?
2. Ordinary people, people untrained in art, have always used visual images
   to reflect important aspects of their lives and to comment upon important events. Can you think of another example of ordinary people using
   art to comment upon their lives? Please explain your example of folk art
   in detail.
3. People, usually young people, sometimes write their names or draw
   images of various types on subways, buses, and the sides of buildings.
   Why do you think they do this? Do you think people should be allowed
   to write or draw on public property? Why? Why not? Why do you think
   young people are the ones usually attracted to this activity? Have you
   ever been tempted to write your name on public property? Explain — if
   you want to.
4. Have you ever used art to express your thoughts and feelings? If so,
   please explain in detail. What did you do and why did you do it? What
   were your feelings later? Did you accomplish what you wanted to accomplish? If not, explain why not. Do you think that one has to be a
   trained artist to use art as a means of expression?
5. What is art? How would you answer this question now that you have
   read the selections in this unit? You may wish to refer to the discussion
   statements at the beginning of the unit in your answer.

TURN TO THE EXPANSION SECTION ON PAGE 187 FOR PRACTICE IN DOING LIBRARY RESEARCH AND REPORT WRITING.

Developing Research Writing Skills

When you finish each unit, you should turn to this section if you are interested in learning how to do basic library research and to write a research paper. Read through this entire section first to give yourself an overview. After that, you should refer to various topics as needed. For example, you will probably need to review the library research topic several times before you understand all of the points mentioned. You may need several study sessions to learn the uses of direct quotation and paraphrasing and the differences between them. Finally, use this section as a resource manual; refer to various parts of it from time to time to help you learn how to do basic library research and to write research papers.

CONTENTS

4.1
CHOOSING A TOPIC

The first step is to choose a topic to research and to write about. The topic should be related to the unit theme so that you can use some of the ideas, information, and vocabulary from the unit. Here are some suggestions. However, you should feel free to suggest your own topic related to the unit theme.

Unit 1: Families and Childcare

Single Parent Families
Childcare in _____ (a country)
Corporate-sponsored Daycare
Fathers and Children

_____ (your suggestion)

Unit 2: Technology and Ethics

Heart Transplants (or transplants of other organs)
Reactions to Surrogate Motherhood by _____ (a particular group, such as a specific religious group, feminists, etc.)
Test-tube Reproduction
The Right to Die

_____ (your suggestion)

Unit 3: Prisons and Punishment

Capital Punishment
Alternative Sentencing
Punishment for Offenders Who Are Minors

A Comparison between Prisons in the United States and Prisons in
_____ (a country)

_____ (your suggestion)

Unit 4: Leisure

Favorite Leisure Activities in _____ (a country)
An Extraordinary Physical Achievement (climbing a mountain, running a
    great distance, etc.)
Changes in Leisure Activities in _____ (a country)
Professional Sports vs. Amateur Sports

_____ (your suggestion)

Unit 5: Art

People's Art in _____ (a country)
[A study of an artist and some of his or her works]
Contemporary Art in _____ (a country)
Political Art in _____ (a country)

_____ (your suggestion)

4.2
EXPLORING YOUR TOPIC

1. *Brainstorming:* Think of your topic, and then spend a few minutes writing down words and phrases that come to mind in connection with the topic.

    > Example: *leisure time* — weekends, recreation, enjoyment, sports, relaxation, fun, social activities, rest, reading

2. *Exploratory writing:* Now, write for 15 or 20 minutes about your topic. Write anything that comes into your mind. After you finish, read your exploratory writing over. Pick out the parts that interest you most so that you can think more about them. If possible, read your exploratory writing to another person and ask that person for his or her opinion on the parts that are most interesting for further research and development.

4.3
NARROWING YOUR TOPIC

Now, think of some specific questions that you want to ask about your topic.

Example: Single-parent Families

1. Are single parent families increasing?
2. If so, what are some of the reasons for the increase?
3. What are some of the problems faced by single-parent families?
4. Do single-parent families have any advantages or strengths?

Example: The Right to Die

1. What is meant by "the right to die"?
2. What is the issue involved? Whose right to die?
3. Why would anyone want to die?
4. What circumstances could cause one to want to die?

You should try to think of at least six or seven questions, more if possible. These questions will help you focus your ideas and provide a direction for your research.

4.4
DEVELOPING YOUR TOPIC

Look at your questions (4.3) above. Which of your questions seem most interesting to you? Which seem most important?

1. Pick out three or four of your best questions. *Note:* You can change your questions at any time if you want — add new ones, combine old ones, restate them in a different way. For example, you may suddenly realize that you have left out a very important question. Just add it to your list at any time.
2. Now, think about where you could get information to answer each question.

Example: Leisure-time Activities

Do people spend more time on leisure-time activities now? If so, why?

Sources of information: Here are some of the places you could find information to answer this question.

Library (books, magazines, newspapers)
Personal observation and experience
Interviews

4.5
DOING LIBRARY RESEARCH

You will probably need to look up information in a library. First of all, if you have never done research in a library before, ask one of the librarians to help you. Ask the librarian where you can find information on your topic. Here are some of the library resources the librarian may suggest.

1. *The card catalog:* This is the place to look up books on your subject. If you look up your general subject area — for example, *leisure* — you can see if there are books on your subject. *Note:* You may need to think of related words and look in several places in the card catalog to find your subject (example: *leisure, activities, free time, weekends, enjoyment*).

   Here are examples of cards from a card catalog. Cards are filed alphabetically according to author, title of book, and general subject area. The first card is filed according to subject (in this case, *leisure*).

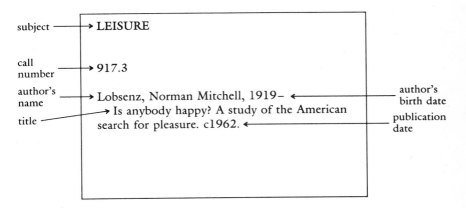

subject ⟶ **LEISURE**

call number ⟶ 917.3

author's name ⟶ Lobsenz, Norman Mitchell, 1919– ⟵ author's birth date

title ⟶ Is anybody happy? A study of the American search for pleasure. c1962. ⟵ publication date

   The *call number* tells you where to find the book in the library. Most libraries have a chart posted showing the location of books by call number areas. However, you can always ask the librarian to tell you where to find a book.

   Note: In many libraries, card catalogs have now been put on computer. You can look things up in exactly the same way in a computerized catalog — alphabetically by author, book title, or general subject area. Ask a librarian to show you how to use the computer.

   The next card is filed according to author. If you knew the name of a particular author, you could look up books by that author by looking through the card catalog for the author's last name.

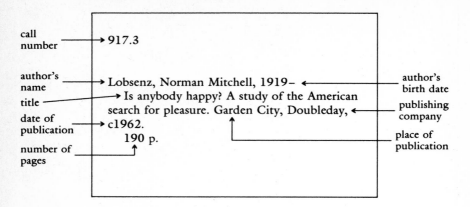

This card is filed according to title.

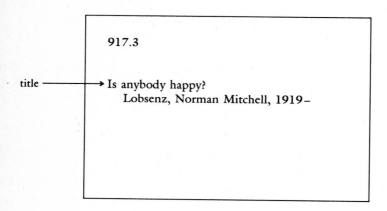

2. *Encyclopedias:* For certain types of subjects, you may be able to find general, background information in an encyclopedia. For example, if you wanted a general, historical overview of crime and punishment, you might look up *punishment* or *penal systems* or *prison* in an encyclopedia. (The first reading in the unit on prisons and punishment came from the *World Book Encyclopedia* under the heading of *Prison*.) There are many specialized encyclopedias on art, music, sports, and other subjects. You can usually get more detailed information in these specialized encyclopedias. *Note:* Encyclopedias provide a good starting point for research —but don't stop there. You need to get more specific information from other sources. Many encyclopedias include a bibliography (a list of related books) at the end of an article.

3. *Readers' Guide to Periodical Literature:* You can look up magazine articles on your subject here. *RGPL* is an alphabetical index by author and

subject of periodicals (magazines) of general interest published in the United States, and it is arranged by year. For example, if you wanted to see what articles relating to single mothers appeared in U.S. magazines in 1987, you would look in the 1987 volume under *Single mothers*. Here is a partial listing of what you would find.

Single mothers
See also
Church work with single mothers
'Don't you talk about my mama!' [adaptation of address, 1987] J. Jordan. *Essence* 18:53+ D '87
Holidays and single moms. V. Gallman. il *Essence* 18:102 D '87
Phantom fathers. K. Richards. il *Progressive* 51:34 Ag '87

Economic conditions
Slum community saves itself [efforts of single mothers to insure survival of low cost housing in Pittsburgh] R. Kahn. *Ms* 15:32 Je '87
A teenage mother's battle to raise her child and pay the bills [Marielle Nelson] M. Maran. il *Sch Update* 119:6 Mr 23 '87

Education
The case for separate schools for pregnant teenagers. J. Buie. *Educ Dig* 53:50-2 D '87
Fort Worth, Texas: a high school that helps teenage mothers shape new lives [New Lives Center] L. Chandler. il *Sch Update* 119:24 Mr 23 '87
Rebuilding lives: a college program for single parents and their kids [Saint Paul's College] R. Brown. il *Ebony* 43:134+ D '87

Employment
Black Boston TV anchor goes public on pregnancy [L. Walker] por *Jet* 72:32 Jl 6 '87
Routes to self-sufficiency: teenage mothers and employment. D. F. Polit. bibl f il *Child Today* 16:6-11 Ja/F '87

Write down the articles that seem to be related to your subject. Be sure to write the name of the magazine and its date of publication.

Look at the other subject categories suggested under "See also." You may find additional information in another subject category.

Ask the librarian if the magazines you want are available in your library. *The Readers' Guide to Periodical Literature* is a good place to look for current information on your topic.

Note: If you are doing research outside of the United States, ask the librarian if the library has some sort of guide to periodical literature.

4. *The New York Times Index:* This is a good place to look for newspaper articles on your topic. *Note:* If your library does not have this particular index, ask the librarian if they have another index of newspaper articles. Many major newspapers have such an index.

This is a sample partial entry under the category **death** of articles that appeared in the *New York Times* in the year 1987. (Some of these articles might be relevant if you were researching the subject, "the right to die.")

DEATH. See also
Deaths
　　Bill that would have set guidelines for when physicians should and should not resuscitate patients is taken off NY State Senate floor during debate when it becomes clear it would not pass. measure discussed (M). Jl 3.II.3:4
　　Feeding tube is removed from stomach of Murray Putzer of West Caldwell, NJ, former laser optics engineer who can do nothing physically except blink his eyes since suffering stroke three years ago. His wife, Dolores, claims it is his decision that he die. State Supreme Court has ruled that patients' wishes supersede those of state and that family members cannot be held criminally lia-

ble for deaths of relatives who want to end treatment that keeps them alive: photo (M). Jl 17.II.2:3

New Jersey Supreme Court justice temporarily bars family of Nancy Ellen Jobes, comatose woman, from removing her feeding tube against wishes of nursing home (M). Jl 19.I.24:1

Murray Putzer, laser optics engineer who received legal permission to have his feeding tube removed, dies on July 9, at age 65, his bodily functions were destroyed after stroke, but he remained mentally competent, portra.: (M). Jl 20.IV.12:5

Nancy Ellen Jobes, 31-year-old comatose woman whose family has New Jersey court permission to remove feeding tubes, is moved to Morristown Hospital from Lincoln Park nursing home where she has been for seven years (S). Jl 21.II.2:4

US Appeals Court upholds New Jersey court ruling that family of Nancy Ellen Jobes may remove life-sustaining feeding tube; family's wish was opposed by Lincoln Park Nursing Home, where Jobes was for seven years until she was moved to Morristown Hospital (S). Jl 25.I.35:4

Again, ask the librarian where the articles you wish to read are located.

4.6
TAKING NOTES

As you look through encyclopedias, newspapers, books, and other sources, you will need to take notes. In every case, you will want to:

■ keep related information together. You should develop a way to keep your notes on each subject separate from notes on all other subjects.
■ be able to organize and reorganize your information in different ways easily. Your notes, when they are all put together, should function as a very rough draft of your report.

There are several ways of taking notes. Two common ways are:

1. *For a short report or composition (two to three pages):*

   On separate pieces of paper, write topic headings, one topic per page (example: types of work women did during World War II, special training programs, benefits for working women).

   As you find information relating to a topic, make notes on the page that deals with that topic. Do not mix topics on one page. If you find that a topic becomes longer or more complex than you expected, divide it onto separate pages, one page for each new subtopic. For each note that you write down, remember to include the source where you got the information (the book/magazine title, author, date of publication, page number).

   When you are finished taking notes, number the points on each page in the order in which you want to use them in your report. You can then organize these pages into the general format of your report. The information on sources will be useful for quotations, footnotes, and references.

2. *Longer reports and general note taking:*

   The most common way to take notes is on 3- by 5-inch index cards. Generally, you use one card per item of information. At the top of each card, write the topic and the source, then use the card to write out the information you want. (Rather than repeating the full information about the source on each card, you may want to keep a separate list with this information — title, author, date of publication — and just write the title and page number on each index card.)

   When you are finished with your research, you may have up to several hundred cards for a long report. You can then organize and reorganize these cards into the format for your report.

   Example: The glossary in this text was developed on index cards, one word per card. Several possible definitions and example sentences were written on each card. The authors then looked over all the cards and selected the definitions and examples they wished to use. Cards for cross-referenced words were added, and all the cards were alphabetized. It was then easy to type the final version.

4.7
QUOTING AND PARAPHRASING

When you are using information from books and articles, it is important to know how to quote and how to paraphrase.

1. *Quoting:* When you are using the *exact words* from a book or article, you must use quotation marks around these words to show that you are borrowing someone else's words.

   Example:

   "Corporations are beginning to discover that more and more of their most valued employees are willing to sacrifice work time, productivity and possibly even careers to devote themselves to family matters."

   Note: The quotation marks (") go at the beginning of the quoted passage and at the end of the quoted passage (". . . . ."). The final quotation mark goes after the period or the question mark.

   Ruth Sidel noted, "The early childhood years comprise one-tenth of humans' lives, and the dignity, respect, and well-being with which persons can live during those years should be of concern to all."

   Directly quoting (using the exact words of someone else) can be quite effective if

   - *the information is very important.*
   - *the ideas are well-expressed.*
   - *the statement is made by an important person,* for example, a recognized expert in the field or a highly placed official.

   Example:

   As **Berit Rollen, under-secretary in the Swedish Ministry of Labour,** stated, "We want to make it possible for everybody to find a paid job and to achieve economic independence. Our aim is to apply this attitude to the whole of society, to working life and also to politics and family life."

   under-secretary   highly placed official.

   On the other hand, *do not quote:*

   - *too much.* A very long quote (a page or more) is not effective. Just pick out the most important information to quote.

■ *everyday, commonplace information:*
"The weather in Belgium is often rainy. However, there were several sunny days in July."
This information is not important enough to directly quote.

■ *too often:* Quotes become ineffective and meaningless if you have too many of them. Save quotes for special information.

2. *Paraphrasing:* When you restate an idea in your own words, you are paraphrasing. Notice the difference between quoting and paraphrasing in the following example.

> *Quoting:* William Broyles said, "I wanted to be tested, mentally and physically; to succeed, but by standards that were clear and concrete, not dependent on the opinion of others."

> *Paraphrasing:* William Broyles said that he wanted to be tested mentally and physically and to succeed by clear, concrete standards . He did not want to be dependent on the opinion of others.

Quoting should be saved for the special situations discussed above (4.7.1). In other situations, it is preferable to paraphrase — to restate an idea in your own words.

Here is another example of the difference between quoting and paraphrasing. You decide which is which.

> Ruth Sidel states that women and their children comprise most of the poor people in the United States today.

> According to Ruth Sidel, "Of poor people in the United States today, the vast majority are women and their children."

4.8
FOOTNOTES AND BIBLIOGRAPHY

You should show your reader where you got your information for your report. You show your sources in the footnotes and the bibliography.

1. *Footnotes:* Your reader often wants to know where you got your information, or you may need to prove where your information came from, particularly if you are dealing with an unusual or surprising bit of information. You should always footnote important information and direct quotes. There are several ways to footnote. Here is one commonly used method. After the statement to be footnoted in your report, you write a

number. The first footnote would be "1", the second one "2", etc. The number should be written above the line.

> The gross national product fell by 0.4 percent between July and September.[1]

At the bottom of the page — or at the end of the paper on a special page entitled *Footnotes* — you cite the reference from which you got this information. In other words, you tell your reader where you got your information. Ask your teacher where you should put your footnotes (at the bottom of the page or at the end of the paper) and which footnote form you should use. Your teacher may refer you to a style sheet such as the *MLA [Modern Language Association] Style Sheet,* which will explain and illustrate how to write footnotes.

Here are some sample footnotes.

Book

> [1]Thomas S. Szasz, *Ideology and Insanity: Essays on the Psychiatric Dehumanization of Man* (Garden City, N.Y.: Doubleday Anchor, 1970), pp. 113–139.

Article

> [2]Robert Pear, "Who Really Needs to Be at St. Elizabeths?" *Washington Star,* August 9, 1971, p. A–1.

Footnotes are sometimes used to give additional information about a point mentioned in the report. Here is an example.

Additional Information

> [3]For more information on this subject, see John Thompson, *The First Cities* (London, 1983), pp. 18–71.

2. *Bibliography:* A bibliography is a complete list of all sources of information you have used in the report: books, articles, interviews. The bibliography (sometimes called *References*) goes at the end of your paper. At the top of the page, you should write the word *Bibliography* (or *References*). Then you should list all of your sources alphabetically by the author's last name. Ask your teacher what bibliographic form you should use. Here is a sample of a partial bibliography.

Bibliography

> Dickens, Mary Ellen, and Margaret Haddad. "New Models of Reading Instruction." *The Reading Journal,* 19:26–29. March, 1989.

Gardiner, John. *Patterns of Immigration in the 1980s.* New York: Harper & Row Publishers, 1988.

Gonzales, David. Personal Interview. London, May 12, 1989.

4.9
INTERVIEWING

In addition to doing library research on your topic, you can get information about your topic by interviewing people. Here are some important points to keep in mind when you are setting up and conducting an interview.

1. *Deciding on interview information areas:* Think about what kind of information you want to get in an interview. Let us suppose that your topic is single-parent families. You could interview some single parents to get information about their experiences as single parents.

   If your topic were "the right to die," you could interview a person who had had a terminally ill person in the family at some point. You could ask your interviewee how he or she felt about a patient's right to choose to die in certain, terminal conditions.

2. *Making up interview questions:* After you have decided upon what kind of information you want to get in an interview (Section 4.9.1 above), you should always make up a general list of interview questions. Try to think of questions that might elicit interesting answers that are related to your choice.

   You should have some yes-no questions —

   > **Example:**
   > **Do you find it difficult to be a single parent?**

   AND some open-ended information-gathering questions (Why . . . ? What do you think about . . . ? How would you . . . ?, etc.)

   > **Example:**
   > **What are some of the most difficult aspects of being a single parent?**

   Show your list of questions to two or three other people, if possible, and ask for their suggestions.

3. *Selecting people to interview:* Now you should choose some people to interview. Generally, two or three interviews are enough unless you are doing a long, in-depth study. Then you will need more. Ideally, the

people you interview should have

- some direct experience related to the topic (e.g., experience as a single parent)

OR

- some important information or knowledge related to the topic. In other words, the person could be an expert in the area or an official who would have access to such information.

4. *Conducting the interview:* Always try to arrange your interviews at a time that is convenient for the interviewee. You will get better results if you do. To make your interviewees feel at ease, try to be as relaxed and cordial as possible when you conduct your interviews. Listen carefully and be sure to ask additional questions if something interesting but unexpected comes up. Make brief notes to help you remember important responses. Jot down just enough information to help you reconstruct the essential information later.

> **Example:**
> **What are some of the problems you face as a single parent?**
>
> *financial problems, no sharing of responsibility, too much responsibility, lack of emotional support.*

Be sure to thank your interviewee for taking the time for the interview and ask if you may check back with him or her later for additional information. You may find that you would like to ask another question or two later as you are looking over your notes.

Try to write up your interviews in some form as quickly as possible so that you don't forget essential information.

5. *Using interview information:* When you are writing your paper, in the body of the paper you can include information from your interviews.

- *Explain who you interviewed and why you interviewed this person*

  Gina Rollins, a student at Davis College, is a single parent with two young children. In a recent interview, Ms. Rollins stated that. . . .[2]

  You should footnote this information so that your reader will know when and where the interview was conducted.

■ *Quote sparingly and paraphrase extensively:*

Write up most of the interview in third-person, narrative form. In other words, paraphrase most of the interview. If your interviewee made a statement that was particularly important or well-expressed, then directly quote that statement. But, remember, don't quote too much! (You may wish to review the guidelines for quoting and paraphrasing in Sections 4.5.1 and 4.5.2 above.)

5.1
MAKING AN OUTLINE

After you have gathered information from a variety of sources, you can then begin to write your paper. Some people find it useful to make a general outline of how they want to organize their paper. Here is an example of an outline.

EMPLOYMENT OF WOMEN DURING WORLD WAR II

I. Introduction — General overview of the subject
  A. *When:* 1939 – 1945
  B. *What:* Increased employment of women in industry
  C. *Why:* Men away fighting in the war
II. Body
  A. Women working in industry during WWII
    1. Examples of types of industries
    2. Numbers of women employed
    3. Kinds of work they did
  B. Government encouragement of women in WWII
    1. Training programs — describe one or two in detail
    2. Benefits designed for women
      a. childcare facilities
      b. some flexibility in working hours
      c. clinics for women and children
  C. Achievements of women during WWII
    1. Examples of outstanding achievements
    2. Examples of other achievements
    3. Recognition by society
  D. Employment of women following WWII
    1. Decline — give specific figures
    2. Men returned from war and took over jobs
    3. Change in attitude toward working women
III. Conclusion

Note: Many people find it useful to make a general outline before they begin writing. They believe the process of making an outline helps them plan and organize their ideas. When they are writing their paper or report, they can refer to their outline to make sure that they have not forgotten any parts. On the other hand, other people believe that they can organize and express their ideas more clearly if they do not make an outline before they begin.

Make an outline of your topic now, but DON'T be afraid to change it as necessary once you begin actually writing. DON'T be locked in by your outline. Use the outline as a guide and as a way of thinking about the organization and content of your report.

5.2
THE PARTS OF A COMPOSITION

Most compositions and reports have four main parts, and each part has a specific function.

■ *Title:* This is the name of your report or composition, and it should give the reader some idea of what the report or composition will cover.

Example:

EMPLOYMENT OF WOMEN DURING WORLD WAR II

■ *Introduction:* Here is where you give the background of your subject and a general overview of what the paper or report will be about. It should give the reader a basic idea of what you will cover in general terms. Your thesis (the main idea of the composition) should be clearly stated in the introduction.

Example of a thesis statement:

During World War II, the United States government encouraged women to work in industry, and women entered the workforce in unprecedented numbers.

■ *Body:* Here is where you give reasons and examples to support your thesis statement. Generally, you state a reason, explain it if necessary, and then give specific examples to illustrate this reason. It is a good idea here to put in as many facts and relevant figures as possible.

Example:

With the outbreak of World War II, women entered the workforce in greater numbers than ever before. For example, more than six million

women entered the paid labor force between 1940 and 1944, an increase of about 50 percent. As Ruth Sidel points out,

> The most dramatic gains were in the 'war industries' such as metals, chemicals, and rubber, in which female employment rose 460 percent. The percentage of women in the auto industry jumped from 6 percent in 1940 to 24 percent in 1944; in electrical manufacturing it rose from 32 percent to 49 percent during the same period.

Note: If a quote is longer than five lines, it should be indented and presented as a separate paragraph. Quotation marks should NOT be used. If the quote is five lines or shorter, it does not have to be indented and presented as a separate paragraph. It simply continues as part of the text, and quotation marks are used around the quote.

Example:

> As Ruth Sidel points out, "The most dramatic gains were in the 'war industries' such as metals, chemicals, and rubber, in which female employment rose 460 percent."[3]

The body is the longest part of a composition. It contains the specific information and concrete examples (see the paragraph above). The length of the body varies according to the length of your report or composition. In a short composition, the body might be two or three paragraphs. In a long report, the body would be many pages long.

■ *Conclusion:* You restate the thesis, briefly review the major points of your report and make a few general remarks about the thesis. Do NOT introduce any new information here. You may want to draw some conclusions of your own that compare, contrast, or highlight some information that you thought was especially important. *Remember:* The conclusion is a kind of brief summary; keep it short. If the reader has not read the whole report or composition, he or she should be able to read the conclusion and get a general idea of its contents.

Example:

> In conclusion, women had a variety of economic opportunities during World War II. The goverment encouraged women to work in nontraditional as well as traditional jobs in order to meet the labor needs of society while men were away at war. Although women succeeded admirably in their wartime jobs, once men returned to the labor force in numbers, women were discouraged from active participation in the labor force. Society once again told women, "Your place is in the home."

5.3
WRITING THE FIRST DRAFT

Beginning with any part of your report, write the first draft. *Note:* You do not have to write the introduction first. If you find it easier to begin with the body, start there. You may wish to write in pencil and double or triple space so that you have room to make changes as you go along.

Show your draft to at least one other person. Ask the person to tell you what parts he or she liked best and what parts need to be changed. Where do you need to have more information? More examples? Which points are unclear? Be sure to discuss problem areas thoroughly so that you can decide how to rewrite them. Concentrate primarily on ideas and making sure they are expressed clearly.

5.4
WRITING THE SECOND DRAFT

Write your report again taking particular care to make the revisions suggested in Section 5.3 above. Concentrate on stating your ideas clearly. Make sure your examples relate closely to the points you are trying to make.

Show your second draft to the person or persons who read your first draft. Make sure your revisions are clear.

When the meaning is clear, check over grammar, punctuation, and spelling with the person or persons reading your draft. *Note:* Don't worry about grammar, punctuation, or spelling until the meaning is clear.

5.5
WRITING THE FINAL DRAFT

Write or type your final draft. If you write your final draft by hand, be sure to use a pen. Write neatly and clearly on lined paper. Skip lines. If you type, double space. Hand in your final draft to your teacher.

One final note: GOOD WRITING IS REWRITING. If you write several drafts of a paper, the final product will be much better. Also, remember to concentrate on content (clear expression of ideas) first and then work on form (grammar, punctuation, and spelling).

Glossary

In this glossary, words are defined as they are used in the readings. Since many of these words may also have other meanings, please check further in your own dictionary for the full range of meanings of a specific word. Page numbers refer to the page on which a word appears in the text.

abjectly *adv.* In a humble manner; deferentially. *Ex.* The naughty child stood abjectly in front of his mother. (p. 70)

absurd *adj.* Foolish; nonsensical. *Ex.* That story is so absurd I can't believe it. (p. 154)

acclimatize *v.* To adapt; to get used to. *Ex.* The scientists had to acclimatize themselves to the Antarctic cold before they could do their outdoor research. (p. 144)

accommodate *v.* To provide for; to support, to handle. *Ex.* This cafeteria can accommodate over 2000 people a day. (p. 99)

across the board *adv. phrase.* In all respects, including everyone or everything. *Ex.* Across the board, the entire staff got a raise in pay. (p. 134)

adverse *adj.* Negative; unfavorable. *Ex.* She had an adverse reaction to the medicine. (p. 180)

advocate *n.* A supporter; one who urges something. *Ex.* Clean air advocates want the government to control industrial pollution. (p. 13)

affluence *n.* Wealth; prosperity. *Ex.* Australia and West Germany are among the nations in the world with the greatest affluence. (p. 124)

aggravate *v.* To make worse. *Ex.* The hot sun aggravated my headache. (p. 48)

agony *n.* Extreme pain. *Ex.* He was in agony after he broke his leg. (p. 49)

alien *n.* A being from outer space; an outsider. *Ex.* Do you believe that aliens exist who can travel through space in flying saucers? (p. 167)

alleviate *v.* To relieve; to lighten. *Ex.* Aspirin should alleviate your muscle pain. (p. 89)

allsided *adj.* On all sides; complete. *Ex.* Did the debate present an allsided view of the daycare issue? (p. 4)

ambivalent *adj.* Undecided. *Ex.* Many people are still ambivalent about the need for child care centers. (p. 14)

anguished *adj.* Extremely sad; in despair. *Ex.* She gave an anguished cry when she heard the terrible news. (p. 181)

annihilation *n.* Total destruction. *Ex.* The World Health Organization is working towards the annihilation of malaria in the world. (p. 168)

anonymity *n.* An absence or lack of identification, leaving out the name of a person. *Ex.* Is the anonymity of wearing uniforms at school a good or bad thing? (p. 111)

anticipate *v.* To expect. *Ex.* She anticipates graduating from college next year. (p. 48)

apprehension *n.* Anxiety; worry. *Ex.* Most people feel some apprehension before a job interview. (p. 33)

archive *n.* Records of past history. *Ex.* City Hall contains archives of all births, deaths, and marriages that occurred here. (p. 6)

asinine *adj.* Foolish; stupid. *Ex.* Her behavior was so asinine that I didn't want to be seen with her! (p. 100)

aspiration *n.* Ambition; hope. *Ex.* She has aspirations to become a lawyer. (p. 180)

at one's disposal *adv. phrase.* The ability or power to do something or to use something. *Ex.* The bank has at its disposal lots of money to loan. (p. 4)

at stake *adv. phrase.* Depending on the result; at risk. *Ex.* The future of the team is at stake if they don't win the championship. (p. 46)

at the mercy of *adv. phrase.* Under the power of; without any defenses against. *Ex.* Sailing across the ocean, our ship was at the mercy of the weather. (p. 19)

avail *v.* To take advantage of; to have access to. *Ex.* I availed myself of every opportunity to see plays when I was in London. (p. 99)

ban *v.* To prohibit. *Ex.* Do you think personal ownership of guns should be banned? (p. 180)

be all over *v.* To be finished. *Ex.* The party was all over by the time I got there. (p. 168)

bedlam *n.* Great uproar and confusion. *Ex.* On a busy day, it's bedlam in my office — phones keep ringing, lots of people need help, everyone has questions. (p. 110)

bellwether *n.* The leader of a group, one who sets the pace. *Ex.* Picasso was the bellwether of the Cubist movement in art. (p. 135)

below par *adv. phrase.* Below normal; inferior. *Ex.* This report is below par; please redo it. (p. 76)

bent on *adv.* Inclined towards, determined to. *Ex.* They were bent on finishing the project by the end of the month. (p. 125)

best interests of *adv. phrase.* Well-being; for the good of. *Ex.* It is in the best interests of the committee for you to be the chairperson. (p. 29)

binding *adj.* Compulsory; required. *Ex.* She signed a binding agreement to pay back the money in two years. (p. 58)

biped *n.* An animal that has two feet. *Ex.* Is the ostrich the largest biped in the world? (p. 154)

bizarre *adj.* Weird; strange. *Ex.* Everyone wore bizarre clothes to the Halloween party. (p. 171)

blend into the woodwork *v.* To fade into the background and not be noticed. *Ex.* At the big party, the shy child was so quiet he just blended into the woodwork. (p. 111)

block *n.* An obstacle; a barrier. *Ex.* There is a roadblock up ahead because of the accident. (p. 169)

bracing *adj.* Stimulating; brisk; sharp. *Ex.* The cool wind felt strong and bracing. (p. 110)

brutal *adj.* Cruel; fierce. *Ex.* The heat can be brutal in the desert. (p. 90)

bundle up *v.* To dress warmly. *Ex.* Be sure to bundle up before you go out in the cold! (p. 33)

burden *n.* A heavy responsibility. *Ex.* It is quite a burden to work and go to school at the same time. (p. 122)

burst *v.* To break; to explode. *Ex.* The balloon burst with a loud noise. (p. 109)

by default *adv. phrase.* Because of a lack of anything else; because of the absence or failure of another. *Ex.* She was the only person on the ballot, so she won the election by default. (p. 135) ˙

cache *v.* To put away safely; to store. *Ex.* We cached our suitcases in a locker at the train station and looked around the town for a few hours. (p. 144)

clean slate *n.* An empty space where one can start fresh. *Ex.* Let's forget about the past and start with a clean slate from today. (p. 31)

coercion *n.* Enforcement under pressure; threat. *Ex.* It is illegal to use coercion to force someone to do something. (p. 58)

coherent *adj.* Consisting of related parts; unified. *Ex.* They developed a coherent plan for conducting the research. (p. 14)

collective spirit *n.* A group feeling. *Ex.* After the terrible earthquake, the whole city joined in a collective spirit to help the people whose homes were destroyed. (p. 5)

come to terms with *v.* To accept; to submit to. *Ex.* I finally came to terms with the fact that I will never be a great tennis player. (p. 101)

comply *v.* To obey; to do what one is told. *Ex.* It will be easy to comply with your request. (p. 30)

compulsion *n.* A feeling that you have to do something; an obsession. *Ex.* Peter always had a compulsion to be the best at whatever he did. (p. 123)

conceivable *adj.* Believable; possible. *Ex.* Your plans are not conceivable without a great deal of money and help from your friends. (p. 7)

concrete *adj.* Specific; precise. *Ex.* These instructions are written in such concrete language that they are easy to follow. (p. 142)

condemn *v.* To disapprove of strongly; to say that something is not good. *Ex.* The authorities condemned the old building as unsafe to live in. (p. 47)

confine *v.* To shut in; to limit the freedom of. *Ex.* My neighbors confine their dog to the backyard when they are away. (p. 87)

conscientiously *adv.* Attentively; seriously. *Ex.* She worked so conscientiously that she was promoted to general manager. (p. 102)

consistency *n.* Uniformity; things remaining the same. *Ex.* Without some consistency in the rules, it is hard to know what to do. (p. 101)

constraint *n.* Restriction; limit. *Ex.* Are there any constraints on how I may use this money? (p. 61)

contemplative *adj.* Thoughtful; focusing one's attention on. *Ex.* People with contemplative minds often become writers or musicians. (p. 144)

contraband *adj.* Forbidden. *Ex.* You are not allowed to bring such contraband items as ivory or tortoise shells into the United States. (p. 100)

contrary *adj.* Opposite; opposed. *Ex.* The opinions of a conservative person are generally contrary to those of a liberal. (p. 59)

conventional *adj.* Ordinary; usual. *Ex.* It is conventional for a man to wear a suit and tie when he works in an office. (p. 48)

cope with *v.* To manage; to take care of; to handle. *Ex.* I can cope with most problems on my job, but sometimes I need help. (p. 6)

corpse *n.* A dead body. *Ex.* The corpse was placed in a coffin and buried. (p. 69)

creche *n.* The French word for day nursery for young children. *Ex.* Creches were organized in nineteenth-century France to care for the children of working mothers. (p. 4)

critique *v.* To comment on; to criticize. *Ex.* She asked me to critique her speech while she rehearsed it. (p. 28)

crooked *adj.* Dishonest. *Ex.* The crooked employee stole money by falsifying the account books. (p. 110)

crystallize *v.* To solidify; to take on a definite form or shape. *Ex.* After she read the travel brochure, her trip to Brazil crystallized. (p. 46)

dawn *v.* To begin to understand; to occur. *Ex.* It finally dawned on him that he was driving in the wrong direction. (p. 170)

deem *v.* To consider; to have an opinion. *Ex.* Do you deem it important to have a college education? (p. 29)

default See *by default*.

degradation *n.* Loss of dignity or respect; humiliation. *Ex.* The prisoners of war suffered great degradation. (p. 59)

degrading *adj.* *Ex.* Don't you think it is degrading to beg for money? (p. 58)

dehydration *n.* The condition in which the body has lost too much fluid. *Ex.* If you are working in the sun on a hot day, drink lots of water to prevent dehydration. (p. 143)

deplorable *adj.* Disgraceful; bad; regrettable. *Ex.* She changed jobs because of the deplorable working conditions in the factory. (p. 18)

deprive of *v.* To take away from; to withhold. *Ex.* If you deprive a plant of water, it will die. (p. 88)

derivative *n.* A modification; a borrowing. *Ex.* The symbols that we use for numbers (1, 2, 3) are derivatives of traditional Arabic numerals. (p. 135)

derive *v.* To receive. *Ex.* I derive great pleasure from playing my guitar. (p. 4)

deserts See *just deserts*.

despair *v.* To feel hopeless. *Ex.* They despaired that the terrible snowstorms would never end. (p. 160)

destitute *adj.* Very poor. *Ex.* The family became destitute after the fire destroyed all their belongings. (p. 16)

deterrent *n.* Something that discourages or prevents. *Ex.* Some people consider Vitamin C a good deterrent to colds. (p. 111)

devastation *n.* Total destruction. *Ex.* The devastation caused by the forest fire was shown on the evening news. (p. 169)

dichotomy *n.* Division into two contradictory parts. *Ex.* There was a strange dichotomy between the nice things he said to people and the terrible way he treated them. (p. 180)

diligent *adj.* Industrious; hardworking. *Ex.* If you are diligent in school, you will get good grades. (p. 5)

diminish *v.* To reduce; to lower. *Ex.* Nothing will ever diminish my love for you. (p. 59)

dire *adj.* Extremely terrible. *Ex.* The victims of the drought in the Sahara Desert live in dire poverty. (p. 180)

directly *adv.* Exactly; precisely. *Ex.* His house is directly opposite the bus stop. (p. 59)

discern *v.* To recognize; to detect. *Ex.* She discerned his meaning even though she didn't understand all the words. (p. 124)

disposal See *at one's disposal.*

disquieting *adj.* Making one feel uneasy or anxious. *Ex.* Being alone in a strange place can be a disquieting experience. (p. 153)

distinction See *questionable distinction.*

do time *v.* *(slang)* To spend time in prison. *Ex.* He did time in prison for robbing a bank. (p. 109)

drift *v.* To wander; to think of other things. *Ex.* The lecture was so boring that my mind began to drift. (p. 33)

dumping ground *n.* Literally, a place to put garbage; idiomatically, a place for one's excuses or problems; a place to put the blame for things. *Ex.* He used his dissatisfaction with his job as a dumping ground for all his problems. (p. 100)

ebb and flow *v.* To go out and in like the tide. *Ex.* The ebb and flow of the seasons creates great changes in the scenery. (p. 179)

eliminate *v.* To get rid of; to end. *Ex.* I eliminated sugar from my diet and lost five pounds. (p. 18)

endurance *n.* The ability to keep going; perseverance. *Ex.* Camels are well known for their endurance in the desert. (p. 142)

enterprise *n.* A business, a large project. *Ex.* As the scientific enterprise grew, more and more researchers were hired. (p. 4)

entrust *v.* To give responsibility to; to give to someone for care or protection. *Ex.* The accountant was entrusted with paying all the company's bills. (p. 3)

era *n.* A time period. *Ex.* The twentieth century has been an era of great technological change. (p. 18)

erode *v.* To disappear little by little; to wear away. *Ex.* As the soil was eroded from the hills, there was great danger from landslides. (p. 145)

escrow *n.* (legal) Something (often money) that is held by a neutral person (often a bank) until a condition is fulfilled. *Ex.* The landlord will put your apartment deposit in an escrow account and return it to you when you move out. (p. 49)

ethical *adj.* Moral; based on social principles. *Ex.* Plato believed that society can function only if people live according to ethical behavior. (p. 46)

evolve out of *v.* To be created from; to develop out of something else. *Ex.* Lions and cats evolved out of the same prehistoric ancestor. (p. 16)

exasperation *n.* Annoyance; arousing anger. *Ex.* She had a look of exasperation on her face because no one believed her story. (p. 153)

execution *n.* Production; performance. *Ex.* The ice skater's execution of the difficult jump was superb. (p. 157)

exploit *v.* To take advantage of; to use unfairly. *Ex.* The workers felt they were being exploited and went on strike. (p. 15)

extramural *adj.* Outside (of the walls or the institution). *Ex.* Some prisoners are allowed to do extramural work during the day and return to prison at night. (p. 110)

exultant *adj.* Extremely happy. *Ex.* The winners were exultant. (p. 46)

facilitate *v.* To be helpful in, to make easier. *Ex.* This letter will facilitate your getting an appointment with the Director. (p. 13)

fathom *v.* To comprehend; to understand after deep thought. *Ex.* No one could fathom why they moved out of town. (p. 121)

flagrant *adj.* Very noticeable and bad; shameless. *Ex.* The child told a flagrant lie and was punished. (p. 14)

(the) flip side *n.* The reverse side; the other side. *Ex.* When this side of the record is over, let's play the flip side. (p. 121)

forgo *v.* To give up; to do without. *Ex.* My doctor told me to cut down on caffeine, but it is hard to forgo coffee. (p. 122)

for good *adv. phrase.* Permanently; finally. *Ex.* I'd like to retire for good before I'm 60 years old. (p. 144)

forum *n.* A public meeting for discussion and debate. *Ex.* I attended a forum where all the candidates presented their views. (p. 46)

frustrating *adj.* Filled with dissatisfaction because one is prevented from reaching one's goal or purpose. *Ex.* It was so frustrating to not be able to talk to the foreign visitors; they spoke only Russian, we spoke only English. (p. 181)

furtive *adj.* Done secretly. *Ex.* Their eyes met in a furtive glance. (p. 46)

gap *n.* An opening; an empty space. *Ex.* There is a great gap in my knowledge about computers, so I plan to take some classes. (p. 143)

get by *v.* To manage; to get what you need. *Ex.* I can just get by on my current income, but I'd rather be earning more. (p. 179)

get it *v.* To understand. *Ex.* It took me a long time to get it, but I finally understood the joke. (p. 170)

glamorous *adj.* Highly desirable; fascinating; attractive. *Ex.* The movie star led a glamorous life. (p. 142)

go by *v.* To follow; to obey. *Ex.* You must go by the rules of the club if you want to be a member. (p. 153)

grandstand *n.* The best place to sit at a sports event. *Ex.* The view of the race will be best from the grandstand. (p. 170)

grant *v.* To acknowledge. *Ex.* I grant that you are right. (p. 159)

grasp the reality *v.* To understand what is really happening. *Ex.* After the accident, it took him a moment to grasp the reality of how badly his car was damaged. (p. 34)

gravity *n.* Seriousness. *Ex.* She was worried about the gravity of her illness. (p. 75)

grim *adj.* Without pleasure; harsh. *Ex.* The firefighters went about the grim work of rescuing the victims of the fire. (p. 97)

grossly *adv.* Terribly; very badly. *Ex.* He was grossly underpaid, so he found a better job. (p. 18)

gruesome *adj.* Horrifying and terrible. *Ex.* I hate those gruesome horror movies where strange-looking creatures rise out of graves. (p. 172)

handicapped *adj.* Disadvantaged; burdened. *Ex.* In Mexico, I was handicapped by my inability to speak Spanish. (p. 16)

hang in *v.* *(slang)* To not give up; to persevere. *Ex.* The losing team tried to hang in until the very last moment. (p. 34)

hang out *v.* *(slang)* To loiter; to pass the time doing nothing. *Ex.* The teenagers like to hang out in front of the ice cream store on summer nights. (p. 102)

harmonious *adj.* In agreement; without conflict. *Ex.* The Smiths have a very harmonious marriage; they never argue. (p. 4)

harrowing *adj.* Very distressing or painful. *Ex.* The refugees lived through a harrowing experience. (p. 110)

have one's work cut out for one *v.* To be naturally suited for, to be arranged ahead of time. *Ex.* My friend loves to fix things, so he has his work cut out for him restoring that old house to its former beauty. (p. 125)

hedonism *n.* The love of pleasure. *Ex.* That book poetically describes the hedonism of youth. (p. 135)

heyday See *in its heyday.*

highlight *v.* To emphasize; to shine a strong light on. *Ex.* Students often highlight important facts in their textbooks by underlining or using a colored marking pen. (p. 14)

hold sway *v.* To have a controlling influence; to extend power over a wide area. *Ex.* The Roman Empire held sway over most of Europe 2000 years ago. (p. 135)

homogeneous *adj.* All alike; consisting of similar elements. *Ex.* Korea is an example of a homogeneous society. (p. 17)

howl *v.* To cry loudly; to complain. *Ex.* Why do dogs howl when they hear a siren? (p. 30)

impending *adj.* About to occur. *Ex.* The dark sky and thick clouds were signs of an impending thunderstorm. (p. 168)

impressively *adv.* Causing great admiration or a strong positive effect. *Ex.* That swimmer can hold her breath under water for an impressively long time. (p. 111)

inadequate *adj.* Insufficient; unsatisfactory. *Ex.* Inadequate housing is a major problem in many large cities around the world. (p. 15)

indifference *n.* Unconcern; lack of interest. *Ex.* I am surprised at your indifference to your family's problems. (p. 135)

indispensible *adj.* Essential; necessary. *Ex.* A microscope is indispensible for the study of cellular biology. (p. 6)

inducement *n.* Incentive; temptation. *Ex.* The belief that South America was rich in gold was a great inducement to explorers in the sixteenth century. (p. 58)

inevitable *adj.* Unavoidable; cannot be prevented. *Ex.* It was inevitable that they would get married someday. (p. 34)

in its heyday *adv. phrase.* In good times; in a time of great prosperity or popularity. *Ex.* In its heyday, the Renaissance in Europe produced splendid architecture. (p. 17)

innocuous *adj.* Insignificant; bland. *Ex.* I had a pleasant but innocuous conversation with the person sitting next to me on the airplane. (p. 180)

innovation *n.* A new idea; a new way of doing something. *Ex.* Computers have created many innovations in office work as well as in technology. (p. 17)

in retrospect *adv. phrase.* Looking back. *Ex.* In retrospect, would you do it all over again? (p. 48)

institution *n.* An organization; a building used for a specific activity (especially public or business purposes). *Ex.* Colleges are institutions of higher learning. (p. 87)

insufficient *adj.* Not enough. *Ex.* He has insufficient time to do his homework. (p. 18)

intact *adj.* Together; preserved; undamaged. *Ex.* The Town Hall remained intact after the flood, but the train station was badly damaged. (p. 110)

interpret *v.* To explain the meaning of; to make clear. *Ex.* Can you interpret the instructions on this application form? (p. 168)

in the long run *adv. phrase.* As a final result; in the end. *Ex.* In the long run, I'm glad I went to college first instead of getting a job right after high school. (p. 111)

intimately *adv.* Very closely. *Ex.* We know each other intimately because we've been best friends since childhood. (p. 181)

intolerably *adv.* Unbearably; too much to be endured. *Ex.* The party next door was so intolerably loud that I couldn't sleep. (p. 18)

intrusion *n.* Entering by force; interference. *Ex.* I consider that question an intrusion on my privacy, so I won't answer it. (p. 135)

irrevocable *adj.* Unchangeable; absolute. *Ex.* She made an irrevocable decision to leave Poland and emigrate to Canada. (p. 58)

isolated *adj.* Separated from others; alone. *Ex.* He lived an isolated existence while he worked on an Alaskan fishing boat. (p. 17)

isolation *n. Ex.* Many artists tend to work in isolation. (p. 89)

jolt *n.* A sudden shake or surprise. *Ex.* The jolt of the earthquake woke me up. (p. 154)

jumble *n.* Things all mixed together. *Ex.* That box contains a jumble of clothes, shoes, and books. (p. 182)

just *adj.* Honest; impartial. *Ex.* The judge gave a fair and just opinion. (p. 4)

just deserts *n.* What one deserves; fair compensation. *Ex.* Their comfortable retirement years were the just deserts of a life of hard work. (p. 110)

keep your eyes and ears open *v.* To be alert. *Ex.* Keep your eyes and ears open for news of the big sale. (p. 98)

kill time *v.* To spend one's time doing nothing. *Ex.* When I'm tired, I sometimes kill time by just looking out the window. (p. 100)

lag behind *v.* To fall behind, to come after. *Ex.* I got so tired on the bicycle ride that I lagged behind everyone else. (p. 133)

laid back *adj. (slang)* Very relaxed; unconcerned. *Ex.* He had such a laid back attitude toward his job that he got fired. (p. 135)

laminate *v.* To encase in plastic. *Ex.* My ID cards and driver's license are laminated. (p. 98)

laxness *n.* Relaxed style; looseness. *Ex.* Do you believe that strictness, laxness, or something in between is the best way to raise children? (p. 123)

layman *n.* An ordinary person; not a specialist. *Ex.* As a layman, I don't know legal terminology, but I can explain the case to you in ordinary words. (p. 153)

lever *n.* A handle. *Ex.* If you pull that lever, the alarm will ring. (p. 169)

linger *v.* To wait for a while; to be slow to leave. *Ex.* We lingered in the park all afternoon because the flowers and trees were so beautiful. (p. 146)

long-standing *adj.* Enduring; traditional. *Ex.* My friend and I have a long-standing arrangement to have coffee together every Sunday morning. (p. 180)

lowest common denominator *n.* A mathematical term; idiomatically, the most generally acceptable thing (often something bland and uninteresting). *Ex.* The music in elevators represents the lowest common denominator in musical tastes. (p. 159)

ludicrous *adj.* Foolish; ridiculous. *Ex.* One hundred years ago people thought that the idea of airplane flight was ludicrous. (p. 171)

luscious *adj.* Very delicious. *Ex.* Viennese pastry always looks so luscious. (p. 69)

manual *adj.* Done by hand. *Ex.* Digging with a shovel is manual labor. (p. 156)

material *adj.* Concrete; pertaining to things that exist. *Ex.* Countries with a high standard of living generally have more material goods for consumers. (p. 5)

meager *adj.* Poor; slight. *Ex.* The Andean Indians earn a meager living growing potatoes and other crops. (p. 103)

means *n.* Ways; resources; ability. *Ex.* Do you have the means to buy a new car? (p. 157)

mercy See *at the mercy of.*

mere *adj.* Only; nothing more than. *Ex.* These paintings are mere images of the real thing. (p. 135)

migration *n.* Movement from one place to another (often in great numbers). *Ex.* Many birds follow a migration route to warm climates in the winter. (p. 17)

mitigating *adj.* Becoming less severe; reducing. *Ex.* There was no excuse for his rude behavior; the only mitigating factor was that he was very tired. (p. 59)

modus operandi *n. (Latin phrase)* The way of doing things. *Ex.* The brush seller's modus operandi was to go into a town and knock on every door. (p. 100)

mold *v.* To shape. *Ex.* The potter molded the clay into a beautiful bowl. (p. 159)

monitor *v.* To watch over; to check regularly; to pay attention to. *Ex.* The doctor monitored her progress. (p. 18)

monogram *n.* The initials of one's name used as a decoration. *Ex.* The tailor sewed the monogram "LMH" onto the pocket of my sweater. (p. 101)

multitude *n.* A crowd; a great number. *Ex.* I have a multitude of questions about life in India. (p. 7)

murky *adj.* Unclear; cloudy; dark. *Ex.* He refused to swim in the murky water. (p. 13)

mutual aid *n.* Cooperation; help for each other. *Ex.* Good friends provide mutual aid and support whenever they have problems. (p. 14)

mystifying *adj.* Puzzling; not understandable. *Ex.* At the time her actions were mystifying, but now I understand what she was doing. (p. 170)

mythologize *v.* To turn into a myth; to romanticize; to describe idealistically. *Ex.* Do you suppose that people mythologize "the good old days" because life seemed simpler then? (p. 14)

narrow-minded *adj.* Intolerant of other opinions. *Ex.* It is impossible to discuss politics with him; he's so narrow-minded. (p. 6)

nostalgically *adv.* Wishing for a return to the past. *Ex.* That book nostalgically describes what it was like to grow up in a small town in the 1920s. (p. 14)

nuclear family *n.* The basic family unit of parent(s) and children. *Ex.* Did you grow up in a nuclear family or an extended family? (p. 18)

of long standing *adj. phrase.* Continuing for a long time. *Ex.* The family's custom of long standing is to have a big family reunion every five years. (p. 14)

omnipresent *adj.* Existing everywhere and all the time. *Ex.* There is an omnipresent danger of an earthquake in Los Angeles. (p. 180)

open many doors *v.* To provide opportunities. *Ex.* My uncle opened many doors for me in business. (p. 99)

optimism *n.* The belief that good things in life outweigh the bad; a positive outlook. *Ex.* A person who views the world with optimism is generally happy. (p. 7)

option *n.* A choice. *Ex.* She had the option of taking her vacation in June or July, but not in August. (p. 98)

ordeal *n.* A difficult or painful experience. *Ex.* The operation on her back was a painful ordeal, but it was necessary for her health. (p. 146)

organ *n.* An internal part of the body that performs a special function, such as the stomach, lungs, or intestines. *Ex.* The lungs are the organs of breathing. (p. 73)

outset *n.* The beginning. *Ex.* Let's agree at the outset to share the profits fifty-fifty. (p. 157)

overwhelming *adj.* Far more than one can handle; overpowering. *Ex.* Isn't it overwhelming to work, study, and raise a family all at the same time? (p. 7)

painstaking *adj.* Done very carefully. *Ex.* He moved the delicate sculpture with painstaking care. (p. 156)

pallid *adj.* Pale; having very little color. *Ex.* The feverish child looked weak and pallid. (p. 69)

par See *below par.*

paradox *n.* Something that contradicts itself. *Ex.* It is a paradox that the more some people have, the unhappier they are. (p. 159)

paradoxically *adv.* Contrary, opposite of what you expect. *Ex.* She is a talented singer, but paradoxically, she has never taken voice lessons. (p. 71)

passionate *adj.* Enthusiastic; devoted to. *Ex.* The art collector was passionate about modern art. (p. 122)

peer *n.* A person who is an equal or at the same stage as you. *Ex.* In Japan, you graduate with your peers, work with your peers, and retire with your peers. (p. 122)

peer *v.* To look into; to examine closely. *Ex.* The scientist peered into the microscope. (p. 122)

penetrate *v.* To enter sharply or by force. *Ex.* It was very painful when the sharp rock penetrated my foot. (p. 158)

phenomenon (*plural:* **phenomena**) *n.* Something you can observe; a real thing. *Ex.* The Great Wall of China is one of the greatest man-made phenomena in the world. (p. 154)

pitfall *n.* A hidden danger; a trap. *Ex.* Read the contract carefully to make sure there are no pitfalls. (p. 154)

poignantly *adv.* A mixed feeling of sadness, sympathy, and pity. *Ex.* The old man spoke poignantly of his childhood in Romania. (p. 48)

poise *v.* To put in position; to hold steadily without motion. *Ex.* The bee poised over the flower for a few seconds and then flew away. (p. 168)

potential *adj.* Possible in the future. *Ex.* The doctors discussed the potential uses of the new drug. (p. 169)

precondition *n.* A condition that must exist before something else can happen. *Ex.* Being an excellent bicyclist is a precondition for entering a bicycle race. (p. 7)

predominant *adj.* Major; most important. *Ex.* What is the predominant religion in Italy? (p. 59)

preliminary findings *n.* Early results; first conclusions. *Ex.* The preliminary findings were so promising that the Institute gave him a grant for three more years of research. (p. 133)

preoccupation *n.* Involvement; taking one's attention. *Ex.* That child has a great preoccupation with mathematics; she may grow up to be an engineer. (p. 6)

prescribed *adj.* Established; predetermined. *Ex.* If you want to play tennis with us, you will have to follow the prescribed rules. (p. 123)

prestigious *adj.* Esteemed; highly regarded. *Ex.* What is the most prestigious career in your country? (p. 15)

prevail *v.* To win; to predominate. *Ex.* In Japanese business, the decision of the group prevails. (p. 101)

priority *n.* The most important thing; the order of importance. *Ex.* What is the greatest priority in your life right now? (p. 17)

profane *adj.* Worldly (as distinguished from spiritual); not religious. *Ex.* Many churches now include profane music as well as sacred music in their services. (p. 135)

proliferate *v.* To multiply; to increase. *Ex.* Fast food stores are proliferating all over the world. (p. 71)

propel *v.* To push forward. *Ex.* That type of jet airplane is propelled by four engines. (p. 121)

pseudonym *n.* A false name; not someone's real name. *Ex.* Norma Jean Baker's pseudonym was Marilyn Monroe. (p. 46)

purport *v.* To claim (often not quite accurately). *Ex.* He is purported to be the wealthiest man in the world. (p. 57)

pursuit *n.* Activity; area of interest. *Ex.* John enjoys athletic pursuits on the weekends. (p. 135)

put in time *v.* To spend time. *Ex.* I put in lots of time in my garden during the summer. (p. 109)

put in touch with *v.* To help establish contact with. *Ex.* Could you put me in touch with someone who knows about real estate law? (p. 102)

quasi- *adv.* To a certain degree; resembling. *Ex.* The City Arts Council is made up of volunteers who have some quasi-official responsibilities. (p. 122)

questionable distinction *n.* A status that one is not sure one wants. *Ex.* Scandinavia has the questionable distinction of having one of the highest suicide rates in the world. (p. 97)

refine *v.* To improve. *Ex.* The violinist constantly refines his technique by practicing. (p. 47)

rehabilitation *n.* Moving a person back into regular society; activities designed to help someone with a problem move into a better situation. *Ex.* The Physical Rehabilitation Center helped my father walk again after he had a heart attack. (p. 89)

relative *adj.* Comparative. *Ex.* They examined the relative value of four different cars before deciding which one to buy. (p. 124)

relentlessness *n.* Perseverance; persistence. *Ex.* The mountain climber kept going with a relentlessness until he reached the peak. (p.121)

reliable *adj.* Secure; can be trusted. *Ex.* Daycare workers must be reliable people. (p. 6)

relish See *with relish.*

remorse *n.* A feeling of regret and guilt for having done something wrong. *Ex.* The guest was filled with remorse after breaking the expensive vase, and she promised to replace it. (p. 110)

remote *adj.* Distant. *Ex.* The hermit lived in a remote village high in the mountains. (p. 135)

replete *adj.* Filled up, well supplied. *Ex.* My trip to Spain was replete with interesting sights, warm people, and good food. (p. 157)

reservoir *n.* A source; a storage place. *Ex.* There is a great reservoir of talent among our young people. (p. 122)

resolve *v.* To be determined; to make a decision. *Ex.* After much hesitation, she resolved to start her own business. (p. 143)

rest *n.* The remainder. *Ex.* I did some sightseeing, and now I'll go fishing for the rest of my vacation. (p. 87)

retaliate *v.* To take revenge; to get even with. *Ex.* The soldiers retaliated with a surprise attack after the enemy shot at them. (p. 49)

rhetoric *n.* Opinionated speech or ideas. *Ex.* Political rhetoric tries to create strong public opinion. (p. 14)

ridiculously *adv.* Unbelievably. *Ex.* She is so skilled at juggling that she makes it look ridiculously easy. (p. 156)

risky *adj.* Dangerous; uncertain; taking a chance. *Ex.* Climbing a mountain is risky even if you are very skilled at it. (p. 157)

rural *adj.* Farm and small town. *Ex.* There are very few rural areas left in Europe. (p. 3)

sacred *adj.* Holy; set apart as something special (often referring to religion). *Ex.* He considers his new car sacred; be careful not to scratch it. (p. 135)

sacrifice *n.* Giving up some desirable thing; depriving oneself of something one wants. *Ex.* The Lees made many sacrifices to send their three children through college. (p. 122)

sanctimonious *adj.* Appearing to be sincere but really not caring. *Ex.* The candidate made sanctimonious statements about the need for more jobs, but he didn't create any after he was elected. (p. 15)

sanction *n.* A means of enforcing a law; a policy. *Ex.* The courts established sanctions against people who violate the law. (p. 111)

scheme *n.* A plan. *Ex.* I have a scheme that will make me a millionaire. (p. 110)

scrawl *v.* To write quickly or carelessly. *Ex.* He scrawled his name on the list and sat down to wait. (p. 46)

scurry *v.* To move quickly; to rush. *Ex.* The children scurried to the table when the cake was served. (p. 71)

second-guess *v.* To predict or anticipate what someone else is thinking. *Ex.* Don't try to second-guess his thoughts. (p. 27)

self-denial *n.* Not satisfying one's own desires. *Ex.* In Buddhism, simplicity and self-denial are respected values. (p. 122)

self-imposed *adj.* Taken on oneself by choice; voluntary. *Ex.* He exercises every day according to a self-imposed schedule. (p. 169)

senile *adj.* Showing a loss of mental ability (often associated with old age). *Ex.* While many people worry about becoming senile, very few people actually lose their memory when they grow old. (p. 146)

sheer *adj.* Pure; absolute; perfect. *Ex.* He learned how to fly a small plane for the sheer pleasure of being alone in the air. (p. 146)

shock *v.* To startle; to offend. *Ex.* I was shocked when I saw how thin he had become. (p. 171)

shoddy *adj.* Poorly made. *Ex.* The shoddy furniture fell apart quickly. (p. 159)

short shrift *adv. phrase.* Too little attention. *Ex.* If you don't have all your documents with you, you will get short shrift from the bank officer. (p. 99)

shrift See *short shrift.*

shuttle *v.* To move back and forth from place to place. *Ex.* That train shuttles between the north end and the south end of town. (p. 46)

skimp *v.* To economize very much. *Ex.* We skimped and saved in order to buy a new car. (p. 13)

slacken off *v.* To reduce; to slow down. *Ex.* We worked hard all day and slackened off around 4:30 P.M. (p. 78)

slate See *clean slate.*

smithereens *n.* Tiny pieces. *Ex.* The glass broke into smithereens when it hit the floor. (p. 168)

snatch *v.* To grab. *Ex.* He snatched up his coat as he ran out the door. (p. 100)

snobbish *adj.* Thinking you are better than everyone else. *Ex.* John has become so snobbish since he inherited lots of money; he won't talk to any of his old friends. (p. 6)

solitary confinement *n.* Being kept alone and not allowed to talk to anyone. *Ex.* Today prisoners are put into solitary confinement only if they are a threat to other prisoners. (p. 89)

squat *adj.* Low and wide. *Ex.* The shape of an Eskimo igloo is squat and round. (p. 69)

stable *adj.* Firmly established; unchanging. *Ex.* The population of Great Britain has remained stable for many years. (p. 134)

stake See *at stake.*

standing See *of long standing.*

stark *adj.* Very obvious; complete. *Ex.* That story is stark nonsense; no one could run 100 miles in one day. (p. 124)

stem from *v.* To result from; to arise from. *Ex.* His fear of dogs stems from the time he was bitten by one as a child. (p. 17)

stigma *n.* A sign of disgrace; disapproval. *Ex.* In some countries it is a stigma to have a tattoo on one's body; in other countries a tattoo is considered beautiful. (p. 47)

stint *n.* Something that must be done within a set period of time. *Ex.* He served a stint in the army and then went into business. (p. 110)

stipulate *v.* To specify; to require. *Ex.* This train ticket stipulates that it must be used within 90 days. (p. 48)

straight from the horse's mouth *adv. phrase.* From the original source; from the person who knows. *Ex.* I heard straight from the horse's mouth that they're getting married; they told me themselves. (p. 70)

strategic *adj.* Of great importance within the whole plan; carefully arranged. *Ex.* The engineers reinforced the bridge at strategic points to distribute the weight evenly. (p. 180)

streak through *v.* To rush through. *Ex.* The express train streaked through the countryside. (p. 125)

striking *adj.* Noticeable; remarkable. *Ex.* She bears a striking resemblance to her grandmother. (p. 123)

strive *v.* To aim; to make a great effort. *Ex.* Researchers are striving to find a cure for cancer. (p. 6)

subsidize *v.* To help pay for; to give financial support. *Ex.* My son works in a supermarket after school to subsidize his college expenses. (p. 45)

subsidy *n.* *Ex.* The research laboratory receives subsidies from the government. (p. 16)

substantiate *v.* To confirm. *Ex.* The tests substantiated the doctor's opinion that I am very healthy. (p. 97)

summarily *adv.* Swiftly; without delay. *Ex.* He was summarily requested to go to the Director's office. (p. 100)

superfluous *adj.* Unnecessary; extra. *Ex.* Don't carry any superfluous clothes on your trip; your suitcase is already too heavy. (p. 76)

surrogate *n.* A substitute; an alternate. *Ex.* If you can't attend the meeting, please send a surrogate in your place. (p. 46)

sustain *v.* To continue to support something; to keep up. *Ex.* Gandhi sustained his belief in nonviolence throughout his life. (p. 30)

swath *n.* A long, wide area. *Ex.* The Grand Canyon cuts a wide swath across Arizona. (p. 135)

tangible *adj.* Capable of being touched; real. *Ex.* His tangible assets include his furniture and car. (p. 154)

tentative *adj.* Subject to change; not final. *Ex.* I made tentative plans to go skiing next weekend if it snows. (p. 159)

ticklish *adj.* Very delicate or sensitive; requiring careful handling. *Ex.* It was a ticklish situation when the hostess asked the guest if he liked the soup, but he thought it tasted terrible. What could he say? (p. 78)

toil *n.* Hard work. *Ex.* The farmer spoke of his toil and the uncertainty of the weather. (p. 135)

torpor *n.* Lethargy; extreme slowness. *Ex.* The heat of the midday sun filled everyone with torpor. (p. 135)

traditionally *adv.* Handed down from the past. *Ex.* The French traditionally drink wine with their meals. (p. 3)

trauma *n.* Shock; psychological stress. *Ex.* The parents suffered terrible trauma after the death of their child. (p. 180)

tremulous *adj.* Shaking; quivering. *Ex.* Gypsy music is characterized by the tremulous sound of violins. (p. 72)

turn in *v.* To give up; to return. *Ex.* She turned in her badge when she retired from the police force. (p. 101)

universal *adj.* Covering the entire world; existing everywhere. *Ex.* A desire for peace is universal. (p. 134)

unsettling *adj.* Disturbing; causing anxiety. *Ex.* It was a very unsettling experience when I lost my wallet. (p. 157)

urging *n.* Strong encouragement. *Ex.* I don't need any urging to try that pie; it looks delicious. (p. 122)

valid *adj.* Legal; authorized. *Ex.* My driver's license is valid for four years. (p. 7)

vast *adj.* Very large. *Ex.* The National Library has a vast collection of books. (p. 122)

venture *v.* To proceed; to go ahead. *Ex.* I ventured into the museum with great anticipation. (p. 98)

verdict *n.* A legal decision; a judgment. *Ex.* What was the verdict in the Baby M case? (p. 97)

viable *adj.* Capable of success; workable. *Ex.* Are there any viable alternatives to that plan? (p. 18)

violate *v.* To disregard; to go against. *Ex.* If you violate the speed limit, you will get a ticket. (p. 90)

virtually *adv.* Almost entirely. *Ex.* Virtually all homes in my native country have a television set. (p. 18)

void *n.* A completely empty space; nothingness. *Ex.* The spacecraft flew past Pluto and out into the void. (p. 135)

voluntary *adj.* Willing; free; independent. *Ex.* Every year, I make a voluntary contribution to the Red Cross. (p. 59)

vulnerable *adj.* Easily damaged; defenseless. *Ex.* If you are vulnerable to colds, don't stay outside too long on a freezing day. (p. 60)

wares *n.* Merchandise; things to sell. *Ex.* At the Saturday village market, craftspeople sell their wares to local residents and tourists. (p. 103)

wary *adj.* Suspicious; distrustful. *Ex.* You should be wary of advertisements that promise to make you rich. (p. 110)

wastage *n.* The part you throw away or don't need. *Ex.* After the hunters cut up the deer, they fed the wastage to their dogs. (p. 74)

wayward *adj.* Lawless; refusing to do the right thing. *Ex.* John was a wayward child, but he became responsible in high school. (p. 110)

well-heeled *adj.* *(slang)* Wealthy; having plenty of money. *Ex.* Her family is well-heeled and can send her on trips abroad every year. (p. 110)

whim *n.* A humorous or unusual idea. *Ex.* On a whim, I decided to go roller skating. (p. 6)

with relish *adv. phrase.* Enthusiastically. *Ex.* "I'm going to use my raise to buy a new car, " he said with relish. (p. 73)

woodwork See *blend into the woodwork.*

yearning *n.* A great desire. *Ex.* I had a yearning for some ice cream on that hot day. (p. 58)

zealous *adj.* Eager; hardworking. *Ex.* The zealous student read all the books and finished her homework early. (p. 70)